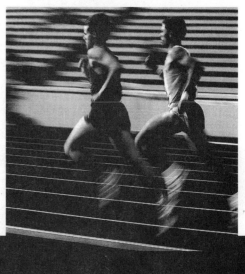

RUNNING

Microsoft® POWERPOINT® 4

FOR WINDOWS™

Microsoft
PRESS

STEPHEN W. SAGMAN

PUBLISHED BY
Microsoft Press
A Division of Microsoft Corporation
One Microsoft Way
Redmond, Washington 98052-6399

Library of Congress Cataloging-in-Publication Data
Sagman, Stephen W.
    Running Microsoft PowerPoint 4 for Windows / Stephen W. Sagman.
        p.   cm.
    Includes index.
    ISBN 1-55615-639-1
    1. Windows (Computer programs)   2. Microsoft PowerPoint for
Windows. I. Title.
QA76.76.W56S24 1994
006.6'869--dc20   94-2358
                                                                               CIP

Printed and bound in the United States of America.

    4 5 6 7 8 9   AG-M   9 8 7 6

Distributed to the book trade in Canada by Macmillan of Canada, a division of Canada Publishing
Corporation.

A CIP catalogue record for this book is available from the British Library.

Microsoft Press books are available through booksellers and distributors worldwide. For further
information about international editions, contact your local Microsoft Corporation office. Or
contact Microsoft Press International directly at fax (206) 936-7329.

Acquisitions Editor: Lucinda Rowley
Project Editor: Ina Chang
Manuscript Editing and Technical Review: Online Press Inc.

Formatting Toolbar

Graph's Standard Toolbar

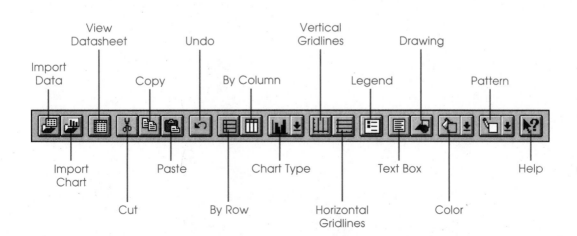

Chapters at a Glance

Table of Contents

Table of Contents

Table of Contents

Table of Contents

Acknowledgments

Many thanks to Glenn Hobin, Ellen Fetty, John Tafoya, and the other members of the Microsoft Graphics Business Unit, who develop PowerPoint, for their encouragement and assistance during the creation of this book.

At Microsoft Press, I had the true pleasure of working with Lucinda Rowley, Ina Chang, Mary DeJong, Peggy McCauley, Sandi Lage, and Susanne Freet, who shepherded the project and me with great concern.

My endless thanks go to Joyce Cox, Polly Fox Urban, and Christina Dudley at Online Press for their infinite care, professionalism, and perseverance as they nursed my words back to health after the sorry state in which I left them. Thanks also to Lisa Chase, who took such pains to review every procedure for technical accuracy and reproduce many of the illustrations. And many thanks to Bill Teel, who worked so hard to ensure that every page and every picture look perfect.

Thanks, finally and not least, to Eric and Lola for their love and support.

Introduction

Since its introduction in 1987, Microsoft PowerPoint has pioneered new ways of working with presentation graphics. PowerPoint introduced the concept of a presentation as a single entity rather than discrete slides, and it has introduced innovations with each new release.

PowerPoint 4 for Windows carries on the tradition, adding dozens of features designed to make creating presentations even easier and more intuitive. At the same time, it has grown more like its colleagues in the Microsoft Office suite of Windows-based applications, sharing on-screen controls like menus and dialog boxes, and techniques like drag and drop. PowerPoint has even mastered the common language of communication shared by the Office applications, so you can now effortlessly pass text, numbers, and graphics among the applications using drag and drop.

What's New in PowerPoint 4

Whether you're a new user or a veteran, you'll appreciate PowerPoint's many new features. And if you're already familiar with other Microsoft Office applications, such as Microsoft Word or Microsoft Excel, you'll recognize many of these innovations. Here is a partial list of the new features in PowerPoint 4:

- Dozens of usability enhancements, which make working in PowerPoint a breeze. These enhancements include shortcut menus that appear when you select an object, text, a toolbar, or an element in a graph and then click the right mouse button; and customizable toolbars that display the most popular commands as buttons you can click on the screen.

- Wizards, which assist you in laying the groundwork for a presentation. The AutoContent Wizard helps you develop the ideas you'll present, and the Pick a Look Wizard helps you design the look of your slides.

- Autolayouts, which offer a variety of preset slide layouts for title slides, bulleted lists, and slides with graphs, organization charts, tables, clip art, and other objects.

- Placeholders, which you can click to add titles, bulleted text, graphs, tables, clip art, and more.

- Microsoft Graph 5, the newest version of the graphing application shared by other Microsoft Windows-based applications. Graph 5 offers many new features, including new chart types and new menus and toolbars.

- In-place editing, which lets you create and edit tables or worksheets using all the powers of Word or Excel, and create graphs using all the capabilities of Graph 5 without leaving PowerPoint.

- Automatic exchange of outlines between Word and PowerPoint, which allows you to click a single button in either application to send the outline to the other application.

- Text Drag and Drop and Automatic Text Selection, which make it easier to move and copy text and to select just the text you want.

- "Mark-up" mode, which lets you annotate slides by drawing on them with the mouse pointer during a slide show.

About This Book

The object of this book is to give you the broadest possible understanding of PowerPoint in the shortest possible time. It serves as a tutorial as you're learning PowerPoint and as a reference for looking up topics. This book assumes that you have a working knowledge of Windows.

The parts and chapters of this book are organized in the order that you're likely to need information as you create presentations in PowerPoint. Part 1, which includes Chapters 1 and 2, introduces PowerPoint. You learn the basics of the PowerPoint environment, and you get off on the right footing by learning the essential steps to follow whenever you create a presentation.

Part 2, which includes Chapters 3 through 8, provides guidelines for creating the basic elements of the presentation. You learn how to start a presentation and how to work in Outline view and Slide view to enter and organize the text and add graphs, organization charts, and tables.

Part 3, which consists of Chapters 9 through 11, offers important information on adapting the basic presentation to your specific needs. You learn how to change the overall presentation design, format the graphs you've created, and use Slide Sorter view to view presentation-wide alterations.

Part 4, which includes Chapters 12 through 14, shows you how to embellish a presentation with text annotations, drawings, clip art, and bitmapped images.

Part 5, which consists of Chapters 15 and 16, gives you the information you need to produce the fruits of your labor: printed pages, audience handouts, and 35-mm slides. You also learn how to prepare and deliver electronic on-screen presentations called slide shows, complete with transitions, builds, sound, music, and video.

Part 6, which includes Chapters 17 and 18, covers advanced topics such as using PowerPoint with other Windows-based applications and customizing PowerPoint to suit the way you like to work. Part 6 also includes the Appendix, where you'll find samples of the dozens of design templates that come with PowerPoint.

Using This Book

In this book, when you see a key combination with a plus sign, like this:

Ctrl+Z

it means "Hold down the first key and then press the second key." For example, Ctrl+Z means "Hold down the Ctrl key and then press the Z key."

A NEW! icon appears next to descriptions of features that are new to PowerPoint 4 or that have been extensively revised from version 3.

Tips that contain helpful suggestions for getting more out of PowerPoint are marked with this icon:

Tips that contain suggestions for enhancing the visual appeal of your presentations are marked with this icon:

 See Also: Whenever you see a note that looks like this, you'll find a reference to another section of the book that provides additional, related information.

Introducing
PowerPoint

Setting the PowerPoint Stage

A word processor prepares the text in your everyday life. A spreadsheet calculates the numbers you need. And a database stores the text and numeric information you've compiled. But to communicate your knowledge and achievements, and to persuade the world at large, you need the power of Microsoft PowerPoint 4 for Windows.

What Is PowerPoint?

PowerPoint is a presentation processor that takes the text and numbers you've collected and hands back graphs and slides with the professional polish that today's sophisticated audiences demand.

PowerPoint follows the premise that you've never used presentation graphics software. That's probably helpful even if you've used such programs before. Unlike a word processor or spreadsheet that you might use daily, a presentation graphics program gets pulled off the electronic shelf only occasionally, so it must always seem familiar and easy to use.

PowerPoint 4 is the newest version of Microsoft's presentation graphics software for Windows. You can buy it separately or as part of the Microsoft Office bundle of Windows-based applications. In many large organizations, PowerPoint is the standard-issue presentation graphics software.

PowerPoint takes you by the hand at the very first screen and gently guides you through the process of creating a presentation. It asks for the text and numbers it needs—you can type them in or import them from other applications—and it asks you to select from a palette of designs for the presentation. Then PowerPoint produces the kind of vivid graphics and dazzling images you'd expect from a professional artist.

Once the presentation is complete, you can print pages to hand out at a meeting, add speaker's notes, or create transparencies to project with a standard overhead projector. You can even produce bright, crisp, 35-mm photographic slides (if you have slide-making equipment or are willing to hand the presentation to a slide-making company). And that's not all. You can also leave the images in a PowerPoint file, add special effects, and display them right on your computer screen—or, with a computer projector, on a large audience-sized screen. Electronic presentations like these are the hottest thing today, and PowerPoint's capabilities for creating and controlling electronic presentations are state-of-the-art.

Best of all, to create professional-quality visuals in PowerPoint, you don't have to be an artist. The program's built-in design templates take care of the presentation's appearance. And you don't have to be a computer expert to use all of PowerPoint's features. There's always an on-screen prompt to lead you to the next task, and often, when you have choices to make, one of PowerPoint's "wizards" appears to guide you through the preliminary decisions. About the only thing PowerPoint cannot do is help you enunciate while speaking, but the professional quality of the visuals will help give you the confidence to be at your very best.

PowerPoint's special presentation-making features can make your work easier no matter what your presentation needs:

You need quick and easy, high-impact visuals to accompany a talk. PowerPoint's AutoContent and Pick a Look wizards and templates not only help you design a presentation, but they can give you a basic presentation outline to follow. You simply select a theme and design, and watch as PowerPoint generates eye-catching slides that are organized, consistent, and professional.

You need a fact-filled presentation with plenty of graphs and charts. PowerPoint's Graph, Organization Chart, and Table modules can help you create elaborate visuals that depict numeric information, detail the structure of an organization, and make comparisons among ideas.

You need a sophisticated electronic presentation with lots of razzle-dazzle. Between slides, which can include animated graphs, sound, music, and even embedded video, PowerPoint's slide shows can serve up sophisticated video-inspired transitions. Slide shows can also be interactive—you can branch to a subtopic or call up hidden detail to support a supposition or respond to a viewer's question.

You need team-spirit presentations that display your group's logo and colors. Easily customizable slide masters and color schemes are all part of PowerPoint's repertoire. By editing the slide master, you can place a logo on the background of every slide or select special colors to match the corporate colors.

You need to assemble existing text and graphics from other Microsoft Office applications. PowerPoint can easily integrate text, graphs, numbers, and diagrams from other Microsoft Office applications (such as Microsoft Word and Microsoft Excel) into presentation materials. With object linking and embedding (OLE—pronounced olé without shouting) implemented by the built-in OLE2 software, you can even edit an object within PowerPoint that you created in another application. And while you are editing, you have access to all the editing tools provided by the other application.

See Also: For more information about object linking and embedding, see Chapter 17, "Using PowerPoint with Other Applications," page 407.

PowerPoint Basics (Read This!)

Although PowerPoint is extremely friendly and easy to use, you've got to know a few basics before you can master the program. The rest of this chapter covers the little bit of groundwork you need. But don't worry; you'll soon start creating an actual presentation.

PowerPoint's Views

Unlike early presentation programs, which forced you to create and then save a single slide at a time, PowerPoint creates entire presentations of slides, all similar in appearance and all stored in a single file on your system.

> **NOTE:** PowerPoint uses the word *slide* to refer to each page of visuals in a presentation even though you may print the presentation on paper or transparencies rather than create 35-mm slides.

The early presentation programs created only one slide per file, and thus only one view was necessary. Because PowerPoint can create an entire presentation's worth of slides per file, it must provide more than one way to view the slides. So instead of offering just Slide view, in which you work on a single slide, PowerPoint also offers Outline, Slide Sorter, Notes Pages, and Slide Show views. Each view lets you work on a different aspect of the presentation, and the changes you make in one view show up in all the other views as well.

Slide View

In Slide view, you can refine and embellish an individual slide in your presentation. You can enter and edit text, and you can add a graph, chart, or table to a slide. You can also dress up a slide with drawings, pictures, and text annotations. Figure 1-1 shows a slide in Slide view.

FIGURE 1-1.
Slide view.

For more information about Slide view, see Chapter 5, "Working with Text in Slide View," page 93.

Outline View

In Outline view, PowerPoint displays only the text of the presentation, allowing you to enter additional text or edit existing text without the distractions you might find in Slide view. Figure 1-2 on the next page shows a sample presentation in Outline view. Because you work only with text in Outline view, you can concentrate on the words of the presentation and the flow of ideas through the slides. Outline view provides an excellent environment for organizing your thoughts and materials before you switch to a different view, where you might work on the design elements of the presentation.

For more information about Outline view, see Chapter 4, "Working with Text in Outline View," page 57.

FIGURE 1-2.

Outline view.

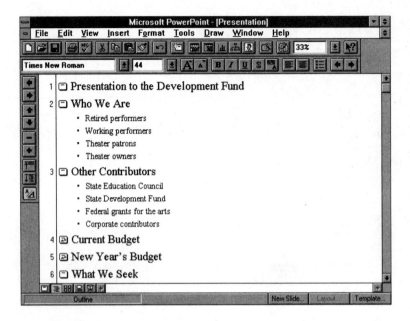

Slide Sorter View

In Slide Sorter view, you see the slides of the presentation laid out in neat rows and columns, as in Figure 1-3. Here you can see the result of sweeping changes to the appearance of the entire presentation, such as a change of the template that supplies the background design and color scheme. You cannot make changes to the content of individual slides, but you can cut extraneous slides, duplicate slides, and shuffle the order of slides just as if you had laid out real 35-mm slides on a tabletop.

By using Slide Sorter view before you print a presentation or generate slides, you can check for inconsistencies among slides and gross errors such as a graph that is positioned on the wrong part of a page. You can also give your presentation a design overhaul by switching to a different template. When you change templates, virtually everything about your presentation's appearance changes too. As a result, a lively, colorful presentation for the sales force can become a stately, elegant presentation for the board of directors. Slide Sorter view is also the place to add and edit the transition effects used between slides during a slide show.

FIGURE 1-3.

Slide Sorter view.

For more information about Slide Sorter view, see Chapter 11, "Using Slide Sorter View," page 303.

Notes Pages View

The fourth PowerPoint view is dedicated to creating speaker's notes that the person giving the presentation can use at the podium. Notes Pages view produces a smaller version of the slide on the top half of a page and leaves the bottom half free for notes that the speaker can use during the presentation. While in Notes Pages view, you can view a reduced version of each slide and type in the accompanying text notes. Figure 1-4 on the next page shows a slide in Notes Pages view.

For more information about Notes Pages view, see "Adding Speaker's Notes," page 326.

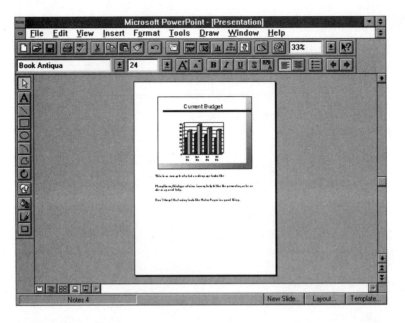

FIGURE 1-4.
Notes Pages view.

Slide Show View

The fifth PowerPoint view, Slide Show view, does not display a single, static image. Instead, it shows the presentation progressing from slide to slide just like a real slide show using projected 35-mm slides. However, unlike a real slide show, which at best can only fade out of one slide before fading into the next, a PowerPoint slide show can use eye-popping special effects to make the transition from slide to slide. As one slide dissolves off the screen, for example, the next slide can reveal itself gradually from top to bottom, and its bulleted lines of text can glide in one by one from the side. Figure 1-5 shows a slide as a new slide sweeps onto the screen from the lower right in Slide Show view.

See Also: For more information about Slide Show view, see Chapter 16, "Creating Slide Shows," page 387.

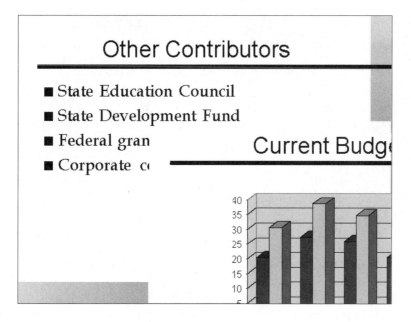

FIGURE 1-5.
Slide Show view.

Starting PowerPoint

Before you can see how easy it is to switch from one view to another, you must get PowerPoint up and running. After the program is installed, a PowerPoint icon should appear in one of the program group windows displayed by Program Manager (the first program you see when you start Microsoft Windows). Every Windows installation is different, however. Many people create their own custom arrangement of icons and windows in Program Manager. Other people are given a standard arrangement of icons by their supervisor or by the computer department at their workplace. Still others use special programs within Windows that let them customize their screens and start programs with specific mouse clicks or keyboard commands.

If you used the standard Windows Program Manager when you installed PowerPoint, the Setup program allowed you to specify which Program Manager group the PowerPoint icon would be placed in. If you installed the PowerPoint icon with the other Microsoft Office application icons (the default), then you probably placed its icon in the Microsoft Office group, as shown in Figure 1-6 on the next page. Wherever the PowerPoint icon is, double-click it to launch the PowerPoint application.

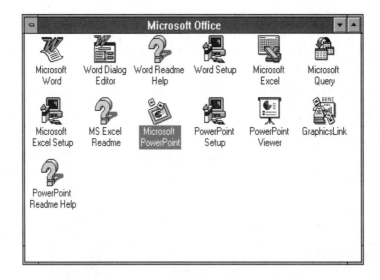

When you start PowerPoint for the first time, you're invited to see a Quick Preview of the software. If you want to skip the preview, simply click the Cancel button. (You can always catch the preview later by choosing Quick Preview from the Help menu.) After the preview ends or you click the Cancel button, the PowerPoint window appears, displaying the Tip of the Day. Read the enlightening tip, and then press Enter to display the PowerPoint dialog box shown in Figure 1-7. You use this dialog box to select a method for creating a new presentation.

TIP   If you get tired of seeing a new Tip of the Day every time you load PowerPoint, deselect the Show Tips at Startup option in the lower left corner of the Tip of the Day dialog box, and then click OK.

To follow along with the rest of this chapter, select the Blank Presentation option and then click OK, or simply double-click the option. As shown in Figure 1-8, the next dialog box to appear is labeled New Slide. You use this dialog box to select a slide layout for your presentation. PowerPoint offers 21 layouts, called *autolayouts*, from which to choose. For now, click OK to create the first slide with the default Title Slide autolayout, which is the appropriate slide for the opening of a presentation.

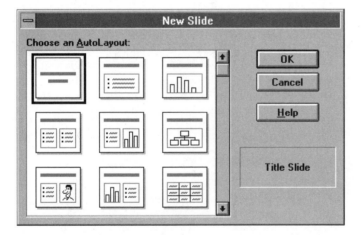

FIGURE 1-8.
The New Slide dialog box.

See Also: For more information about the PowerPoint dialog box and autolayouts, see Chapter 2, "The Essential Steps," page 25.

Switching Views

If you have successfully started a blank presentation and selected the Title Slide autolayout, you are now in Slide view, looking at the first slide. Getting to a different view is simply a matter of clicking one of the five buttons in the lower left corner of the presentation window.

Go ahead and click the first four buttons one by one. When you click the fifth button, the blank first slide of the presentation appears full-screen in Slide Show view. No, your system hasn't crashed. You just haven't created any slides to present in Slide Show view yet. Simply press the Esc key to return to the previous view.

Another way to switch between views is to use the View menu. To open the View menu, click the word *View* in the menu bar, or hold down the Alt key and then press the underlined letter in the menu name, in this case *V*.

The first four entries on the View menu lead you to the first four views. The fifth entry, Slide Show, leads you to the Slide Show dialog box, from which you can run the slide show.

NOTE: If a command on a menu is dimmed, the command is currently unavailable. If a command is followed by an ellipsis, a dialog box appears when you choose the command. If a command is preceded by a dot, it is one of a group of mutually exclusive commands. If a command is preceded by a check mark, the command is currently active and can be toggled on and off.

Controlling the PowerPoint Window

Like all windows in Microsoft Windows, the PowerPoint window has Minimize and Maximize buttons in its upper right corner. The Minimize button shrinks the PowerPoint window to an icon, and the Maximize button expands the window to fill the screen. Clicking the Control button in the upper left corner displays a menu with additional commands for restoring the PowerPoint window to its previous size; moving, sizing, or closing the window; and switching to another open application.

NOTE: When the PowerPoint window is maximized, the Maximize button becomes the Restore button (with up and down arrows). If you click this button, the window is restored to its previous size. To return the window to full size, click the Maximize button or choose Maximize from the Control menu.

TIP   When the PowerPoint window is not maximized, you can use the mouse to move and resize the window. For example, click and drag the window's title bar to move the window to a new location. To change the window's size, position the mouse pointer on one side of the window's frame, hold down the left mouse button, and when the pointer changes to a double-headed arrow, drag the frame in the desired direction.

Manipulating the Presentation Window

When you create a new presentation in PowerPoint or edit an existing one, the presentation window occupies most of the PowerPoint window. To change the presentation window's location or size, you can use its buttons and Control menu commands just like you use the PowerPoint window's buttons and commands.

You can have more than one presentation open at a time so that you can compare presentations or copy graphics or text from one presentation to another. To open more than one presentation, choose Open from the File menu, and when the Open dialog box appears, double-click the filename of the next presentation you want to open. The new presentation window covers any windows that are open, but you can use the commands on the Window menu to rearrange the windows. For example, the Arrange All command places the open windows side by side, as shown in Figure 1-9.

The Cascade command on the Window menu arranges open presentation windows in sequence so that you can see all their title bars. You can then click any title bar to bring a presentation window to the front. The Fit To Page command sizes the currently selected window so that it neatly fits the presentation slide.

NOTE: After you use any of the commands on the Window menu, you can still manipulate each window individually by using the window's buttons and Control menu commands.

FIGURE 1-9.

Two presentations arranged side by side using the Window menu's Arrange All command.

Using the Toolbars

Every command in PowerPoint resides on one of PowerPoint's menus. This fact isn't very comforting, however, when you're in a rush and you'd rather not have to rummage through PowerPoint's menus. Fortunately, to make life a little easier, PowerPoint features several toolbars that contain buttons for the commands you use most often. These toolbars are conveniently displayed in the PowerPoint window so that you can access a command simply by clicking the corresponding toolbar button. As shown in Figure 1-10, the default PowerPoint window displays three toolbars: the Standard, Formatting, and Drawing toolbars. In addition to these toolbars, PowerPoint provides the Custom, Drawing+, Microsoft, and AutoShapes toolbars.

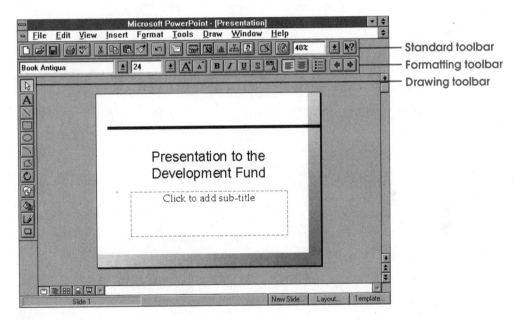

FIGURE 1-10.
The Standard, Formatting, and Drawing toolbars.

Displaying Toolbars

To display a toolbar that doesn't appear by default, choose the Toolbars command from the View menu; when the Toolbars dialog box appears, as shown in Figure 1-11 on the next page, click the check boxes for the toolbars you want. Check boxes like these act as toggles. In other words, you click once to

FIGURE 1-11.

The Toolbars
dialog box.

turn on the option (add the check), and you click again to turn off the option (remove the check).

Try turning on an additional toolbar now by clicking the check box to the left of Microsoft in the Toolbars dialog box. When you click OK, the Microsoft toolbar appears in the PowerPoint window, just below the Formatting toolbar. The Microsoft toolbar contains buttons that you can use to launch other Microsoft applications. To remove the Microsoft toolbar, return to the Toolbars dialog box, and clear the Microsoft check box by clicking it again.

All of PowerPoint's toolbars can be customized to include only the buttons you want. You can also move buttons from one toolbar to another.

See Also: For more information about customizing toolbars, see "Customizing Toolbars," page 428.

Positioning Toolbars

By default, PowerPoint arranges its toolbars where they fit best on the screen, but you can change this arrangement to create a workspace that you find more comfortable. A toolbar can be located along one of the four sides of the PowerPoint window, or it can be free-floating within the window. You might want to leave the default arrangement of toolbars for now. When you become more familiar with PowerPoint, you can position the toolbars to suit your needs.

To move a toolbar, first place the mouse pointer within the borders of the toolbar, but not on top of any button. Then hold down the left mouse button, and drag the toolbar to a new location on the screen. When you release the mouse button, the toolbar drops into its new position, and, if necessary, the presentation window inside the PowerPoint window adjusts to make room. If you drag a toolbar to one side of the PowerPoint window, the toolbar automatically changes shape to fit the space. If you drag the toolbar toward the middle of the screen, the toolbar becomes a box. After you drop a toolbar into place, you can reshape it by dragging its borders just as you reshape a window. Figure 1-12 shows the Drawing toolbar placed within the PowerPoint window.

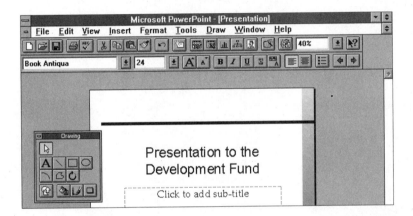

FIGURE 1-12.
The floating Drawing toolbar.

NOTE: You'll find that the Standard and Formatting toolbars refuse to be placed along the left or right side of the PowerPoint window. You can position them only at the top or bottom of the window or display them as floating toolbars within the window.

ToolTips

PowerPoint provides a handy feature called ToolTips to help you keep track of all those toolbar buttons. To see a description of any toolbar button or of any button on the screen, simply place the mouse pointer on the button and pause. A small ToolTip window pops up nearby, displaying the button's name; a brief description of the button appears in the status line at the bottom of the PowerPoint window. Whenever you display a new toolbar in PowerPoint, use ToolTips to get acquainted with its buttons. To turn off ToolTips, choose Toolbars from the View menu, and deselect the Show ToolTips option at the bottom of the Toolbars dialog box.

Moving Through Slides

In Slide view, you see only one slide at a time, but the presentation may contain many slides. To move to another slide in your presentation, use any of the following methods:

- Press PgDn to move forward one slide or PgUp to move back one slide.

- Click the Next Slide button at the bottom of the presentation window's vertical scroll bar (see Figure 1-13) to move forward one slide, or click the Previous Slide button to move back one slide.

- Drag the scroll box down or up in the presentation window's vertical scroll bar (see Figure 1-13) to move forward or backward through the presentation. As you drag the scroll box, the current slide number appears next to the scroll bar.

To practice moving through slides in a ready-made presentation, click the Open button on the Standard toolbar or choose the Open command from the File menu. When the Open dialog box appears, double-click the WIZARDS subdirectory in the Directories list. Then, in the File Name list, double-click the GENERAL.PPT presentation filename to open one of the sample presentations. Next, switch to Slide view by clicking the Slide View button in the lower left corner of the presentation window. Now try moving through the slides in the

FIGURE 1-13.

The vertical scroll bar and scroll box and the Previous Slide and Next Slide buttons in Slide view.

sample presentation by using any of the methods listed on the facing page. When you finish viewing the slides, choose Close from the File menu to close the presentation window.

Saving Your Work

You've heard it before, but it always bears repeating: Save your work often. Don't wait until you've finished a presentation to save it. Save a presentation after you create the first slide. Save it again a little while later. The more frequently you save your work, the less you stand to lose if you fall victim to a power failure, a coffee spill, or a rambunctious child who decides to play piano on your keyboard.

To save a file, click the Save button on the Standard toolbar (that little picture on the button is a disk, not a TV) or choose Save from the File menu. If you have not yet named the file (if the presentation title bar still displays the name *Presentation*), the Save As dialog box appears, as shown in Figure 1-14. Note that the current entry in the File Name edit box is highlighted, so anything you type will replace it. Enter a filename of up to eight characters in the File Name edit box, and then click OK. PowerPoint supplies the PPT filename extension automatically.

The filename you type appears here →

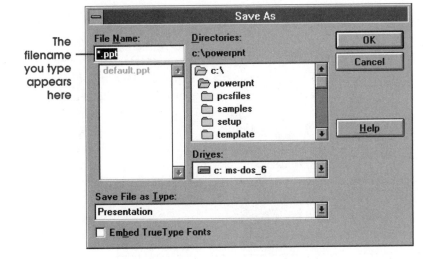

FIGURE 1-14.

The Save As dialog box.

After you enter a filename, PowerPoint displays the Summary Info dialog box shown in Figure 1-15 on the next page. You can use the information that

FIGURE 1-15.

You can use the
information in the
Summary Info
dialog box to search
for specific files.

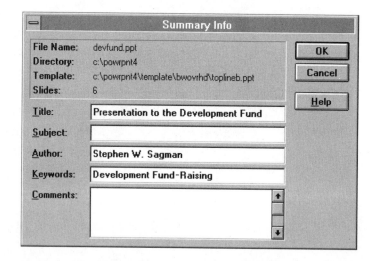

you enter in this dialog box to help you search for files later. For example, if
you always enter in the Keywords edit box the project name for all presentations
belonging to a particular project, you can later use the Find File command to
extract a list of those presentations (see the tip below).

To enter information in the Summary Info dialog box, type text directly in
the edit boxes, using Tab to move to the next edit box and Shift+Tab to move
to the previous edit box. When you've filled in as many edit boxes as you want,
click OK to close the dialog box.

TIP To search for files based on information in the Summary Info dialog box, choose Find File from the File menu to
display the Search dialog box. Select the drive you want to
search from the Location drop-down list, select the Include
Subdirectories option (optional), and then click the Advanced
Search button. In the Advanced Search dialog box, click the
Summary tab, enter the information you want to search for in
the appropriate edit boxes, and click OK twice to perform the
search. If the search is successful, PowerPoint displays the
files in the Find File dialog box.

Getting Help

PowerPoint's online Help system is extensive and easy to use. You can search for a Help topic or select from a list of procedures. You can also use context-sensitive Help to learn about a feature on the PowerPoint screen. In addition, all dialog boxes include a Help button so that you can read about your options before you select them.

To get into the Help system, choose Contents from the Help menu or press F1. The PowerPoint Help Contents window appears, as shown in Figure 1-16. To see a list of Help topics, double-click the Using PowerPoint option. To view helpful shortcuts, keyboard equivalents, and a concise reference to the PowerPoint menus and commands, double-click the Reference Information option. To search for a specific feature, such as Outline view, first click the Search button at the top of the Help Contents window, and then type the name of the feature letter by letter until it appears highlighted in the list below. Next, click Show Topics to see a list of topics related to the feature, select the topic you want, and then click Go To.

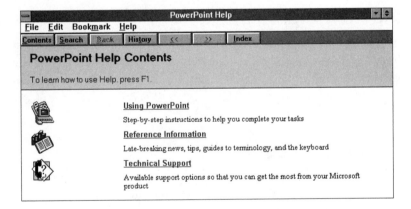

FIGURE 1-16.

The PowerPoint Help Contents window.

As you read a Help topic, you'll see words with dotted underlines and words with solid underlines. A dotted underline indicates that when you click the word, a pop-up definition of the word is displayed. A solid underline indicates that when you click the word, the Help topic for the word is displayed. In addition, you can click the items listed in the See Also section of a Help topic to get information about those items.

Some Help topics have an Examples and Demos button at the top of their window. When you click this button, Help displays a graphical representation of the topic or gives you a step-by-step demonstration of how to carry out a corresponding task.

While in the Help system, you can click the Back button at the top of the Help window to return to the previous topic or click the History button to see a list of topics you've recently visited. You can also click the Index button to access an alphabetical listing of terms associated with PowerPoint.

 TIP   When you find a Help topic pertinent to the task you are trying to accomplish, you can keep the topic on your screen to refer to it while you work in PowerPoint. In the Help window, simply open the Help menu, and then choose Always on Top. To close the Help topic, choose Always on Top again.

Using the Help Button

 To get help about a button or menu command, you can use the Help button on the Standard toolbar. Just click the Help button (or press Shift+F1), and when the pointer displays a large question mark, click the button or menu command you want information on. Help then displays the corresponding topic for the button or menu command you've chosen.

Using Cue Cards

 Help provides cue cards that display step-by-step instructions for some of the most common tasks in PowerPoint. To use cue cards, choose the Cue Cards command from the Help menu, and when the Cue Cards window appears, click the button next to the procedure you want to follow step by step. The cue card remains on the screen while you follow its instructions. (The steps you should follow are numbered and set in indented panels.) To return to the cue cards menu, click the Menu button in the Cue Cards window. To return to the previous cue cards display, click the Back button. You can also minimize the Cue Cards window so that it becomes an easily accessible icon on the Windows desktop. To close the Cue Cards window, double-click the Control button in the upper left corner of the window.

2

The Essential Steps

Like any great software, PowerPoint offers a cornucopia of resources that were designed for a broad range of needs. Uses for the software are limited only by your time and imagination. Yet there's one well-trodden path that most users follow, taking excursions into the finer points of the program only when required. This chapter focuses on the steps that form the basic presentation-making process. Follow these footsteps, and you'll never get lost in the woods.

As you learn to use PowerPoint, you'll discover that it always guides you through the process of creating a presentation. After you start a slide, for example, PowerPoint displays a prompt that tells you to *Click here to add a title*. Simply follow PowerPoint's lead. Remember, the software was written with ease of use in mind. Whenever PowerPoint's designers could anticipate your next logical move, they instructed the software to do the same.

Although this chapter covers the nine steps involved in creating a presentation, you won't actually create one yet. Instead, you'll become familiar with the sequence of the steps, which also forms the structure of this book.

Step 1: Starting the Presentation

The presentation process gets under way as soon as you launch PowerPoint and start a new presentation. (As mentioned in Chapter 1, the first time you use PowerPoint, you can opt to see a Quick Preview of the software. To skip the preview, click the Cancel button.)

After the PowerPoint window opens and you read the Tip of the Day, the PowerPoint dialog box, shown in Figure 2-1 on the next page, is displayed. If you don't see this dialog box, you can always click the New button on the Standard toolbar or choose New from the File menu to start a new presentation. (The New Presentation dialog box offers the same options as the PowerPoint dialog box.)

The first two options in the PowerPoint dialog box activate wizards, which guide you through a series of steps to accomplish a certain task. For example, the AutoContent Wizard asks you to select a presentation type from a list of six predefined types and then loads a set of slides with relevant text already in place. Of course, the text is generic, such as *Details about this topic*, but it nevertheless guides you in structuring the presentation.

The Pick a Look Wizard takes you step by step through the process of selecting a presentation template, which designs the overall look of a presentation.

FIGURE 2-1.
The PowerPoint
dialog box.

It also helps you create the very first slide your audience sees: the title slide. The third option, labeled Template, displays a list of design templates you can choose from. You won't use this option until you're more familiar with Power-Point. The fourth option, Blank Presentation, starts a blank presentation devoid of any design or sample text.

If you've already used PowerPoint to create a presentation, you can select the last option, Open an Existing Presentation. When you select this option, PowerPoint displays the Open dialog box so that you can open a presentation that has already been created and filed away.

Step 2: Choosing the Content and Appearance

Step 2 consists of two tasks that you can perform in either order: entering the presentation content and establishing its design. You can focus on the text of the slides first and leave the design for later, or you can select a design and have it applied to each new slide as you enter the text. The simplest way to take care of the content is to use the AutoContent Wizard. (Figure 2-2 shows one of the AutoContent Wizard's dialog boxes.) One caveat, though: The AutoContent Wizard, which enters sample text on a set of presentation slides, also institutes a presentation design. Of course, you can always change the design at step 6, Tweaking the Presentation.

FIGURE 2-2.

You can use the AutoContent Wizard to help you choose the content and design of your presentation.

You can use the Pick a Look Wizard to select a design template before you enter the content. As shown in Figure 2-3, this wizard provides step-by-step help in selecting a design suitable for the type of output you want to generate.

FIGURE 2-3.

Use the Pick a Look Wizard to get assistance in choosing a design template.

As mentioned, you won't use the Template option in the PowerPoint dialog box until you're more familiar with PowerPoint and you've had a chance to develop your own logos and color schemes for custom design templates.

Step 3: Entering and Editing the Text

Even if you use the AutoContent Wizard rather than type in your own text, you still need to replace the wizard's generic text with your own. You can step through the presentation slide by slide and substitute your words for Power-Point's, or you can work in Outline view, where you can focus on the overall

flow of text as well as the text on individual slides. In Outline view, you can
enter and edit text, rearrange text, and copy or move text from slide to slide. In
fact, Outline view is so useful that when the AutoContent Wizard's job is done,
it leaves you in Outline view, as shown in Figure 2-4.

FIGURE 2-4.
The AutoContent
Wizard leaves you
in Outline view so
that you can enter
and edit text.

**See
Also:**   For more information about Outline view, see Chapter 4, "Working
with Text in Outline View," page 57.

Step 4: Adding Graph,
Organization Chart, and Table Slides

Not every topic is best communicated with written statements. Sometimes
pictures or charts are the ticket, and sometimes tables are most effective. You
can add a graph, chart, or table to a text slide, or you can create a new slide
devoted to a graph, chart, or table. When you request a new slide, PowerPoint

displays the New Slide dialog box, which offers a variety of slide autolayouts, as shown in Figure 2-5. Some slide autolayouts have text only—a slide title and a block of text below, usually with bulleted lines of text—and others have graphs, organization charts, and tables in addition to a title. Some even have combinations of text and graphics on the same slide. You simply click the autolayout you want, and then click OK. The autolayout appears full-screen in Slide view, as shown in Figure 2-6.

FIGURE 2-5.
The New Slide dialog box.

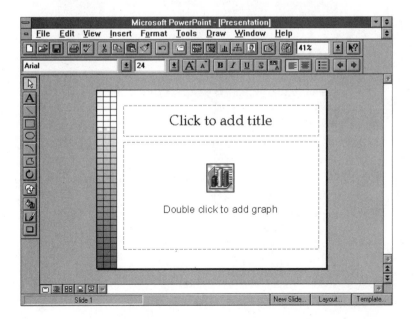

FIGURE 2-6.
After you select an autolayout, it appears full-screen in Slide view.

As you can see, an autolayout contains a combination of *placeholders*, which are dashed, rectangular boxes with text prompts. (Some placeholders, such as graph placeholders, contain icons as well as text prompts.) The text prompt in each placeholder tells you how to use the placeholder. For example, one placeholder tells you to *Click to add title*. Another tells you to *Double click to add graph*. The autolayout shown in Figure 2-7 has three placeholders: one for a title, one for bulleted text, and one for a graph. With placeholders, you can't go wrong. When you click a text placeholder, such as *Click to add title*, PowerPoint displays an insertion point so that you can type text directly in the placeholder. If you double-click a graph placeholder, PowerPoint loads the special module you use to create graphs.

FIGURE 2-7.

An autolayout with title, bulleted text, and graph placeholders.

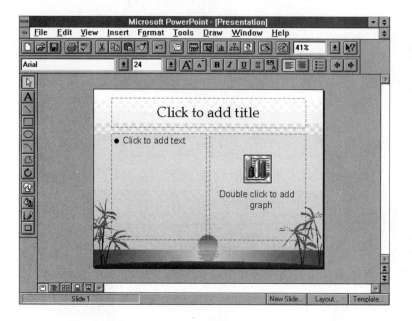

Autolayouts and placeholders are the keys to making your way through a presentation. When you select an autolayout and then click one of its placeholders, PowerPoint displays all the tools you need so that you don't have to hunt around for specific commands or toolbars.

Step 5: Adding Annotations and Graphic Embellishments

By step 5, you're ready to add the finishing touches to your presentation. The text and charts are complete, but you should take a moment to review each slide before continuing. On some slides, a little additional explanation might help the audience. With the Text Tool button on the Drawing toolbar, you can add free-floating blocks of text as annotations that highlight or explain a special feature. You can also use the Drawing toolbar to add graphics to accompany an image or text on a slide. The simplest case is a line that connects a text annotation to the subject it describes, such as the line connecting the label to the pie chart in the slide shown in Figure 2-8. But you can also draw more complex images with PowerPoint's drawing tools and commands.

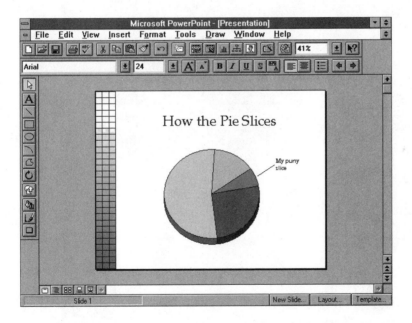

FIGURE 2-8.
A simple line connects a label to the pie chart in this slide.

If drawing is not your thing, you can take advantage of the ClipArt Gallery, which is PowerPoint's extensive library of ready-made images. PowerPoint organizes the images by category in the gallery, as shown in Figure 2-9 on the next page.

As Figure 2-10 shows, you can increase the effectiveness of a slide by adding a clip art image to the text.

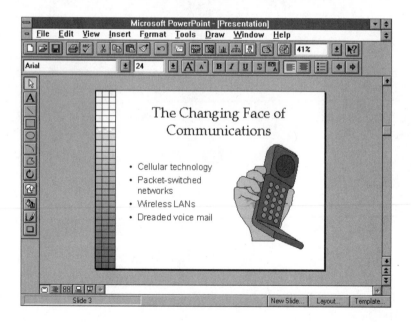

In addition to using clip art, you can also incorporate pictures you've drawn in other software programs and display photos you've scanned with a scanner. PowerPoint can import and display both drawings and bitmapped graphics from other applications.

See Also: For more information about clip art, see "Using the ClipArt Gallery," page 360.

Step 6: Tweaking the Presentation

What would you do with all that extra time if it weren't for last-minute changes? Because your presentation is stored electronically in PowerPoint rather than drawn on paper, you can make changes as easily as you edit a document in a word processor or update numbers in a spreadsheet.

If you started with the AutoContent Wizard, which applies its own design template, or if you started with a blank presentation that had no template attached, you might also want to make more discretionary modifications to the presentation at the last minute. No matter what the circumstances, PowerPoint's Slide Sorter view, shown in Figure 2-11, is the best place to see and make sweeping changes to your slides because you can view an entire segment of the

FIGURE 2-11.

Use Slide Sorter view to make sweeping changes to your entire presentation.

presentation at once. While in Slide Sorter view, you can also adjust the order of the slides or delete extraneous slides.

Step 7: Saving Your Work

To store a completed presentation, you save it in a file by clicking the Save button on the Standard toolbar or by choosing Save from the File menu. Each PowerPoint file holds an entire presentation's worth of slides, so you don't have to worry about lost slides the next time you display a presentation.

Step 8: Generating Printed Output, Slides, and Electronic Presentations

Even if it's just for immediate gratification, you'll probably want to print a set of slides as soon as they're complete. PowerPoint can print your slides on paper with just about any printer you install in Windows. Laser and ink-jet printers, today's business standards, produce especially attractive printouts.

PowerPoint is equally adept at generating 35-mm slides. Unfortunately, slides do not pop out of a slide-making device the same way that pages emerge from a printer. You must either attach a film recorder, which records your slides onto slide film that must then be developed, or you can send the presentation file to a service bureau that can create and develop the slides for you.

A special form of output, the electronic presentation, is quickly overtaking even slides in popularity. An electronic presentation displays images on the computer screen or on a large screen with the aid of a computer projector. Electronic presentations can incorporate fancy fades and slick transitions between slides, and they can play sound and video, too. Electronic presentations can also be interactive, so you can control their flow during the presentation, stepping back to a previous slide or advancing to an additional topic. What's more, in an electronic presentation, you can "drill down" to the spreadsheet file that contains the figures for a graph so that the audience can see the original worksheet. Best of all, electronic presentations can be updated at the very last second. You'd be surprised by how many concluding slides are prepared even while a presentation is in progress.

Step 9: Collecting Accolades

The final step is the easiest. Leave your phone line clear and your door open for the flood of praise that will come your way. With a PowerPoint presentation, you'll not only enlighten an audience but entertain them as well. So say goodbye to the chalkboard, flip chart, and Orator ball.

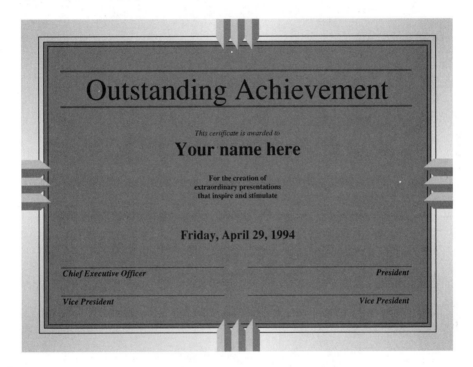

In the next chapter, you'll get an opportunity to try the procedures you've learned about here.

Creating the
Basic Presenation

3

Getting Started on the Presentation

f you're new to preparing presentations, you'll find PowerPoint at your side, ready to help you through the process step by step. If you're a presentation veteran, on the other hand, PowerPoint provides easy-to-use tools for performing familiar tasks. If you're somewhere in between, PowerPoint offers as much assistance as you need.

PowerPoint recognizes that creating a professional presentation involves two initial tasks: drafting the content and coming up with a consistent design. Amazingly, PowerPoint can help you with both of these tasks. It's easy to find a presentation graphics program that comes with a selection of professionally designed templates. But it's rare to find a program that helps you work out what to say and how to say it. So rare that only PowerPoint fits the bill.

In this chapter, you'll learn how to choose from among the options that PowerPoint presents whenever you start a new presentation. These options determine how much assistance PowerPoint provides as you get started creating the presentation. In the remaining chapters of this part of the book, you'll learn the next steps: working with the sample content PowerPoint provides, entering your own text, and adding graphs, organization charts, and other fancy visual effects.

Starting with the Presentation Content

When you have a good idea of the general content of your presentation, you can translate that idea into the beginnings of a PowerPoint presentation in three ways:

- You can use the AutoContent Wizard to help you select a ready-made presentation. It even helps you create the opening slide. The rest of the job—adapting the sample text; dropping in graphs, charts, and other elements; and revising the overall design—is up to you.

- If you've already created a presentation outline in Microsoft Word 6 for Windows, you can import it into PowerPoint's Outline view in one step. This option is often better than using the AutoContent Wizard because you start your work in PowerPoint with a specific outline instead of a generic sample. Adding graphs and other special elements and coming up with a design are still up to you.

■ You can start from scratch in PowerPoint, laying out the text in Outline view, and then dropping in graphs, pictures, annotations, and so forth in Slide view. After you complete the content, you can turn your attention to the design.

The first half of this chapter, which focuses on the content, explains each of these courses of action in more detail.

Using the AutoContent Wizard

PowerPoint can't possibly know what you need to say, but it does know how successful communicators organize their presentations. So, in the AutoContent Wizard, PowerPoint offers half a dozen tried-and-true predefined outlines as starting points for your own presentation. You can select one of these outlines:

■ Recommending a Strategy

■ Selling a Product, Service or Idea

■ Training

■ Reporting Progress

■ Communicating Bad News

■ General

To set up your presentation, the AutoContent Wizard does the following:

■ Asks for the title of the presentation (What are you going to talk about?)

■ Asks for other text for the title slide (a subtitle or footnote)

■ Asks you to select one of the six presentation types

■ Displays a general outline for the presentation in Outline view

To activate the AutoContent Wizard, follow these steps:

1. Start PowerPoint, or if PowerPoint is already on your screen, start a new presentation by clicking the New button on the Standard toolbar

or by choosing New from the File menu. If you just started PowerPoint, you'll see the PowerPoint dialog box shown earlier in Chapter 2. If you clicked the New button instead, you'll see the New Presentation dialog box shown here:

The first four options in the PowerPoint dialog box and the New Presentation dialog box are the same. (The fifth option in the Power-Point dialog box lets you open an existing presentation; the fifth option in the New Presentation dialog box lets you use the format of the current presentation in a new presentation.)

NOTE: PowerPoint can be set up so that you see the New Slide dialog box instead of the PowerPoint dialog box whenever you start a new PowerPoint session. If this is the case, you can redisplay the PowerPoint dialog box by choosing Options from the Tools menu, selecting the Show Startup Dialog option, and clicking OK. (Notice that you can also control the display of the New Slide dialog box.)

2. Be sure the AutoContent Wizard option is selected (click it if it's not) and then click OK, or double-click the AutoContent Wizard option. No matter how you activate the AutoContent Wizard, you see the dialog box displayed here:

The AutoContent Wizard has four steps, and the title bar of the dialog box shows the current step. At the bottom of the dialog box are a set of navigation buttons. Click Next or press N on your keyboard to get to the next step, click Back or press B on your keyboard to get to the previous step, or click Cancel or press Esc to close the AutoContent Wizard. The wizard has a default choice for each step along the way, so you can click Finish or press F on your keyboard at any step to use all the defaults for the remaining steps.

Use the AutoContent Wizard by following these instructions:

1. The Step 1 screen introduces you to the AutoContent Wizard. Click Next or press N to move to the Step 2 dialog box shown here:

2. In the Step 2 dialog box, answer the question *What are you going to talk about?* by typing a title for the presentation in the edit box. The text you enter will become the presentation title on the title slide.

3. Enter your name or your organization's name in the second edit box. The next time you use the AutoContent Wizard, PowerPoint will enter this name automatically. You can always type over the highlighted entry to change it.

> **TIP** You can replace the name in the edit box with text you want to use for a presentation subtitle. The text you enter will appear below the title on the title slide. You can always put your name or your organization's name in the third edit box, under *Other information you'd like to include?*

4. Enter an optional third line of text for the title slide in the third edit box, under *Other information you'd like to include?* This line of text will appear as the third line on the title slide.

5. Click Next or press Alt+N to get to this Step 3 dialog box, where you select a presentation type:

6. Click a presentation type to preview the titles of that presentation's slides in the box on the left.

7. Click the presentation type you want, and then click Next or press N. Or you can save time by clicking Finish or pressing F because Step 4 simply tells you that you've finished and gives you another chance to click the Finish button. The text of the new presentation appears in Outline view, as shown here:

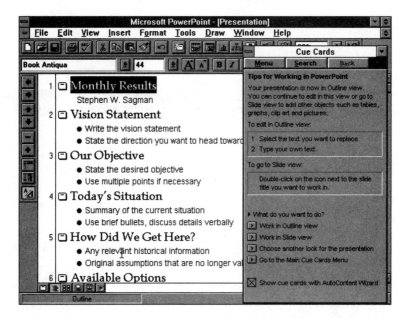

A Cue Cards window appears at the right side of the screen with some guidance about what you can do next. The Cue Cards window remains open to provide help with the task at hand until you close it by double-clicking the Control button at the left end of the window's title bar. After you become comfortable with the AutoContent Wizard, you can deselect the *Show cue cards with AutoContent Wizard* option at the bottom of the Cue Cards window.

You can press the Up and Down arrow keys, press the PgUp and PgDn keys, or use the vertical scroll bar within the presentation window to scroll through the entire presentation. Notice that the presentation includes suggestions for the content of each slide in addition to the slide titles.

See Also: For more information about cue cards, see "Using Cue Cards," page 24.

Behind the Scenes

The AutoContent Wizard is nothing more than a step-by-step procedure for using one of six presentation files stored in the WIZARDS subdirectory of the directory where you keep PowerPoint, and for displaying their text in Outline view. You can accomplish the same task manually by using the Open command on the File menu to open the file and then switching to Outline view. Table 3-1 lists the filenames of the presentation files stored in the WIZARDS subdirectory.

TABLE 3-1.
The presentation files used by the AutoContent Wizard.

Presentation Type	Presentation File
Recommending a Strategy	STRATEGY.PPT
Selling a Product, Service or Idea	SELLING.PPT
Training	TRAINING.PPT
Reporting Progress	PROGRESS.PPT
Communicating Bad News	BADNEWS.PPT
General	GENERAL.PPT

 TIP You can customize any presentation file used by the AutoContent Wizard in the WIZARDS subdirectory by modifying text on the slides or changing the template that gives the presentation its design. To customize an AutoContent presentation, first open one of the presentation files in the WIZARDS subdirectory. Then edit the text and/or change the template, and resave the file in the same directory without renaming it. The next time you use the AutoContent Wizard, you'll get the same six presentation types, but they'll reflect your customized changes.

Using an Outline from Microsoft Word

If you've prepared an outline for your presentation in Microsoft Word 6 for Windows, you can easily send the outline to PowerPoint by viewing the outline in Word and then clicking Word's Present It button. The Outline immediately shows up in PowerPoint's Outline view exactly as it appeared in Word. Level 1 headings become slide titles, and lower-level headings become indented bulleted items on the slides.

For more information about using existing outlines, see "Importing Outlines," page 86.

For more information about the Present It button, see "Installing the Present It Button in Word 6 for Windows," page 88.

Entering the Text from Scratch

When you know what you want to say and you just want to create the slides, you can always jump right into a new presentation and start entering the text from scratch. Simply follow these steps:

1. Start a new presentation by clicking the New button or choosing New from the File menu.

2. Instead of selecting AutoContent Wizard in the New Presentation dialog box, click one of the other three options:

   ❏ Pick a Look Wizard: Starts a wizard that helps you select a presentation design and output type (such as printed pages or an on-screen presentation), and sets up special formatting for the output type you've selected. You'll learn about this wizard in "Starting with the Presentation Design," page 50.

   ❏ Template: Opens the Presentation Template dialog box, where you can select a presentation design from the list of available templates. You'll learn about this dialog box in "Selecting a Presentation Template," page 54.

   ❏ Blank Presentation: Starts a new presentation without any design elements. When you click Blank Presentation, you can develop the content of the presentation first and then select a design later.

TIP If you are using a slower computer or a portable, you may want to select Blank Presentation. You can then enter the content of the presentation without seeing background colors and graphics, which take longer to draw on the screen.

No matter which option you select, PowerPoint displays the title slide of a new presentation in Slide view. You can switch to Outline view and concentrate on the text, or you can stay in Slide view and add slides one by one, entering text and graphics as you go.

For more information about Outline view, see Chapter 4, "Working with Text in Outline View," page 57.

For more information about Slide view, see Chapter 5, "Working with Text in Slide View," page 93.

Starting with the Presentation Design

If you want to see the presentation's design while working on its content, you can select a presentation template first. Each slide you create picks up the design of the template so that your presentation has a consistent look.

You can select a template in two ways:

- You can use the Pick a Look Wizard.

- You can select a template manually from a list.

If you'd rather not use one of PowerPoint's templates and if you're feeling creative, you can create a design from scratch.

Using the Pick a Look Wizard

The Pick a Look Wizard helps you select a template that has a design you like and that is appropriate for the type of output you plan to create. For example, if you plan to print black and white overheads on a laser printer, the wizard gives you a choice of templates that are appropriate for black and white printing. The Pick a Look Wizard also helps you set up a footer that appears on all slides and that can display the date, page number, and any special text you want to include, such as *Confidential*.

To activate the Pick a Look Wizard, follow these steps:

1. Start PowerPoint, or if PowerPoint is already on your screen, start a new presentation by clicking the New button on the Standard toolbar or by choosing New from the File menu.

2. In the PowerPoint or New Presentation dialog box, select Pick a Look Wizard and click OK, or double-click the Pick a Look Wizard option. You then see the first of nine dialog boxes, as shown below.

Use the Pick a Look Wizard by following these steps:

1. Click Next to get to this Step 2 dialog box, where the action begins:

2. Select the type of output you want—Black and White Overheads, Color Overheads, On-Screen Presentation, or 35mm Slides. (You can always switch to a different type of output later.

3. When you've made your selection, click Next or press N to move to this Step 3 dialog box:

4. Select one of the four named templates or click the More button to see a list of all the templates that are appropriate for the type of output you selected in the previous step. The list looks like the one shown here:

You can click any template name once to see a preview of its design in the box on the right. Double-click a name to select the template.

5. Click Next or press N to move to this Step 4 dialog box:

The Step 4 dialog box contains check boxes for four different output types—Full-Page Slides, Speaker's Notes, Audience Handout Pages, and Outline Pages—which are previewed in the boxes on the left. You can select as many of these output types as you plan to use. For each selected output type, the wizard will display another step that allows you to set up the content of the footer that will appear on your slides.

6. Click the check boxes for any output types you do *not* plan to use. (Clicking a check box that is already checked clears it.)

7. Click Next or press N to move to the next step, shown here:

8. Click the check boxes for the options that you do *not* want to appear in the footer of the first output type. If you leave the Name, company, or other text option selected, enter the text for the option in the edit box below.

9. Click Next or press N. If you selected other output types, you are asked to select footer options for them in successive steps.

10. When you get to the Step 9 dialog box, click Finish or press F to create the new presentation with the selected look. You'll see the first slide of the presentation in Slide view.

Selecting a Presentation Template

Selecting a template manually is the best strategy when you know the name of the template you want to use—perhaps you've used that template before, or perhaps someone gave you a special template that is customized for a particular project or for your organization. You can also use this option to select an existing presentation as a template. The custom changes you've made to the appearance of the existing presentation (its background design and colors, for example) will be transferred to the new presentation, but the content of the existing presentation won't. With this technique, you can start a new presentation that has the same design as an earlier presentation.

To select a presentation template manually, follow these steps:

1. Click the New button or choose New from the File menu.

2. In the New Presentation dialog box, select Template and click OK, or double-click the Template option. The Presentation Template dialog box appears, similar to the one shown here:

3. If necessary, double-click the TEMPLATE directory in the Directories list to display these three subdirectories:

Template Subdirectory	Description
bwovrhd	Templates for black and white overheads
clrovrhd	Templates for color overheads
sldshow	Templates for color slide shows

4. Double-click the subdirectory that contains templates for the type of presentation you plan to create.

5. Click each template's filename in the File Name list to see a preview of the template design in the box under the Help button. Then, when you find the template you want, double-click its filename, or click the filename and then click the Apply button.

 TIP To quickly scan through the list of templates, click a template and press the Up or Down arrow key to preview the other templates.

To use an existing presentation as a template for the design of a new presentation, follow one of these procedures:

- Open an existing presentation. Then start a new presentation, and in the New Presentation dialog box, select the Current Presentation Format option.

- Start a new presentation and select Template in the New Presentation dialog box. In the Presentation Template dialog box, navigate to the directory that contains the existing presentation's file, and then select the file by double-clicking its filename or by clicking its filename and then clicking Apply.

PowerPoint transfers the background design of the existing presentation, logos, and other design elements to the new presentation without any of the content, and opens the new presentation in Slide view.

Starting a Design from Scratch

If none of the templates suits your fancy or if you need to create a special presentation with a unique appearance, you can start with a blank presentation and then custom design the background, color scheme, and font choices.

To start with a blank presentation, follow these steps:

1. Click the New button or choose New from the File menu.

2. In the New Presentation dialog box, select Blank Presentation and click OK, or double-click the Blank Presentation option. The title slide of a new presentation appears in Slide view. The slide is completely devoid of design elements.

 For more information about changing the background, color scheme, and fonts of your presentation, see Chapter 9, "Making Overall Changes," page 217.

No matter what choices you make when starting a presentation, your next stop will probably be Outline view, where you can enter and edit the text that will form the backbone of your presentation. Chapter 4, "Working with Text in Outline View," is devoted to this next logical step. But if you want, you can skip Outline view and head straight to Slide view, where you can work on the slides of your new presentation one by one. In that case, Chapter 5, "Working with Text in Slide View," will give you the guidance you need.

4

Working with Text in Outline View

Chapter 3 introduced the three ways of producing the text of a presentation: using the AutoContent Wizard; importing an outline created in Microsoft Word 6 for Windows (or another application); and creating an outline from scratch in Outline view. The second and third methods are the topics of this chapter.

Starting a presentation in Outline view lets you mull over the themes and topics of the presentation, hone the flow of your arguments before you worry about how the presentation will look, and build a case that will be overwhelmingly persuasive. That, after all, is the purpose of a presentation. If you don't start the presentation in Outline view, you can always switch to it to gain these advantages:

- In Outline view, you see only the presentation text—you don't see graphs, tables, or the design elements of the presentation, such as the background design. So you can concentrate on the content of the presentation without being distracted by its appearance.

- In Outline view, you can easily enter the list of main topics of your presentation. Entering the main topics generates all the presentation slides you need because each main topic becomes the title of a slide in other views.

- In Outline view, you can easily rearrange the topics, thereby changing the order in which you will address issues in the presentation. You can enter supporting statements that will become bulleted items on the slides, and you can move the statements from topic to topic until you are sure a discussion point is addressed in just the right spot during the presentation.

Figure 4-1 on the next page shows the topics and supporting statements of a presentation in Outline view. Figure 4-2, also on the next page, shows the resulting titles and bulleted items on slides in Slide Sorter view.

FIGURE 4-1.
A presentation
outline in Outline
view.

FIGURE 4-2.
The slides in Slide
Sorter view.

Switching to Outline View

If you use the AutoContent Wizard to start a new presentation, it leaves you in Outline view automatically because the wizard assumes that you want to customize the presentation's generic text before you go on to other tasks. If you start by using the Pick a Look Wizard or a design template from the library of templates, or if you start with a blank presentation, you may want to switch to Outline view immediately, where you can brainstorm the topics you'll cover in the presentation and enter text to support each topic. After you finish with the text in Outline view, you can turn your attention to creating graphs and tables for information that is not easily communicated with words.

Assuming that you have launched PowerPoint and started a new presentation, here's how to switch to Outline view at any time: With the title slide on the screen, click the Outline View button in the lower left corner of the presentation window or choose Outline from the View menu.

Outline View

If you have been dropped off in Outline view by the AutoContent Wizard, the next step is to edit the sample text. If you have switched to Outline view after starting a new presentation using one of the other methods, you are ready to begin entering text in a new outline.

When you switch to Outline view to begin a new presentation, the insertion point is positioned beside blank slide number 1, as shown in Figure 4-3 on the next page. When you begin typing, PowerPoint inserts your text at the insertion point. A special Outlining toolbar replaces the Drawing toolbar on the left side of the presentation window.

Promote (Indent less)
Demote (Indent more)
Move Up
Move Down
Collapse Selection
Expand Selection
Show Titles
Show All
Show Formatting

Insertion point

FIGURE 4-3.
Starting a new presentation in Outline view.

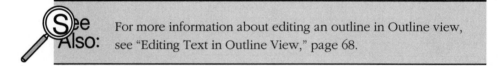

For more information about editing an outline in Outline view, see "Editing Text in Outline View," page 68.

Entering the Main Topics

The first step in creating a presentation in Outline view is to enter a title for the presentation and a list of the topics you plan to discuss. The title and topics become your preliminary slide titles. Don't worry about entering the topics in exact order. You can always rearrange them later.

To enter the topics you'll cover in your presentation, follow these steps:

1. Type the presentation title on the first line of the outline, and then press Enter to move to the second line, where slide number 2 appears, as shown here:

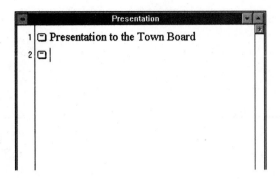

2. Type the first topic, and press Enter. If you don't yet have a topic precisely pinned down, type a two- or three-word placeholder. You can always edit it later.

3. Type the next topic, and press Enter.

4. Type the topic for each successive slide, pressing Enter after each one except the last.

Figure 4-4 shows a completed list of topics for a presentation about the construction of a new store.

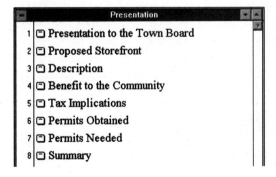

FIGURE 4-4.
A list of topics for the slides of a new presentation.

TIP   On each slide, use the fewest words possible to communicate your message. The fewer words, the more impact the text has, and the larger and more readable it can be. Try to write newspaper-like headlines, not whole sentences. Write *Profits up 26%* rather than *Our profits increased by 26%*.

Next, examine your list of topics to determine the best way to communicate to your audience. Some topics are best conveyed with a few bulleted items you can add below the topics. Other topics involve numeric data. Later, you can switch to Slide view and add graphs or tables to these slides to bring the numbers to life. You can also add organization charts and drawings.

 TIP   If your presentation outline has many topics, you may want to use the Zoom Control box on the Standard toolbar or the Zoom command on the View menu to reduce the magnification of the text so that more of it fits on the screen. For more information about zooming, see the sidebar titled "Zooming In and Out," page 73.

The Outline View–Slide View Connection

Each main topic entered in a presentation in Outline view becomes a title on a slide in Slide view. Similarly, each supporting statement entered under a main topic in Outline view becomes a bulleted item on a slide in Slide view. This connection between Outline view and Slide view is a two-way street. If you edit a title or bulleted item in Slide view, the changes you make show up in Outline view as well.

Adding Bulleted Items

After entering a list of topics, you're ready to enter the supporting statements for those topics.

To add bulleted items under a topic, follow these steps:

1. In Outline view, move the insertion point to the end of the topic that requires bulleted items. (The fastest way is to click at the end of the line, but you can also move the insertion point to the desired line with the Up or Down arrow keys, and then press the End key.)

2. Press Enter to create a new line. PowerPoint thinks you want to insert a new topic, so it adds a slide icon and renumbers the existing topic, as shown here:

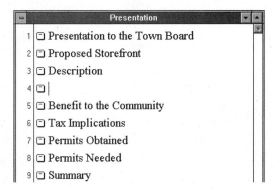

3. Click the Demote button on the Outlining toolbar or press the Tab key to move the insertion point to the right one level. PowerPoint removes the slide icon, readjusts the numbers, and inserts a bullet, as shown here:

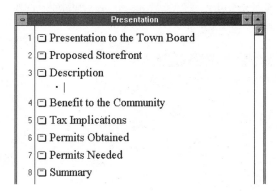

4. Type the first bulleted item. If you type more text than will fit on one line, the text wraps to the next line.

5. Press Enter to start another bulleted item.

6. Repeat steps 4 and 5 until you've added all the bulleted items you need.

Figure 4-5 on the next page shows the completed set of bulleted items for the third slide of the store-construction presentation.

FIGURE 4-5.

A complete set of
bulleted items.

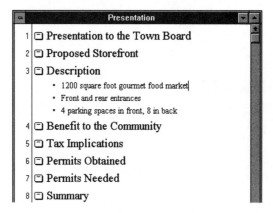

NOTE: Text indented under the presentation title on slide 1 is not given a bullet; it becomes a subtitle on slide 1.

If you add bulleted items below the last topic of your outline and then you want to add a new topic, press Enter at the end of the last bulleted item, and then click the Promote button on the Outlining toolbar or press Shift+Tab to move the insertion point to the left one level. Then type the new topic. For example, Figure 4-6 shows the store-construction presentation with a new topic added after the bulleted items for slide number 8.

FIGURE 4-6.

Press Enter and
click the Promote
button after typing a
bulleted item to add
another slide.

You can have five levels of bulleted items on a slide, as shown in Figure 4-7. Each level is indented from the preceding level and has its own default bullet style. To demote a bulleted item one level, thereby indenting it farther to

FIGURE 4-7.

The five levels of
bulleted items.

7 ☐ **Permits Needed**
- State Permits
  - Retail Certificate
    - Food Handling Approval
      - Servers
      - Food Preparers
        - Chefs
        - Sous Chefs
- County Permits
  - Retail Certificate

the right, click the Demote button on the Outlining toolbar or press Tab before typing the bulleted item. Click the Promote button on the Outlining toolbar or press Shift+Tab to promote a bulleted item one level. With five indent levels, you can have points under the main topics, subpoints under the points, and so on. But don't get carried away. Remember, when it comes to presentations, less is more.

TIP   To demote or promote an existing bulleted item, place the insertion point anywhere in the item, and click the Demote or Promote button or press Tab or Shift+Tab.

TIP   Typing all the topics and then adding bulleted items is one approach to creating the outline. The advantage of this approach is that you can reorganize the list of main topics before adding any detail to the presentation. (For information about reorganizing the outline, see "Reorganizing Text in Outline View," page 77.) Another approach is to enter a topic and then press Tab to enter its supporting bulleted items. Then, after the last bulleted item, press Shift+Tab and type the next topic. When you finish the last topic, you can still reorganize the presentation before switching to Slide view, where the topics become slide titles and where you can add graphs, tables, and other elements.

Editing Text in Outline View

After you've entered topics and bulleted items, you can revise the text to reword entries or make corrections. To edit text in Outline view, you must first move the insertion point to the spot that needs editing. The simplest way is to click an insertion point in the text. For example, clicking to the left of the *B* in *Board* positions the insertion point as shown in Figure 4-8.

FIGURE 4-8.

An insertion point appears where you click.

You can also move the insertion point with the keyboard by using one of the keys or key combinations listed in Table 4-1.

TABLE 4-1.

Keys and key combinations for moving the insertion point.

Key or Key Combination	Moves the Insertion Point
Left, Right, Up, or Down arrow key	One character left or right or one line up or down
Ctrl+Left arrow key	To the beginning of the previous word
Ctrl+Right arrow key	To the beginning of the next word
Ctrl+Up arrow key	To the beginning of the current topic (or to the beginning of the previous topic if the insertion point is already in a topic)
Ctrl+Down arrow key	To the beginning of the next topic
Home	To the beginning of the current line
End	To the end of the current line
Ctrl+Home	To the top of the outline
Ctrl+End	To the bottom of the outline

After correctly positioning the insertion point, simply start typing to insert text. You can press the Backspace key to delete the character to the left of the insertion point, or you can press the Delete key to delete the character to the right of the insertion point. You can also press Ctrl+Backspace to delete the word to the left and Ctrl+Delete to delete the word to the right.

NOTE: Unlike Microsoft Word for Windows, PowerPoint is always in Insert mode. Anything you type is inserted at the insertion point. You cannot press the Insert key to switch to Overtype mode.

Selecting Text for Editing

In PowerPoint, as in other Windows-based applications, the easiest way to make more drastic editing changes is to select the text you want to modify so that your changes affect the entire selection rather than single characters.

To select a block of text with the mouse, click to the left of the first character in the block, hold down the left mouse button, and then drag across the text past the last character in the block. PowerPoint highlights the text as the mouse pointer passes across it, as shown in Figure 4-9. To select more than one line, drag down to the next line. Note that if you select a single word in one topic and then drag down to the next line, the entire first topic is selected.

FIGURE 4-9.
Selected text.

TIP   You can select a single word and its trailing space by double-clicking the word. You can select a series of words by double-clicking the first word, holding down the mouse button on the second click, and dragging across the remaining words. To select all of the text that follows a bullet, click the bullet once; to select a topic and all of its bulleted items, click the slide icon to the left of the topic text. You can select the entire presentation by choosing Select All from the Edit menu or by pressing Ctrl+A.

A special PowerPoint option called Automatic Word Selection makes it easy to select multiple words with the mouse. When you drag across any part of a word and continue to drag to the next word, PowerPoint selects both the first and second words. If you want to select an entire sentence, all you have to do is click anywhere in the first word and then drag to anywhere within the last word. PowerPoint then highlights the first and last words and all of the words in between. This option is on by default. To disable Automatic Word Selection, choose the Options command from the Tools menu, deselect the Automatic Word Selection option, and click OK.

If you have trouble dragging across the text without also selecting part of the line above or below, you're not alone. You may want to use this technique instead: Click anywhere in the first word you want to select, hold down the Shift key, and then click anywhere in the last word of the block you want to select. PowerPoint highlights the first word, the last word, and all of the text in between. This technique does not work if the Automatic Word Selection option is turned off.

 TIP   You can select text with the keyboard by moving the insertion point to the beginning of the text you want to select, holding down the Shift key, and then using the keys and key combinations listed earlier in Table 4-1 to move the insertion point to the end of the desired text block.

To practice selecting and editing text, you can try this example: Start a new presentation, and use the AutoContent Wizard to load the presentation called *Selling a Product, Service or Idea.* When the presentation appears in Outline view, click an insertion point in the *Objective* topic. Press the End key to move the insertion point to the end of the line, and then type an *s* to change the last word to *Objectives.* Next, click the bullet in front of *State the desired objective* to select the entire line, and then type *To make you happy* to replace the selected text.

Later in this chapter, you'll make further changes to the outline, so you might want to save the presentation now by choosing Save As from the File menu and entering a filename.

Moving and Copying Text

Want to take the easiest and most direct approach to moving or copying selected text to another position within the outline? Then drag-and-drop editing is for you.

To move text using drag and drop, follow these steps:

1. Select the text you want to move or copy.

2. Point to the selected text. The I-beam changes to a hollow arrow, as shown here:

3. Hold down the mouse button, drag the pointer to the destination for the selected text, and release the mouse button. The text appears in its new location, as shown here:

To copy text using drag and drop, follow the same procedure, but hold down the Ctrl key while dragging the pointer. With drag and drop, you can drag text clear to another slide.

In addition to using the drag-and-drop techniques, you can move or copy selected text using the following methods:

■ To *move* selected text, start by clicking the Cut button on the Standard toolbar, choosing Cut from the Edit menu, or pressing Ctrl+X. Then move the insertion point to the destination for the text (even if it's on another slide), and click the Paste button on the Standard toolbar, choose Paste from the Edit menu, or press Ctrl+V.

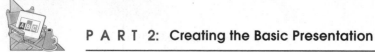

■ To *copy* selected text, start by clicking the Copy button on the Standard toolbar, choosing Copy from the Edit menu, or pressing Ctrl+C. Then move the insertion point to the destination for the text, and click the Paste button, choose Paste from the Edit menu, or press Ctrl+V.

The Cut, Copy, and Paste commands are available on the text shortcut menu as well as the Edit menu. To use a shortcut menu, select an object or text, and then click the right mouse button. A menu pops up with options that are relevant to the object or text.

For example, to use the shortcut menu to move or copy a text selection, follow these steps:

1. Select the text you want to move or copy.

2. Click the right mouse button. This shortcut menu appears:

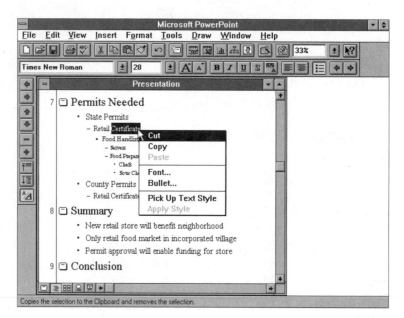

3. Choose Cut or Copy.

4. Move the insertion point to the destination for the text.

5. Click the right mouse button to open the shortcut menu again, and then choose Paste.

Zooming In and Out

While working in Outline view, you can use the Zoom Control box on the Standard toolbar, shown below, to change the magnification level, or zoom percentage, of your view of the outline. When you use a higher zoom percentage, the text becomes larger. Use a smaller zoom percentage to fit more text on the screen.

To change the zoom percentage, click the current percentage number in the Zoom Control box on the Standard toolbar, type a new zoom percentage, and press Enter. To select a preset magnification level, click the arrow to the right of the Zoom Control box, and then select one of the zoom percentages from the drop-down list.

You can also change the zoom percentage by first choosing Zoom from the View menu to display the Zoom dialog box shown below:

Then select one of the Zoom To percentages or edit the number in the Percent edit box. You can also click the arrows to the right of the Percent edit box to adjust the percentage up or down by one. Click OK to implement the new zoom percentage.

By default, Outline view uses a smaller zoom percentage than Slide view so that you can see more of your outline on the screen at one time. If you make Outline view's zoom percentage the same as Slide view's, the text size is identical in both views.

Deleting Text

To delete selected text, simply press the Delete key or the Backspace key. You can also click the Cut button on the Standard toolbar, choose Cut or Clear from the Edit menu, or press Ctrl+X.

Undoing Editing

Retrieving something you've deleted is as simple as clicking the Undo button on the Standard toolbar, choosing Undo from the Edit menu, or pressing Ctrl+Z. You can undo almost anything you've just done in PowerPoint.

Finding and Replacing Text

While editing an outline, you can search for a word or a string of characters and you can replace it with another. For example, you can use the Find command to find a former client's name in a presentation, and then use the Replace command to replace that name with a new client's name throughout the presentation.

To find text, follow these steps:

1. Choose Find from the Edit menu or press Ctrl+F. PowerPoint displays the Find dialog box, shown here:

2. Enter the text you want to find in the Find What edit box.

3. Finally, click Find Next or press Enter.

To have PowerPoint find only those words or strings of characters that match the capitalization entered in the Find What edit box, select the Match Case option. (Then PowerPoint will not find *Man* when you entered *man.*) To have PowerPoint find the text you've entered only when it is a whole word rather than part of a word, select the Find Whole Words Only option. (Then PowerPoint will not find *constitutional* when you entered *constitution.*)

To replace text, follow these steps:

1. Choose Replace from the Edit menu or press Ctrl+H. PowerPoint displays the Replace dialog box shown here:

2. Enter the text you want to replace in the Find What edit box.

3. Enter the replacement text in the Replace With edit box.

4. Click the Find Next button.

5. When PowerPoint locates the Find What text, click the Replace button to substitute the Replace With text.

To replace every occurrence of the Find What text throughout the presentation, click the Replace All button instead of the Find Next button and the Replace button. You may want to use the Match Case option and the Find Whole Words Only option to be sure you do not inadvertently replace text that does not exactly match the Find What text.

PowerPoint keeps a log of the text you have searched for or used as a replacement. To perform the same search or replace again, open the Find dialog box or the Replace dialog box, click the down arrow next to the Find What edit box or Replace With edit box, and then select a previous entry from the drop-down list.

Checking the Spelling of Presentation Text

Before your presentation goes public, take a moment to use PowerPoint's very capable spelling checker. Nothing looms larger than a silly little typo when it is projected full-screen.

To spell-check a presentation, follow the steps on the next page.

1. Click the Spelling button on the Standard toolbar, choose Spelling from the Tools menu, or press F7. PowerPoint checks each word against two dictionaries: the main dictionary and a supplemental dictionary called CUSTOM.DIC, which is empty until you add words to it. When Power-Point finds a word it considers misspelled, it displays the Spelling dialog box shown here:

The questionable word is displayed in the Not in Dictionary edit box. The first and most strongly suggested replacement is highlighted in the Suggestions list and appears in the Change To edit box.

2. Indicate what you want PowerPoint to do next:

   ❏ If you know that the word is spelled correctly—if the word is a company name, for example—then click the Ignore button.

   ❏ If the word is spelled correctly and occurs frequently in this presentation, you may want to click Ignore All instead of Ignore.

   ❏ If the word is spelled correctly and occurs frequently in other presentations, you can click Add to add the word to a custom dictionary. In future spelling checks, the word will not be flagged as a misspelling.

   ❏ If the word is misspelled and you want to change it to the word in the Change To edit box, click Change.

   ❏ If the word is misspelled and you want to make the same change throughout the presentation, click Change All instead.

3. When PowerPoint completes the spelling check of the presentation, it informs you with an on-screen message. Click OK to remove the message and return to your outline.

Using Custom Dictionaries

When you click the Add button to add a word to a custom dictionary, the word is added to the dictionary file listed in the Add Words To box in the Spelling dialog box. The default custom dictionary is CUSTOM.DIC, the same custom dictionary file used by Microsoft Word and other Microsoft Office applications. If you have created custom dictionaries in another Microsoft Office application, you can select one of those dictionaries from the Add Words To drop-down list. If you enter words in a custom dictionary while working in another Microsoft Office application, those words won't be flagged as incorrect in PowerPoint either.

WARNING: PowerPoint cannot check the spelling of text in graphs, organization charts, and tables. It also cannot check the spelling of text in objects created in other applications that are embedded in PowerPoint.

If the presentation you are creating is strictly text, as most presentations are, and you do not need to reorganize the text, then your basic presentation is complete. You can skip ahead to Chapter 9 and beyond. But if you want to format your slides or add graphs, organization charts, or tables to your presentation, take a close look at the next four chapters.

Reorganizing Text in Outline View

The power of Outline view becomes obvious as soon as you need to reorganize the text of a presentation. You can change the order of the topics covered in the presentation, change the order of bulleted items under individual topics, and even move bulleted items from one topic to another. You can also delete topics, duplicate topics, and insert new topics.

Selecting Topics and Bulleted Items

Before you can reorganize a presentation, you must select the element you want to work with. You can select an entire topic (the topic text and its bulleted items), several topics, or one or more bulleted items within a topic.

To select an entire topic, you can use any of the following methods:

■ Click the slide number or click the space to the left of the slide number.

■ Click the slide icon to the left of the topic.

■ Triple-click the topic text.

■ Click the topic text, and press Ctrl+Shift+Down arrow key.

Whichever method you use, the result is similar to that shown in Figure 4-10.

FIGURE 4-10.
A selected topic.

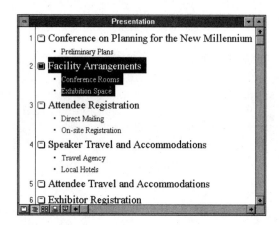

To select multiple slides, you can use one of these methods:

■ Hold down the Shift key while clicking each slide's icon.

■ If the slides are consecutive, point to the left of the first slide number, hold down the mouse button, and drag downward in the space to the left of the slides you want to select.

To select a bulleted item, as shown in Figure 4-11, you can do one of the following:

■ Click in the space to the left of the text but to the right of the vertical line that separates the slide number and the slide icon. This method selects the bulleted item and any items indented below it.

■ Triple-click a word to select the entire bulleted item. Any items indented below it are also selected.

■ Drag through the text of the bulleted item with the mouse.

■ Click the first word of the bulleted item, hold down the Shift key, and then click the last word.

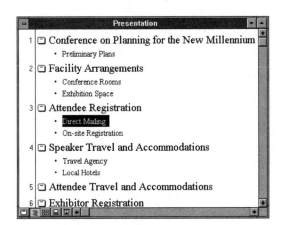

FIGURE 4-11.
A selected bulleted item.

■ Position the insertion point at the beginning of the bulleted item, hold down the Shift key, and use the keyboard to move the insertion point to the end of the bulleted item.

Reordering Topics and Bulleted Items

After you select a topic or a bulleted item, you can move it up or down in the outline to solidify the logic of your presentation. For example, you can move a touchy topic to the front of a presentation to get it over with early. Then move some good news to the end so that your audience can leave on a high.

To move an entire topic, follow these steps:

1. Point to the slide icon for the selected topic.

2. Hold down the mouse button, and drag up or down. When you drag, the pointer becomes a double arrow, and a horizontal line indicates where the topic will drop when you release the mouse button.

3. Release the mouse button. The topic and its bulleted items move to the new position.

For example, Figure 4-12 on the next page shows the result after the Attendee Registration topic is moved down in the New Millennium Conference presentation.

You can also move the selected topic up or down by clicking the Move Up or Move Down button on the Outlining toolbar at the left side of the presentation window. In fact, if you've selected multiple topics, you *must* use the Move Up or Move Down button to move them.

FIGURE 4-12.

Dragging a selected topic's slide icon moves the topic within the presentation.

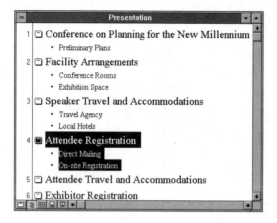

```
┌─────────────────────────────────────────┐
│  ▫              Presentation        ▼ ▲  │
├─────────────────────────────────────────┤
│ 1 │▭ Conference on Planning for the New Millennium │
│        • Preliminary Plans               │
│ 2 │▭ Facility Arrangements               │
│        • Conference Rooms                │
│        • Exhibition Space                │
│ 3 │▭ Speaker Travel and Accommodations   │
│        • Travel Agency                   │
│        • Local Hotels                    │
│ 4 │▣ Attendee Registration               │
│        • Direct Mailing                  │
│        • On-site Registration            │
│ 5 │▭ Attendee Travel and Accommodations  │
│ 6 │▭ Exhibitor Registration              │
└─────────────────────────────────────────┘
```

You can change the order of entire topics just as easily in Slide Sorter view. But what makes Outline view special is that you can reorder bulleted items under a topic and move them from topic to topic, as well as reorder entire topics. To move a bulleted item up or down, follow these steps:

1. Select the bulleted item.

2. Click the Move Up button or the Move Down button until the bulleted item is positioned where you want it. Alternatively, point to the left of the bulleted item, hold down the mouse button, and drag up or down in the outline. Release the mouse button when the bulleted item is in the correct position.

Using either the mouse or the button technique, you can move the selected bulleted item all the way to another topic if you want. Working this way in Outline view saves you from having to cut and paste text from one slide to another in Slide view.

TIP   If you want to use the keyboard to organize the outline, you can press Alt+Shift+Up arrow to move selected text up and Alt+Shift+Down arrow to move selected text down. (These are the same key combinations used to reorganize outlines in Microsoft Word for Windows.)

Now try reorganizing the outline you've started. Load the presentation you created earlier in this chapter, and click the slide icon for slide 2. All the text related to the *Objectives* topic is now selected. Point to the slide icon, hold down the mouse button, and drag down to just below the last text item on slide 3. As you drag, a horizontal line shows where the text will drop. Release the mouse button. *Objectives* becomes slide 3, and *Customer Requirements* becomes slide 2.

Now try moving a bulleted text item from one topic to another. Click the bullet at the beginning of *This section may require multiple slides,* on slide 4. Drag the bullet up and drop it under *Customer Requirements* on slide 2. Be sure to save the presentation again because you'll have the opportunity to make further changes later in this chapter.

Promoting and Demoting Topics and Bulleted Items

Earlier in the chapter, you learned that *promoting* text moves it to the left one level and *demoting* text moves it to the right one level. If you need to split a topic into two slides, you can promote one of the bulleted items to the main topic level to start a new slide. When an existing topic should be a supporting statement for the previous topic, you can demote it to a bulleted item.

To promote a bulleted item, select it and then do one of the following:

■ Click the Promote button.

■ Click just to the left of the item, hold down the mouse button, and drag to the left.

■ Press Alt+Shift+Left arrow.

Figure 4-13 on the next page shows the result after the second bulleted item under Facility Arrangements in the New Millennium Conference presentation is promoted to a topic. As you can see, a new slide number and slide icon appear to the left of the promoted text, which becomes the title of a new slide in Slide view.

To demote a topic or bulleted item, select it and do one of the following:

■ Click the Demote button.

FIGURE 4-13.

Promoting a
bulleted item
creates a new topic
on a new slide.

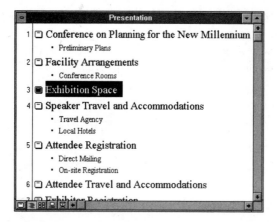

- Click to the left of the selected text, hold down the mouse button, and drag to the right.

- Press Alt+Shift+Right arrow.

All of the promotion and demotion techniques discussed so far promote or demote not only the selected text but also bulleted items below the selected text. What if you want to promote or demote a line but leave any subpoints at their current levels? You can click once anywhere in a topic or bulleted item, and then press the Tab key to demote the line, or press Shift+Tab to promote the line without affecting any subordinate text.

> **WARNING:** Don't select any text on the line before pressing Tab or Shift+Tab. If you do, the selected text will be replaced by a tab when you press the Tab key.

Be aware when you are organizing topics and bulleted items that you can fit only a certain amount of text on any one slide. For example, in the presentation on the left in Figure 4-14, the list of bulleted items under the topic *What I Love About New York* is far too long. To get all these points across, move the insertion point to the end of *The action,* and press Enter to start a new bulleted item. Then type *What I Love to Do in New York* as a new bulleted item. Finally, drag the bullet in front of the new bulleted item to the left one level so that the bulleted item becomes a new main topic. The outline then looks as shown on the right in Figure 4-14.

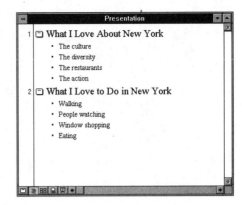

FIGURE 4-14.
A long list of bulleted items (left) divided between two slides for greater impact (right).

Hiding and Revealing Detail

Sometimes you need to step back to see the big picture while working on a presentation outline. If the entire outline is displayed, the volume of detail can muddle the big themes. By *collapsing* bulleted items, you can temporarily hide them from view and show only the larger topics. To redisplay the bulleted items, you *expand* them. You can collapse and expand outlines using the Collapse Selection button and the Expand Selection button on the Outlining toolbar:

To collapse bulleted items under a topic, follow these steps:

1. Click anywhere in the topic or click the slide icon to the left of the topic.

2. Click the Collapse Selection button or press Alt+Shift+Minus. Power-Point draws a gray line under the topic to indicate the presence of collapsed bulleted items, as shown here:

To expand the collapsed bulleted items, follow these steps:

1. Click anywhere in the topic.

2. Click the Expand Selection button or press Alt+Shift+Plus.

> **TIP** When you collapse bulleted items under a topic, they remain an intrinsic part of the topic. If you move that topic, the collapsed bulleted items also move. In fact, you may find it easier to reorganize a presentation with many bulleted items if you collapse them under their topics and then re-order the topics.

To quickly collapse all bulleted items under their topics, click the Show Titles button or press Alt+Shift+1. Then to expand all of the items again, click the Show All button or press Alt+Shift+A.

Try hiding detail in this chapter's sample presentation. With the presentation displayed on your screen in Outline view, click the Show Titles button on the Outlining toolbar to show only the main topics. Drag topic 2, *Customer Requirements,* to just after topic 3, *Objectives.* Then click the Expand Selection button on the Outlining toolbar to see that the collapsed bulleted items have come along for the ride. Finally, click the Show All button on the Outlining toolbar to redisplay all the presentation text.

You may want to save the sample presentation you've made for posterity, but you'll be making no further changes to it in this chapter.

Formatting Text in Outline View

Slide view is usually the best place to format the text of a presentation because you can see how the text fits with the background design. However, while entering and editing the presentation in Outline view, you can format any words or characters that are sure to need it. For example, you can italicize a special term or superscript a character in a formula name.

To format text in Outline view, you must first select it. Then you can use the character formatting buttons on the Formatting toolbar or the character formatting commands on either the Format menu or the shortcut menu. For example, choosing the Font command from the Format menu or the shortcut menu displays the Font dialog box shown in Figure 4-15. The character formatting buttons and commands work the same way in both Outline view and Slide view.

FIGURE 4-15.
The Font dialog box.

NOTE: The Shadow option and Emboss option in the Font dialog box are not available in Outline view. These effects can only be applied in Slide view.

Whether you apply character formatting in Outline view or in Slide view, you can display the outline in Outline view without character formatting. Just click the Show Formatting button on the Outlining toolbar or press the slash key above the numeric keypad on your keyboard. The Font box and Font Size box on the Formatting toolbar still show accurate information about the selected text, but the entire outline is displayed in a standard font and size (Arial, 28 points). To redisplay the character formatting in Outline view, click the Show Formatting button or press the slash key again.

 See Also: For more information about selecting text, see "Selecting Text for Editing," page 69.

For more information about formatting text, see "Formatting Text in Slide View," page 105.

Importing Outlines

If you have already created a perfectly good outline in another application, it would be tedious to have to recreate it in PowerPoint. And you don't have to. You can import the outline as a starting point for your presentation.

Importing a Microsoft Word 6 for Windows Outline

You can generate a presentation outline in Microsoft Word 6 for Windows and then easily export the outline to PowerPoint. Developing the outline in Word for Windows lets you take advantage of Word's sophisticated text capabilities. For example, you can use the thesaurus to replace ordinary outline words with vibrant, vigorous, pulsating, dynamic, energetic words.

Because PowerPoint imports Word outlines so easily, anyone can generate an entire text presentation in Word and hand the file over to you. You can then import the outline, give the presentation a distinctive look, and generate slides in no time.

To import a Word 6 for Windows outline:

1. View the outline in Word.

2. Click the Present It button. (If you don't see the Present It button, you must install it on the Standard toolbar by following the procedure described in the next section.) Word opens PowerPoint if necessary, opens a new presentation in Outline view, and "exports" the outline to PowerPoint.

For example, Figure 4-16 shows an outline in Word 6 for Windows. Figure 4-17 shows the same outline after it has been imported into PowerPoint.

 TIP A super-slick method you can use to create a new PowerPoint presentation from a Word outline is to drag and drop the Word outline file from the Windows File Manager to the PowerPoint window. A new presentation opens in PowerPoint with the Word outline in place.

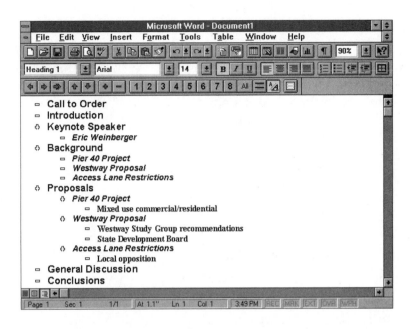

FIGURE 4-16.
An outline in
Microsoft Word 6
for Windows.

FIGURE 4-17.
The Word outline in
PowerPoint.

NOTE: Imported outlines can have up to nine indent levels.
However, when you import the outline into PowerPoint, levels
beyond level five are converted to fifth level entries.

Installing the Present It Button in Word 6 for Windows

The Present It button does not appear on a Word 6 for Windows toolbar until you put it there. The fairly long installation procedure involves copying the Present It toolbar and PresentIt macro from a template called CONVERT.DOT that ships with Word. You can copy the toolbar and macro to an existing document to make the Present It button available while you are working on the document. Or you can copy the toolbar and macro to the NORMAL.DOT template so that you can use the Present It button whenever you are working in Word.

To copy the toolbar and macro to the NORMAL.DOT template, you must first open the NORMAL.DOT template for editing. Follow these steps:

1. Start Word.

2. From the File menu, choose the Open command, and in the Open dialog box, select Document Templates (*.dot) from the List Files of Type drop-down list.

3. In the Directories list, double-click the TEMPLATE subdirectory of the directory in which you keep the Word files (probably WINWORD or WINWORD6), and in the File Name list, double-click NORMAL.DOT. The NORMAL.DOT template opens in a window, ready for editing.

The second step is to copy the Present It toolbar and PresentIt macro from CONVERT.DOT to NORMAL.DOT. Follow these steps:

1. From the File menu, choose Templates.

2. In the Templates and Add-ins dialog box, click the Organizer button.

3. On the Styles tab of the Organizer dialog box, click the Open File button on the right.

4. In the Open dialog box, double-click NORMAL.DOT in the File Name list.

5. Click the Close File button on the left to close NORMAL.DOT.

6. Now click the Open File button on the left.

7. In the Open dialog box, double-click the directory where you keep the Word 6 for Windows files (probably WINWORD or WINWORD6).

8. Double-click the MACROS subdirectory.

9. Double-click CONVERT.DOT in the list of filenames in the MACROS subdirectory.

10. Click the Toolbars tab in the Organizer dialog box.

11. In the CONVERT.DOT list box, click Present It and then click the Copy button to copy the toolbar to NORMAL.DOT on the right.

12. Click the Macros tab in the Organizer dialog box.

13. In the CONVERT.DOT list box, click the PresentIt macro, and then click the Copy button to copy the macro to the NORMAL.DOT list box on the right.

14. Click Close to close the Organizer dialog box.

Next, you must move the Present It button to Word's Standard toolbar. Follow these steps:

1. From the View menu, choose Toolbars.

2. Select the Present It option, and click OK. The Present It toolbar appears, displaying its single button.

3. Hold down the Alt key, and drag the Present It button from the Present It toolbar to any location on the Standard toolbar.

4. From the View menu, choose Toolbars, deselect the Present It option, and click OK.

The last step is to save the NORMAL.DOT template with the new button and macro.

1. From the File menu, choose Save.

2. From the File menu, choose Close to close the NORMAL.DOT template.

Importing an Outline from Another Application

You can import an outline from just about any word processing program as well as from other presentation applications that can export their presentation outlines. If the application can generate an RTF (Rich Text Format) file, you should use that format when saving the outline on disk. When you import the file, PowerPoint uses the styles in the file to determine the outline structure. For example, a Heading 1 style becomes a slide title, a Heading 2 style becomes an indented bulleted item, and so on. If the file contains no styles, PowerPoint uses the paragraph indents to determine the outline structure.

If the application cannot generate an RTF file, you should generate a plain ASCII text file. PowerPoint then picks up the outline structure from the tabs at the beginning of paragraphs. A paragraph preceded by no tabs becomes a slide title, a paragraph preceded by one tab becomes an indented bulleted item, and so on.

To import an outline file, follow these steps:

1. Click the Open button on the Standard toolbar or choose Open from the File menu.

2. In the Open dialog box, select Outlines from the List Files of Type drop-down list.

3. Navigate through the Directories list, select the file you want to import from the File Name list, and then click OK. PowerPoint opens the file and displays it as a PowerPoint outline.

Inserting an Outline in an Existing Presentation

In addition to importing an outline created in an application such as Word as a starting point for a presentation, you can also insert an outline file created with another application into an existing PowerPoint presentation.

To supplement a PowerPoint outline with an imported outline, follow these steps:

1. In Outline view, click the topic after which you want the imported outline to appear.

2. Choose Slides from Outline from the Insert menu. PowerPoint displays the dialog box shown here:

3. In the Insert Outline dialog box, navigate through the directories and filenames, select the outline file you want to insert, and then click OK. PowerPoint inserts the imported outline in the current outline, assigning numbers, slide icons, and indent levels to create a seamless presentation. If you import an outline with more than five levels, PowerPoint converts all levels beyond five to fifth level entries.

NOTE: You can also import an outline in Slide view. First move to the slide after which you want the outline to appear, and then follow steps 2 and 3 above. PowerPoint imports the outline into the presentation as slides.

After you import an outline from another application as a new presentation or insert an imported outline in an existing PowerPoint presentation, you can manipulate it just like an outline created from scratch in Outline view.

In this chapter, you learned how to develop and modify a presentation outline in Outline view—the best place to concentrate on the text and the flow of ideas. In the next chapter, you'll learn how to create the text for a presentation in Slide view, where you can see the design of each slide but cannot easily see the progression of the presentation from one slide to the next.

5

Working with Text in Slide View

C reating and organizing a presentation in Outline view may be the best way to focus on the text of your presentation, but you may prefer to create the slides of your presentation one by one in Slide view—especially if you know what you want to say and how you want to say it. In Slide view, you can devote your energies to crafting a single slide at a time. Slide view may also be the best place to start when your job is not to conceive a presentation but to produce slides for someone else from handwritten notes and napkin sketches. Figure 5-1 below shows a completed slide as it appears in Slide view.

FIGURE 5-1.
A slide in Slide view.

In this chapter, you'll learn how to create text slides in Slide view. By the time you finish, you'll be just as far along as if you'd entered the presentation text in Outline view and then switched to Slide view. The task still remaining is to drop in the graphs, tables, and drawings you want to include in the presentation. You'll learn how to do this in the next several chapters.

Creating a New Presentation in Slide View

After you start a new presentation by using the Pick a Look Wizard or by selecting a presentation template, you are dropped off in Slide view with a blank title slide displayed on your screen. When you start a new presentation by selecting the Blank Presentation option or the Current Presentation Format option (which only appears when another presentation is already open), PowerPoint displays the New Slide dialog box. The first autolayout in the first row, called the Title Slide autolayout, is selected by default, so you can simply click OK to move to Slide view with a blank title slide displayed. If PowerPoint is correct in assuming that you plan to create a complete presentation, you should fill out this title slide.

> **NOTE:** If you're using PowerPoint to create a single slide, you may want to use a slide layout other than the Title Slide layout. To work with a graph chart layout or organization chart layout, for example, click the Layout button in the lower right corner of the PowerPoint window, and select a different slide layout in the Slide Layout dialog box. (For more information about selecting a slide layout, see "Adding a New Slide," page 100.)

If you need to switch to Slide view from another view, click the Slide View button in the lower left corner of the presentation window or choose Slides from the View menu.

Slide View

See Also: For more information about the New Slide dialog box, see "Adding a New Slide," page 100.

Creating the Title Slide

As shown in Figure 5-2, the Title Slide layout displays two text *placeholders*—dashed boxes that show the location for an object on a slide. All placeholders contain a prompt that tells you to click (or double-click) to add text, a graph, or another presentation element. In this case, you're prompted for a title and a subtitle for the new presentation.

FIGURE 5-2.
The Title Slide layout that appears when you create a new presentation based on the BLACKB.PPT template.

To enter a presentation title in the Title Slide layout, follow these steps:

1. Click the *Click to add title* placeholder. The dashed box disappears, a gray bar surrounds the placeholder frame, and the insertion point appears within the frame, as shown on the next page.

NOTE: When you add a new slide, you can start typing without clicking the *Click to add title* placeholder. The first text you type is automatically entered in the placeholder.

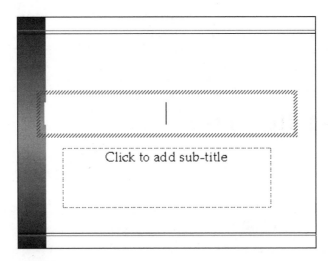

2. Type the presentation title.

3. If you want to enter a subtitle, click the *Click to add sub-title* place-holder, and type the subtitle.

4. Click anywhere outside the placeholder frame to see a completed slide, like the one shown below.

TIP   After typing text in a placeholder, you can press Ctrl+Enter to move to the next placeholder. If the current slide has no more placeholders, PowerPoint creates a new slide and puts the insertion point in the *Click to add title* placeholder on that slide.

NOTE: The formatting of the text (its font, size, color, and so on) is determined by the formatting of the text on the slide master. To change the appearance of the text on any single slide, you can apply your own formatting, which overrides the slide master's formatting. (For more information, see "Formatting Text in Slide View," page 105.) To change the appearance of the text on all the slides of a presentation, you must change the formatting of the slide master. (For more information, see "Editing the Slide Master," page 232.)

If you want to try creating the sample title slide shown in Figure 5-3, start a new presentation by clicking the New button or by choosing New from the File menu. In the New Presentation dialog box, click Template so that you can select a design for the presentation, and then click OK. In the Presentation Template dialog box, select the BRKNBARB.PPT template, and click Apply. (You'll find this template in the TEMPLATE\BWOVRHD subdirectory of the

FIGURE 5-3.
A sample title slide.

> ### Person to Person
>
> Our New Care-Giving Partnership

directory in which you installed PowerPoint.) When the New Slide dialog box appears, select the Title Slide autolayout, and click OK. Then click the *Click to add title* placeholder, and type *Person to Person*. Click the *Click to add sub-title* placeholder or press Ctrl+Enter, and type *Our New Care-Giving Partnership*. Finally, click anywhere outside the subtitle frame to see the completed title slide.

Adding a New Slide

After completing the title slide, you are ready to add the next slide. Before you add a slide, however, you must select an autolayout from the New Slide dialog box. Like the Title Slide autolayout, PowerPoint's other autolayouts also contain placeholders. For example, the Bulleted List autolayout has a *Click to add title* placeholder and a *Click to type text* placeholder; the Graph autolayout has a *Click to add title* placeholder and a *Double click to add graph* placeholder; and so on. PowerPoint offers 21 autolayouts that should meet nearly all your presentation needs.

To add a new slide to your presentation, follow these steps:

1. Click the New Slide button at the bottom of the PowerPoint window. The New Slide dialog box appears, as shown here:

Use this scroll bar to scroll through the display of autolayouts

The name of the selected autolayout appears here

2. Scroll through the display of autolayouts using the scroll bar. To see the name of an autolayout, click the autolayout once to display its name in the box in the lower right corner.

3. When you've decided which autolayout you want, either double-click it or click it once and then click OK. A new slide with the selected autolayout appears on the screen.

The rest of this chapter focuses on entering text in text slides. (In the chapters that follow, you'll learn about creating slides for graphs, organization charts, and tables.) When you finish one slide, you can repeat the previous steps to create the next one. If you need to look at a slide you've already completed, you can move back to the slide by pressing the PgUp key. Press the PgDn key to move forward through your slides. You can also move from one slide to another by dragging the scroll box in the vertical scroll bar up or down.

Entering Text in a Bulleted List AutoLayout

If you add a new slide with a layout that has bulleted text, such as the Bulleted List autolayout or the 2 Column Text autolayout, a *Click to add title* placeholder appears on the new slide along with one or more *Click to add text* placeholders. Figure 5-4 shows a Bulleted List layout as it appears on a new slide.

FIGURE 5-4.
The Bulleted List autolayout on a new slide.

To complete a slide with bulleted items, follow these steps:

1. Type a slide title. (You don't have to click the *Click to add title* placeholder first.)

2. Click the *Click to add text* placeholder or press Ctrl+Enter.

3. Type the first bulleted item, press Enter, type the next item, and so on.

4. After typing the last bulleted item, click outside the placeholder frame to see the completed slide.

> **NOTE:** Don't worry if you want text without bullets (for a paragraph that is a quote, for example). You can always turn off the bullets later. For more information about turning off bullets, see "Adding and Removing Bullets," page 113.

As an example, try creating the bulleted slide shown in Figure 5-5. Click the New Slide button, and then double-click the Bulleted List autolayout—the second layout in the first row. Type *Activities* in the title placeholder frame. Then click the *Click to add text* placeholder or press Ctrl+Enter, type *Home visits*, and press Enter. Type *Hospital bedside visits*, and press Enter. Finally, type *County Community Center work*, and click outside the placeholder frame.

FIGURE 5-5.
A sample slide with bulleted items.

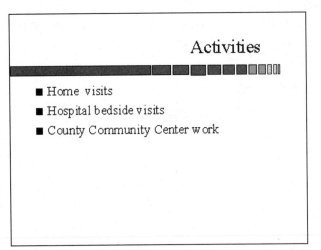

As in Outline view, you can create up to five levels of bulleted items in Slide view, using the same buttons and keystrokes that you use in Outline view. The Demote and Promote buttons are available on the Formatting toolbar, and you can also press Tab to demote an item and Shift+Tab to promote it.

Editing Text in Slide View

While creating presentation text in Slide view, you can use all the text editing techniques available in Outline view. In fact, everything you type flows through to the presentation outline; you see the presentation as an outline if you switch to Outline view.

To edit text directly on a slide in Slide view, first position the insertion point in the spot that you want to edit. The keyboard methods of moving the insertion point in Slide view are nearly the same as those used in Outline view. The notable exceptions: Pressing Ctrl+Up arrow or Ctrl+Down arrow moves the insertion point to the previous or next paragraph, respectively, rather than to the previous or next topic; and pressing Ctrl+Home or Ctrl+End moves the insertion point to the beginning or end of the current *text object* (all the text in a single placeholder) rather than to the beginning or end of the entire outline.

After clicking an insertion point or positioning the insertion point with the keyboard, you can type to insert text, press the Backspace key to delete characters to the left of the insertion point, or press the Delete key to delete characters to the right of the insertion point. As in Outline view, you can make larger edits most efficiently by first selecting the text you want to edit.

Selecting text with the mouse is the same as it is in Outline view: Position the insertion point at the beginning of the text, hold down the left mouse button, and drag to the end of the text. (Automatic Word Selection is active in Slide view, so when you drag across any part of a word, the entire word is selected.) Selecting text with the keyboard is also the same: Move the insertion point to the beginning of the text, hold down the Shift key, and then use the appropriate keys to move the insertion point to the end of the text. To select all the text in one bulleted item, click the bullet. Any text indented under that bulleted item is also selected, as shown on the left side of Figure 5-6 on the next page.

To select an entire text object, click anywhere in the object, and choose Select All from the Edit menu or press Ctrl+A. PowerPoint highlights all the text in the current placeholder, as shown on the right side of Figure 5-6. (By the way, the slide on the right has the 2 Column Text autolayout.)

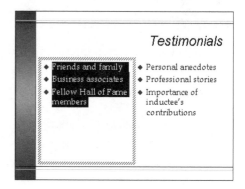

FIGURE 5-6.

A selected bulleted item (left) and a selected text object (right).

After you select text on a slide, you can delete, move, or copy it using the same buttons, commands, and key combinations you use in Outline view. You can also use drag-and-drop editing, but this technique works only within one placeholder. To move or copy text from one placeholder to another, you must use the cut and paste or copy and paste method.

See Also: For information about editing text, see "Editing Text in Outline View," page 68.

Reorganizing Text in Slide View

Reorganizing bulleted items is not quite as easy in Slide view as it is in Outline view, but it's not that difficult, either. Because the Outlining toolbar, with its Move Up and Move Down buttons, is not present, you must select bulleted items and then press Alt+Shift+Up arrow or Alt+Shift+Down arrow to move them.

To convert a slide title to a bulleted item or vice versa, use the Demote or Promote buttons on the Formatting toolbar. You can also press Alt+Shift+Right arrow or Alt+Shift+Left arrow to achieve the same effect.

See Also: For more information about reorganizing text, see "Reorganizing Text in Outline View," page 77.

Formatting Text in Slide View

The appearance of the text on all text slides is determined by the slide master for that particular presentation. By editing the slide master, you can change the formatting of text throughout the presentation. You can also override the slide master's control of the text on any individual slide by applying your own formatting. This section discusses formatting that you apply to individual slides.

Many of PowerPoint's text formatting options are available as buttons on the Formatting toolbar or as key combinations. Others are available only as menu commands. You'll soon get a feel for the quickest way to apply specific types of formatting.

For more information about changing the slide master, see "Editing the Slide Master," page 232.

Selecting Text for Formatting

You can apply two types of formatting to the text on your slides: character formatting that affects individual characters, and a broader type of formatting that affects an entire text object. Selecting text for character formatting is just like selecting text for editing. You drag across characters to select them, and then make your formatting changes.

You can also drag to select entire text objects, but you might want to take advantage of a special technique to select all the text in the object containing

the insertion point. Either press Ctrl+A to highlight all the text within the object, as shown on the left side of Figure 5-7, or press F2 to select the text object
itself, as shown on the right side of Figure 5-7. When you press F2 to select a
text object, the object is surrounded by handles. Press F2 again to select the
text within the object. After you select a text object, you can press Tab to select the next text object on the slide either before or after you make formatting
changes. (You can select the previous text object by pressing Shift+Tab.)

FIGURE 5-7.
Selected text within a text object (left) and a selected text object (right).

TIP   Instead of pressing F2 to select the object, you can click
the fuzzy gray border that surrounds the text object.

Changing the Font,
Font Style, Size, Color, and Font Effects

You can emphasize individual characters, words, or phrases by changing their
font, font style, size, or color. You can even apply special font effects, such as
shadows or embossing, to selected text. All of these options are available in the
Font dialog box.

To make formatting changes using the Font dialog box, follow these steps:

1. Select the text you want to format. You can select an individual character, you can place the insertion point in a word to format the entire
   word, or you can select several words or sentences.

2. Choose Font from the Format menu, or click the right mouse button and choose Font from the shortcut menu to display the Font dialog box shown below:

3. Select a Font, Font Style, and Size from the lists in the Font dialog box. The Font list includes all the fonts installed on your Windows system. The sizes are measured in points (with 72 points comprising 1 inch).

4. Select any combination of Effects options by clicking the appropriate check boxes. If you turn on Superscript or Subscript, you can change the percentage by which the text is set above or below the line by increasing or decreasing the Offset setting.

5. To change the color of the selected text, first click the down arrow next to the Color box. Then click one of the eight colors available for the current color scheme, or click Other Color to select from the full palette of available colors.

6. Click the Preview button if you want to see the changes you've made, and then click OK to implement the changes.

 TIP Limiting the number of fonts on a slide is as important as limiting the number of fonts in a document. Try to stick to just two fonts. Also, remember to use a light text color against a dark background and vice versa for legibility.

Try formatting some text on the bulleted slide you created earlier in this chapter. Select *County Community Center work*, click the right mouse button, and choose Font from the shortcut menu to display the Font dialog box. Then select Bold Italic as the Font Style option, and click OK.

You might want to think of the choices you make for the selected text in the Font dialog box as cumulative. You might make certain changes during one pass, such as changing the font and font style, and then come back later and make more changes, such as changing the color. When you select already formatted text and return to the Font dialog box, all the changes you've made to the formatting up to that point are reflected in the dialog box's settings.

After you select the text you want to format, you can also change the font and font size by using the Font and Font Size drop-down lists on the Formatting toolbar. The Increase Font Size or Decrease Font Size button increases or decreases the font size by specific increments. The increments become larger as the font size increases. The largest theoretical font size is 4000 points, but you'll probably run out of paper long before you can print a character that large.

You can apply the bold or italic font styles by clicking the Bold button or the Italic button on the Formatting toolbar, and you can apply the underline or shadow effects by clicking the Underline button or the Text Shadow button. Clicking the Text Color button drops down a palette of the eight colors available with the current color scheme. Most text formatting options are available as keyboard shortcuts, too. Rather than using menus or the Formatting toolbar, you can select the text and then use one of the keyboard shortcuts listed in Table 5-1.

TABLE 5-1.
Text formatting
keyboard shortcuts.

Text Formatting	Keyboard Shortcut
Change font	Ctrl+Shift+F
Change font size	Ctrl+Shift+P
Increase font size	Ctrl+Shift+>
Decrease font size	Ctrl+Shift+<
Bold	Ctrl+B
Underline	Ctrl+U or Ctrl+Shift+U
Italic	Ctrl+I or Ctrl+Shift+I
Subscript	Ctrl+=
Superscript	Ctrl+Shift+=
Plain text	Ctrl+Shift+Z
Restore default formatting	Ctrl+Spacebar

Changing the Indents, Alignment, and Spacing

You can perform certain types of text formatting only on entire text objects, not individual characters or words. These formatting types include changing the left and first-line indents of paragraphs, changing the alignment of paragraphs, and changing the spacing between and within paragraphs.

Remember, a text object includes all the text in a single placeholder. For example, a bulleted list slide has only two text objects, the title and the bulleted list, even though the bulleted list probably consists of more than one paragraph. Any change you make to a text object affects all the paragraphs within it.

Changing the Left Indent and First-Line Indent

Increasing the left indent of a bulleted list text object pushes all the text to the right, increasing the space between the bullets and the text for each bullet. To change the indents of a text object, you must click anywhere in the text object and then drag the corresponding markers in the top ruler.

First-line indent

Left indent

If the ruler is not visible, you can display it in one of the following ways:

- Choose Ruler from the View menu.

- Point to the slide background, click the right mouse button, and choose Ruler from the shortcut menu.

  NOTE: If a text object has bulleted items at two or more levels, the ruler contains a pair of markers (a left indent marker and a first-line indent marker) for each level.

To increase the space to the right of the bullets, follow these steps:

1. Click any of the text in the object.

2. Drag the left indent marker to the right.

TIP Be sure to drag the lower, triangular marker that points upward. Dragging the rectangular marker located below the left indent marker moves the first-line indent marker and the left indent marker at the same time.

Dragging the first-line indent marker (the upper, triangular marker that points downward) to the left or the right changes the starting position of the first line relative to the rest of the paragraph. Because a bullet starts the first line of a bulleted list paragraph, dragging the first-line indent marker to the right moves the bullet to the right. Figure 5-8 shows the indent settings on several rulers and the corresponding indents of the text below.

FIGURE 5-8.

Notice how the ruler settings correspond to the text on these three slides.

If a text object contains paragraphs that have no bullets, drag the first-line indent marker to the left to create a hanging indent, as shown in Figure 5-9.

FIGURE 5-9.
Paragraphs with hanging indents.

Changing Paragraph Alignment

The *alignment* of a text object determines the horizontal placement of its lines. The alignment options are as follows:

Option	Effect
Left	Text within a text object is flush with the left edge of the object.
Center	Text within a text object is centered horizontally within the object.
Right	Text within a text object is flush with the right edge of the object.
Justify	Extra spaces are added between the words within a text object to make the text flush with both the left and right edges of the object.

To change the alignment of the paragraphs in a text object, follow these three steps:

1. Click any of the text in the object.

2. Choose Alignment from the Format menu, or click the right mouse button and choose Alignment from the shortcut menu.

3. Select the alignment option you want from the Alignment submenu.

You can also use one of the keyboard shortcuts listed in Table 5-2.

TABLE 5-2.
Alignment
keyboard shortcuts.

Alignment	Keyboard Shortcut
Left-align	Ctrl+L
Center	Ctrl+E
Right-align	Ctrl+R
Justify	Ctrl+J

Changing Line and Paragraph Spacing

The *line spacing* determines the amount of vertical space between paragraphs within a text object and between lines within a paragraph. You may want to add extra space between paragraphs to separate them or add extra space between the lines of a paragraph to make the paragraph easier to read, for a design effect, or to make the text fill more vertical space on the page.

To change the line spacing in an object, follow these steps:

1. Click any of the text in the object.

2. Choose Line Spacing from the Format menu. This dialog box appears:

3. In the Line Spacing dialog box, you can change the line spacing by hundredths of a line or by a single point. First select either Lines or Points from the drop-down list in the Line Spacing section of the dialog box, and then enter a new number in the edit box to the left. You can click the up or down arrows to increase or decrease the number.

The other two options in the Line Spacing dialog box allow you to add extra space before or after each paragraph. By using the Before Paragraph and After Paragraph options, you can spread out the paragraphs vertically.

Adding and Removing Bullets

Each bullet that appears at the beginning of a text line emphasizes the statement that follows. In addition, bullets are only appropriate when a slide contains a series of statements. As a result, there may be times when you don't need bulleted text, such as when a slide contains a single phrase. Fortunately, you can easily add and remove bullets in PowerPoint by using the Bullet On/Off button on the Formatting toolbar.

To remove the bullet from a line of text:

1. Click anywhere in the line.

2. Click the Bullet On/Off button on the Formatting toolbar.

For example, in Figure 5-10, the bullet has been removed from the second of two text statements. To remove the bullets from all the text in a placeholder, first select the text by pressing Ctrl+A, or select the placeholder's text object by pressing F2 or by clicking the object's gray border, and then click the Bullet On/Off button. The Bullet On/Off button is a toggle, so if you select the text and press the Bullet On/Off button again, PowerPoint restores the bullets.

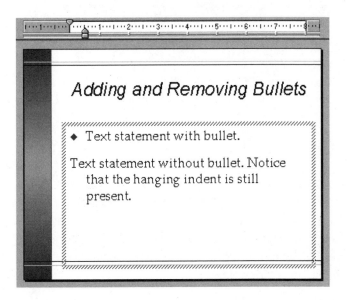

FIGURE 5-10.
The bullet has been removed from the second text statement.

Another way to add or remove bullets is to select the text to the right of the bullets, and choose Bullet from the Format menu or the shortcut menu. Then, when the Bullet dialog box appears, select or deselect the Use a Bullet option to turn the bullets on or off.

When you remove the bullet from a bulleted paragraph that contains more than one line of text, you'll notice that the first line of text shifts to the left. The paragraph's hanging indent is still present, as you can see in the second text statement in Figure 5-10.

To remove the hanging indent in a nonbulleted paragraph, simply follow these steps:

1. Check that the ruler is visible. (If it is not, choose Ruler from the View menu or the shortcut menu.)

2. Drag the left indent marker to the left so that it aligns with the first-line indent marker, as shown below. Be careful to drag the triangular part of the left indent marker, not the rectangular part, which moves both the first-line and left indent markers simultaneously.

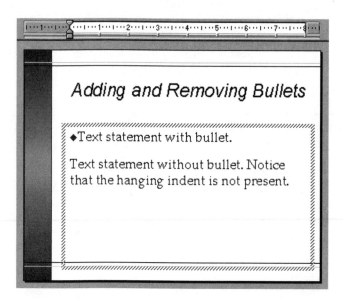

Notice that the text in the second bulleted item is now properly left-aligned, but the top bulleted item has been affected, too. Changing indents affects all the paragraphs in a text object.

Changing the Bullet Shape, Color, and Size

The default bullets that precede the text on your slides are only one of the almost limitless options for bullet shape, color, and size. You can use any character from any TrueType font on your system, and you can change the color and size of the bullets on any slide.

To select a special bullet character, follow these steps:

1. Select the text following the bullet or bullets you want to change.

2. Choose Bullet from the Format menu, or press the right mouse button and choose Bullet from the shortcut menu. The Bullet dialog box appears, as shown here:

3. Select a font from the Bullets From drop-down list. The special characters available for the selected font are then displayed in the dialog box. As you can see, the Wingdings font is a good source of graphic bullet shapes.

4. Click any of the characters displayed. The character will be magnified temporarily so that you can see it better.

5. If you want to change the bullet color, select a color from the Special Color drop-down list.

6. If you want to change the bullet size, type a new size in the Size edit box, or click the up or down arrows to the right of the edit box to increase or decrease the size of the bullet as a percentage of the text size.

7. Click the Preview button at the bottom of the Bullet dialog box to see the changes you've made, or click OK to implement the changes.

Figure 5-11 shows a bulleted list slide with bullets that are far more interesting than the defaults.

FIGURE 5-11.
Check boxes used
as bullets.

> ## Media Contacts
>
> ☑ Local newspapers
> ☑ Local TV and radio news
> ☑ Network news
> ☑ Cable news
> ☑ Industry magazines

Creating Numbered Lists

PowerPoint cannot automatically number paragraphs in a text object. You must first turn off the bullets, and then type a number at the beginning of each paragraph. After the number, enter one space rather than a tab. (Pressing Tab moves the paragraph to the next indent level.) Then align the text of the numbered paragraph by changing the indents of the paragraph.

Setting Tabs

Creating tables in PowerPoint is so easy that you'll probably want to use a table whenever you need to place text in columns on a slide. But you can also place tab stops in a text object and follow a more traditional approach for spacing text horizontally across a slide.

As described in Table 5-3, PowerPoint provides four different types of tab stops. All of these are available on the ruler.

Tab Button	Tab Stop	Description
Left-aligned tab stop	Left-aligned tab stop	Aligns the left edge of text with the tab stop
Centered tab stop	Centered tab stop	Aligns the center of text with the tab stop
Right-aligned tab stop	Right-aligned tab stop	Aligns the right edge of text with the tab stop
Decimal tab stop	Decimal tab stop	Aligns the decimal points of numbers at the tab stop

TABLE 5-3.
PowerPoint's tab stops.

To switch from one tab type to the next, click the Tab Alignment button at the left end of the ruler until the tab type you want appears on the face of the button. Figure 5-12 shows the location of the Tab Alignment button and the appearance of text entered at a set of tab stops.

Tab Alignment button

FIGURE 5-12.
The Tab Alignment button and text entered at various tab stops. (The ruler shows the current tab stops.)

To enter tab stops, follow these steps:

1. Click anywhere in the text within a text object. (All of the text in the object will be formatted with the same tab stops.)

2. Click the Tab Alignment button until the tab stop you want appears.

3. On the ruler, click the position for the tab stop.

4. Continue clicking different positions in the ruler to add tab stops of the same type, or select a different tab type and then click the ruler.

WARNING: To move from one tab stop to the next while entering text, you must press Ctrl+Tab. Pressing the Tab key without pressing Ctrl moves the current paragraph to the next indent level.

Changing the Case of Text

To change the capitalization of text on a slide, select the text you want to modify, and then, from the Format menu, choose Change Case. Figure 5-13 shows the Change Case dialog box, which offers five case options for the selected text. You might want to take a moment and try out each of the options to see their effects. Simply select an option, and then click OK. You can also cycle between uppercase, lowercase, and title case for the selected text by pressing Shift+F3.

FIGURE 5-13.
The Change Case
dialog box.

Adding and Removing Periods

To add or remove periods from the text on a slide, select the text, and then, from the Format menu, choose Periods. In the Periods dialog box, shown in Figure 5-14, select either Add Periods or Remove Periods, and click OK.

FIGURE 5-14.
The Periods
dialog box.

118

You can also use the Periods command in Outline view. But no matter what view you're in, you cannot use the Periods command to add or remove periods from a slide title.

Transferring Text Styles

After you format one selection of text, you can transfer the same formatting, called the *text style,* to another selection of text. By simply transferring a text style, you save time because you don't have to reopen menus, reselect options, and so on.

To transfer the formatting of one text selection to another text selection, follow these steps:

1. Select the text whose formatting you want to transfer, as shown below.

2. From the Format menu, choose Pick Up Text Style, or click the right mouse button and choose Pick Up Text Style from the shortcut menu.

3. Select the text that you want to transfer the formatting to.

4. From the Format menu, choose Apply Text Style, or click the right mouse button and choose Apply Text Style from the shortcut menu. As shown on the next page, the formatting of the original text selection is transferred to the other text selection.

Ceremony Schedule

5:00 PM Technical rehearsal
Sound and video check
Lighting check
7:30 PM Doors open
8:00 PM Ceremony begins
9:30 PM Ceremony concludes

Moving and Resizing Text Objects

The text you enter in a placeholder appears at the position of the placeholder text. But after you enter all the text you need, you may want to move the text object or change its size, perhaps to make room on the slide for a chart or graphic.

To move or resize a text object, you must select the object with one of these procedures:

- Choose Edit Object from the Edit menu.
- Press F2.
- Click the fuzzy gray border that surrounds the object.

In each case, a set of handles appears around the selected object, as shown in Figure 5-15.

After you select the text object, position the mouse pointer on the object's border, hold down the left mouse button, and drag the object to a new position; or press the arrow keys to move the object incrementally. To resize the object, drag one of the object's handles.

NOTE: By dragging one of the object's corner handles, you can change the object's scale. That is, both the object's width and height are resized proportionally.

FIGURE 5-15.

Handles around a selected text object allow you to move and resize the object.

Turning Word Wrap On or Off

When you resize an object, the text inside wraps to fit the new size, as shown in Figure 5-15. Words in a paragraph that can no longer fit on a line within the object move to the following line. Words in a paragraph that can fit on the previous line after the object is resized move to the previous line.

You can turn word wrap off by first selecting the text object or any of the text within the object, and then choosing Text Anchor from the Format menu. The Text Anchor dialog box appears, as shown in Figure 5-16.

FIGURE 5-16.

The Text Anchor dialog box.

The Word-wrap Text in Object option controls word wrapping. Click the option's check box to turn word wrapping on or off.

When word wrapping is turned off, any text you add to a paragraph continues across the slide, beyond the borders of the text object, and even beyond the edge of the slide if necessary.

Changing the Box Margins

The two Box Margins settings in the Text Anchor dialog box, shown in Figure 5-16, let you adjust the horizontal and vertical margins of the text object. When you increase the margins, you add space within the object, between the text and the borders of the object.

Increasing the box margins is helpful when you add an actual graphic box to the borders of a text object, as you'll learn in the section titled "Special Text Object Formatting." Larger margins pad the interior of the box so that the text does not appear so cramped in the box. Figure 5-17 shows the same text within two text objects. The text object in the right box has larger box margins.

Text inside a text object fits within the box margins.

Text inside a text object fits within the box margins.

FIGURE 5-17.
The text object on the right has larger box margins.

Fitting Text Objects to the Text

Sometimes, the text you enter in a placeholder does not completely fill the placeholder. For example, the right border of the text object shown on the left in Figure 5-18 is still some distance from the text. To automatically shrink the text object to fit the text you've entered, select the text, and then select the Adjust Object Size to Fit Text option in the Text Anchor dialog box. The text object immediately shrinks to fit the text inside. If you enter additional text, the text object will grow vertically to accommodate the new text, as shown on the right in Figure 5-18.

When the Adjust Object Size to Fit Text option is turned on, you can stretch the sides of a text object horizontally, but the bottom border of the object always snaps to fit the last line of the text. When Adjust Object Size to Fit Text is turned off, newly typed text overruns the bottom border of the text object, and you have to resize the object manually.

Decreasing the box margins while the Adjust Object Size to Fit Text option is turned on brings the borders of the text object closer to the text.

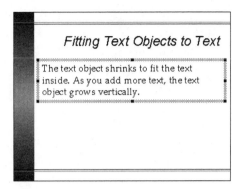

FIGURE 5-18.
The right border of the text object on the left is still some distance from the text. The text object on the right has grown vertically to accommodate the new text.

Special Text Object Formatting

Because a text object is just like any other object on a PowerPoint slide, you can surround it with a line, add a shadow to it, fill it with color, rotate it, and scale it. In fact, you can use any of the commands that you use to change the appearance of other objects (such as drawings) to change the appearance of a text object. For example, you can add a border to a text object by first selecting the object and then choosing the Colors and Lines command from the Format menu. Or you can add a shadow to a text object by choosing the Shadow command from the Format menu.

One special command you may find helpful is Scale. After selecting a text object, you can change its size by choosing Scale from the Draw menu and then revising the Scale To percentage setting in the Scale dialog box, which is shown in Figure 5-19. You can make a text object 90 percent of its former size, for example, to make room for a graphic.

FIGURE 5-19.
The Scale dialog box.

Microsoft WordArt 2

When your presentation title needs a little pizzazz, you can use Microsoft WordArt 2 to create spirited titles with one or more eye-catching special effects. WordArt can create shadowed, stretched, rotated, and skewed text of any size, and text that has been contoured to fit a number of predefined shapes.

To add WordArt text to a title slide, or to any slide, choose Object from the Insert menu, select Microsoft WordArt 2.0 from the Insert Object dialog box, and click OK. (Before you choose the Object command, you can delete the *Click to add title* placeholder on the title slide so that it doesn't get in your way.) When WordArt's menus and toolbar appear on the screen, type the desired text in the Enter Your Text Here dialog box, and then click Update Display. Next, use WordArt's Format menu and toolbar to add special formatting effects. For example, click the arrow next to the first box on the WordArt toolbar to display a palette of shapes that you can use to contour the text.

To return to PowerPoint after you finish formatting the text, click outside the WordArt frame. To return to WordArt, double-click any WordArt text.

If the presentation you are creating is strictly text, as most presentations are, then you have now done everything required to create the presentation, and you can skip ahead to Chapter 9. But if you want to add graphs, organization charts, and tables to your presentation, go on to the next three chapters.

6

Adding Graph Slides

You can reel off numbers until you're blue in the face, but nothing gets your message across like a graph. PowerPoint's powerful Graph module offers 14 different chart types with all the pizzazz you could want, and it makes the process of creating graphs simple and automatic. In this chapter, you'll learn how to use the Graph module to create the graphs you need and add them to presentation slides. You'll also learn how to enter and edit the data that supports your graphs, and you'll make the acquaintance of the AutoFormat command. Finally, you'll discover ways to incorporate data and graphs from other sources into your PowerPoint graph slides.

Because a graph is a visual representation of data, it can have a much greater impact than words alone. For example, the statement "We outproduced our nearest competitors by 2 to 1" is impressive, but not nearly as impressive as this graph:

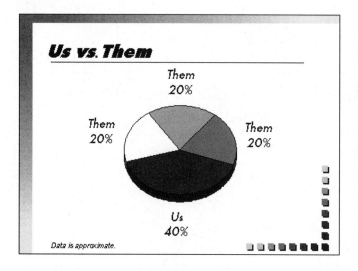

A graph can communicate any information that can be quantified, so don't hesitate to pull a graph from your arsenal whenever your message is numeric—even if your numbers aren't precise.

Graphs are your best bet for illuminating trends, deviations, and other measurements that don't require a great deal of explanation. If an explanation is needed, you can simply add text to the graph or include a text slide. By the time you finish this chapter, you'll probably think of new ways that you can use graphs to enhance your PowerPoint presentations.

For information about creating custom graphs, see Chapter 10, "Formatting Graphs," page 241.

What Is Microsoft Graph?

Microsoft Graph 5 is a special module that creates graphs for use in Windows-based applications like Microsoft Word, Microsoft Excel, and, of course, Power-Point. If you're already familiar with graphing in Excel, you'll find it easy to jump to graphing in PowerPoint because both programs use the same Graph module. If you're not familiar with graphing in Excel, don't worry. At every step of the way, Graph guides you through the process of converting raw numbers into professional, colorful, and illuminating graphs.

When you create or modify a graph, Graph's menus and Standard toolbar replace PowerPoint's menus and toolbars, as shown in Figure 6-1, so only the commands and controls you need are on the screen.

FIGURE 6-1.
Graph's menus and Standard toolbar take over the screen when you create a graph.

The graph you are creating in Graph appears on the current slide. When you are entering or editing the graph's data, a datasheet containing the numbers overlays the graph. Any change to the numbers in the datasheet is reflected immediately in the graph.

Graph Basics

When it's time to back up an assertion with numeric data, you can create a special graph slide devoted to an entire graph, or you can add a graph to an existing slide to enhance a text message. Then you can select from 14 different chart types to ensure that the graph presents your data in the best possible light.

> **NOTE:** The words *graph* and *chart* are used interchangeably throughout this chapter. In general, the word *chart* is reserved for option and button names.

Creating a Graph Slide

To create a graph slide in an existing presentation, follow these steps:

1. In Slide view, switch to the slide that the new slide should follow, and click the New Slide button at the bottom of the PowerPoint window or choose New Slide from the Insert menu to display the New Slide dialog box shown below:

2. In the New Slide dialog box, click the third autolayout in the first row if you want only a graph on a slide, or click the second autolayout in the second or third row if you want a bulleted list along with a graph. These are the only autolayouts that provide graph placeholders.

3. Click OK. A graph placeholder on the new slide displays the text *Double click to add graph*.

4. Double-click the graph placeholder to start Microsoft Graph. A sample graph appears within the placeholder, and the datasheet window, which contains the sample data for the graph, overlays the graph as shown earlier in Figure 6-1.

Adding a Graph to an Existing Slide

To add a graph to an existing slide, click the Insert Graph button on PowerPoint's Standard toolbar or choose Microsoft Graph from the Insert menu. Either way, Graph loads and displays a sample graph and datasheet on the current slide. Don't worry about the positioning or size of the graph at this point. After you enter your data, you can move and size the graph as needed.

Selecting a Chart Type

After you create a graph slide or add a graph to an existing slide, you can select a chart type from PowerPoint's 14 chart options. Selecting a chart type before you begin entering data is a good first step because you are compelled from the start to consider the message your data conveys. It also modifies the appearance of the datasheet window to show how the data will be represented. You'll see bars in the datasheet window if you select a bar chart and pie slices if you select a pie chart. Of course, PowerPoint always lets you change your mind at any time, so you can begin with the default chart type and change to any other chart type later.

Keep in mind that PowerPoint can produce stock variations, called *subtypes*, of most of the 14 basic chart types. You can also go way beyond these subtypes and modify any chart to a virtually unlimited degree. You can even mix chart types within the same graph, showing some data with lines and some with bars, for example.

To select a chart type for a graph, follow these steps:

1. Select the sample graph on your slide.

2. Click the down arrow to the right of the Chart Type button on Graph's Standard toolbar. A palette of chart types appears, as shown on the next page.

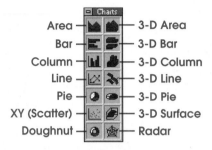

3. Click the chart type you want.

> **TIP** You can "tear off" the palette of chart types and drop it on an unused part of the screen for easy access later. Simply click the arrow next to the Chart Type button to drop down the palette. Next, position the mouse pointer over the palette, hold down the left mouse button, and drag the palette away from Graph's Standard toolbar. You can close the Charts palette by double-clicking the Control button at the left end of the palette's title bar.

You can also use the Chart Type command on Graph's Format menu or shortcut menu to select a chart type. When you choose this command, Graph displays the Chart Type dialog box shown in Figure 6-2. Note that the names of the chart types and their pictures appear in large and easy-to-see panes. Click

FIGURE 6-2.

The Chart Type dialog box.

2-D or 3-D in the Chart Dimension section, and then select a chart type from the display of chart options.

You can further refine your selection by clicking the Options button in the Chart Type dialog box and selecting a chart subtype. For example, Figure 6-3 shows the Format Column Group dialog box that appears when you select the 2-D Column chart option and then click Options. You can select one of the subtypes displayed in large panes on the Subtype tab of the dialog box. After you select a subtype, a preview of your data plotted according to the selected chart subtype appears in the bottom section of the dialog box. You can then click OK to implement the selected chart subtype, or click another Subtype option and click OK. To return to the Chart Type dialog box, simply click the Chart Type button.

FIGURE 6-3.

You can use the Format Column Group dialog box to select a chart subtype.

TIP You can select a chart type, a subtype, and special chart formatting options all at once by choosing AutoFormat from Graph's Format menu or shortcut menu. For more information, see "Selecting an AutoFormat," page 144.

The following sections discuss PowerPoint's 14 basic chart types and explain how each chart type presents information. Figure 6-4 provides an example of each chart type.

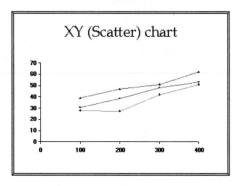

FIGURE 6-4.

PowerPoint's 14 basic chart types.

(continued)

Figure 6-4. *continued*

(continued)

Figure 6-4. *continued*

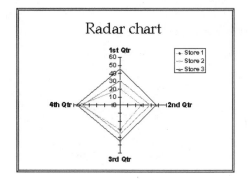

Area Charts

Area charts show the amount of change in a set of values during an interval of time. Line charts are similar, but they emphasize the *rate* of change rather than the *amount* of change.

Bar Charts

Bar charts compare measurements at intervals. They emphasize measurements at discrete times rather than the changes over time. Their bars run horizontally. The stacked bar subtype shows the relative contributions of several measurements to a whole. The 100% stacked bar subtype shows the relative percentage of contributions of several measurements to the whole without identifying specific numeric contributions.

Column Charts

Column charts are much like bar charts except their bars run vertically rather than horizontally. Like bar charts, they compare measurements at intervals and provide snapshot views of data taken at specific moments rather than offer a depiction of the change of data over time. Column charts also have stacked and 100% stacked subtypes.

Line Charts

Line charts show changes in data or trends over time. You can show the same data with bars or columns, but lines emphasize change rather than comparisons at intervals. Two subtypes of line charts, high-low-close and open-high-low-close, are used to depict stock prices and other data that have a high and low during an interval, such as the temperature or barometric pressure.

Pie Charts

Pie charts show the breakdown of a total. You can separate slices of the pie to emphasize certain values. The values depicted by slices are contained in a single series on the Graph datasheet.

XY (Scatter) Charts

XY (scatter) charts show the degree of correspondence between two series of numbers. Generally used for scientific data, XY charts also let you depict two sets of numbers as one set of XY coordinates.

Doughnut Charts

Doughnut charts show breakdowns of totals, like pie charts do, but they let you depict several breakdowns in successive rings around a doughnut hole.

3-D Area Charts

3-D area charts are area charts depicted in three dimensions. The third dimension has no significance except to make the chart more interesting.

3-D Bar Charts

3-D bar charts are bar charts shown in three dimensions. Again, the third dimension has no significance except to make the chart look more visually appealing than the standard 2-D bar chart.

3-D Column Charts

3-D column charts come in two varieties. The standard 3-D column chart, shown in Figure 6-4, is a three-dimensional view of a column chart. The 3-D perspective column chart, shown in Figure 6-5, creates a far more visually striking chart. But

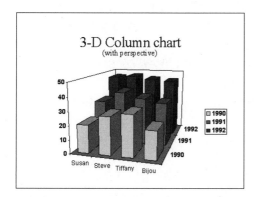

FIGURE 6-5.
A 3-D perspective column chart.

beware of the difficulty of interpreting 3-D perspective column charts. Gauging the true relative and absolute heights of the bars can be very difficult. Use this chart type to give a general impression of the data, not the specific values.

3-D Line Charts

3-D line charts display lines as ribbons. They provide a more interesting view than 2-D line charts, but like 3-D bar charts, 3-D line charts make it difficult to interpret change over time.

3-D Pie Charts

3-D pie charts offer a more visually appealing view of a breakdown than standard 2-D pie charts. Otherwise, they are identical. You can separate slices of 3-D pie charts from the pie just as easily as you can in 2-D pie charts.

3-D Surface Charts

3-D surface charts emphasize the relationships among large quantities of numbers. Colors or patterns designate the areas with the same value. Two subtypes, contour charts and wire-frame charts, show a 2-D view of the surface chart from above and the surface chart without color, respectively.

Radar Charts

Radar charts simultaneously compare the relationship of several different values of a subject. Each value is measured on an axis that radiates from the center of the chart and depicts another aspect of the subject.

Entering the Data

The generic set of data you see in the datasheet window when you start Microsoft Graph provides an example of how text and numbers should be arranged in a datasheet. The graph peeking out from behind the datasheet window displays the text and numbers graphically, and it is updated immediately as you enter and edit data in the datasheet. Figure 6-6 shows the datasheet.

The datasheet is made up of *cells*, which are the rectangular spaces at the intersections of the rows and columns. In Figure 6-6, text labels appear in the leftmost and topmost cells of the datasheet. The actual numbers to be graphed occupy the cells below and to the right of the labels. Each cell in this section

Labels   Cell pointer   Column letter button

Row number button

Marker

FIGURE 6-6.
The datasheet.

has an *address* that consists of a column letter and row number. For example, the address of the cell at the intersection of column A and row 1 is *A1*.

> **NOTE:** In most spreadsheet programs, every cell in a worksheet has an address. But in Microsoft Graph, the cells reserved for text labels in the datasheet (the leftmost and topmost cells) do not have cell addresses.

To create a proper graph, PowerPoint must know whether the *series* (the sets of related numbers) are entered in rows or columns. By default, PowerPoint assumes the series are arranged in rows. If you've arranged the series in columns instead, you can click the By Column button on Graph's Standard toolbar. To return to a by-row arrangement, simply click the By Row button.

PowerPoint places small pictures of the *markers* that will be used in the graph (the bars, columns, lines, or other graphic shapes) on either the row number or column letter buttons in the datasheet. If the markers are on the row number buttons, the data is organized in the graph by row. If the markers are on the column letter buttons, the data is organized by column.

Entering the Labels

Your first step in entering the data for a graph is to replace the text labels in the first row and first column of cells. To replace a label, use the mouse or the arrow keys to move the *cell pointer*, the highlight surrounding a single cell, to the cell containing the label, and then type over the existing entry. You can also double-click or press F2 to place an insertion point in a selected cell and then edit its contents. Keep in mind that you can use the same text editing techniques that you use elsewhere in PowerPoint to edit the contents of a cell in the datasheet.

Because PowerPoint's default setting arranges graph data by row, each label entered in the leftmost cell of a row appears in the graph's legend. (Displaying the legend is optional.) The labels entered in the topmost cells of columns often have time or date designations, such as a specific year or month, but they can be any other text that distinguishes the individual data points in a series of numbers. Remember, if you want the column labels to appear in the graph's legend rather than the row labels, you can click the By Column button on Graph's Standard toolbar.

To try your hand at entering labels, start by creating a new graph:

1. Click the New Slide button at the bottom of the PowerPoint window.

2. In the New Slide dialog box, select an autolayout that includes a graph placeholder.

3. In Slide view, double-click the *Double click to add graph* placeholder to start Microsoft Graph.

Stick with the default chart type when the graph and datasheet appear, and then follow these steps, using the suggested labels or your own:

1. Select the first cell in row 1 (the cell that contains the label *East*).

2. Type *Regular mail* and press Enter. Don't worry that the label is too long to fit in the cell. The length of the label won't affect the resulting graph, and you can widen the entire column to accommodate the label at any time (see the sidebar titled "Changing the Widths of Columns," on the facing page).

3. Now replace *West* with *Overnight* and press Enter.

4. Replace *North* with *Courier,* and then select the first cell in column A, and replace *1st Qtr* with *Package*.

5. Press Tab to move to the cell to the right, replace *2nd Qtr* in column B with *Box*, and press Tab again.

6. Replace *3rd Qtr* in column C with *Letter*. Leave the text in Column D as is—you'll plot only three columns of data in the graph. Here's how the datasheet should look now:

Presentation - Datasheet					
		A	B	C	D
		Package	Box	Letter	4th Qtr
1	Regular m	20.4	27.4	90	20.4
2	Overnight	30.6	38.6	34.6	31.6
3	Courier	45.9	46.9	45	43.9
4					

Changing the Widths of Columns

When the label you enter in a cell exceeds the width of the cell, you won't be able to see the entire label. To solve this problem, widen the entire column by placing the mouse pointer between the current column letter button and the column letter button to the right (the pointer changes to a double arrow). Then hold down the left mouse button, and drag to the right. In the datasheet shown below, the mouse pointer is in position, and the first column has been widened to accommodate the longest label.

Presentation - Datasheet					
		A	B	C	D
		Package	Box	Letter	4th Qtr
1	Regular mail	20.4	27.4	90	20.4
2	Overnight	30.6	38.6	34.6	31.6
3	Courier	45.9	46.9	45	43.9
4					

To change the width of more than one column, click the column letter button for the first column, hold down the mouse button, and drag across the other column letter buttons. Then, when you widen the first column using the technique described above, the other selected columns are also widened.

In addition, you can double-click between two column letter buttons to automatically adjust the width of the first column to accommodate the column's longest entry. Select several columns and double-click between any two to automatically fit them all to their longest entry.

Entering the Numbers

After you enter the labels to create a framework for the data, you must replace the sample numbers with your own. You can select any single cell, type over the cell's contents, and then move to the next cell. However, the best way to quickly enter all the numbers is to select the range of cells that will contain the numbers and then begin typing columns of replacement numbers. To select a range of cells, place the mouse pointer on the first cell, hold down the mouse button, and then drag across to the cell at the opposite corner of the range. You can also move the cell pointer to the first cell, hold down the Shift key, and then use the arrow keys to move to the cell at the opposite corner.

When you type a number and press Enter, the cell pointer moves to the cell below. When you type a number in the last cell of a selected range of cells and press Enter, the cell pointer returns to the first cell in the range.

To enter the data for the graph you created on the previous page, follow these steps. (Again, you can use the suggested data or supply your own.)

1. Place the mouse pointer on cell A1, which is located at the intersection of column A and row 1.

2. Hold down the left mouse button, and drag the pointer to cell C3.

3. Release the mouse button. The rectangular range of cells from A1 to C3 is selected, as shown here:

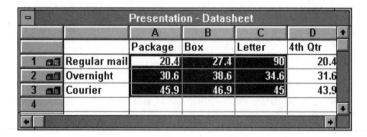

4. Type the columns of numbers shown below, pressing Enter after each number. Be sure to enter the numbers by column, *not* by row.

8.60	10.75	.29
17.90	22.00	9.95
48.00	56.00	17.50

The datasheet now looks like this:

Presentation - Datasheet				
	A	B	C	D
	Package	Box	Letter	4th Qtr
1 Regular mail	8.6	10.75	0.29	20.4
2 Overnight	17.9	22	9.95	31.6
3 Courier	48	56	17.5	43.9
4				

NOTE: To use the quick data-entry technique, you must enter the numbers in columns, even if you're charting the data by rows.

TIP You can control whether the cell pointer moves to the next cell or remains on the selected cell when you press Enter by first choosing Options from Graph's Tools menu. Then click the check box next to the Move Selection After Enter option to deselect it, and click OK.

Formatting the Labels and Numbers

You can use Graph's Formatting toolbar (shown below) to select a different font and numeric format for a datasheet. The changes you make to the font are displayed only in the datasheet, whereas the changes you make to the numeric formatting appear in both the datasheet and the graph.

NOTE: If Graph's Formatting toolbar is not present, choose Toolbars from Graph's View menu, select the Formatting option, and then click OK.

Text formatting buttons   **Number formatting buttons**

From Graph's Formatting toolbar, you can select a font, point size, and character formatting attributes such as bold, italic, and underline for the text and numbers in your datasheet. You cannot change the alignment while working in the datasheet because the paragraph alignment buttons are inactive, but you should keep in mind that text is always left-aligned in the datasheet and numbers are always right-aligned.

In addition to Graph's Formatting toolbar, you can use the Font command on Graph's Format menu or shortcut menu to change the formatting of the data in the datasheet. When you choose the Font command, the Font dialog box is displayed so that you can make your formatting selections.

To change the numeric formatting of the numbers in a datasheet, you must first select the numbers, and then use the number formatting buttons on Graph's Formatting toolbar or choose the Number command from Graph's Format menu or shortcut menu. You can select one set of numbers and format them as decimal and then select another set and format them as percentages, for example.

The five number formatting buttons are located at the right end of Graph's Formatting toolbar. You use the first three buttons to apply a general format to your numbers, and the last two buttons to increase or decrease the number of decimal places. For additional number formatting options, choose Number from Graph's Format menu or shortcut menu. Then in the Number Format dialog box, shown in Figure 6-7, select a formatting category from the list at the left, and select a formatting code from the list at the right. The code you select appears in the Code edit box, and a sample number at the bottom of the dialog box shows the effect of your selection. Click OK to implement your changes.

FIGURE 6-7.
The Number
Format dialog
box.

To format the numbers in your sample graph, follow these steps:

1. Select the rectangular range of numbers from cell A1 to cell C3.

2. Click the Currency Style button on Graph's Formatting toolbar. The numbers should look like this:

Presentation - Datasheet						
		A	B	C	D	
		Package	Box	Letter	4th Qtr	
1	Regular mail	$8.60	$10.75	$0.29	20.4	
2	Overnight	$17.90	$22.00	$9.95	31.6	
3	Courier	$48.00	$56.00	$17.50	43.9	
4						

To remove formatting from the data in your datasheet, select the data, choose Clear from Graph's Edit menu, and choose Formats from the Clear submenu. Choosing Contents from the Clear submenu removes the data from selected cells without deleting the cells. (You can also remove the data from selected cells by choosing Clear from Graph's shortcut menu.)

 See Also: For more information about formatting graphs, see Chapter 10, "Formatting Graphs," page 241.

Viewing the Graph

As you revise the data in the datasheet, the graph adjusts to reflect the changes. To see the graph, close the datasheet window by clicking the View Datasheet button on Graph's Standard toolbar, by double-clicking the Control button at the left end of the datasheet's title bar, or by clicking any visible part of the graph window. Figure 6-8 on the next page shows the graph created from the sample datasheet. If you close the datasheet window, you can always reopen it by clicking the View Datasheet button again or by choosing the Datasheet command from Graph's View menu.

> **NOTE:** Before closing the sample datasheet window, we double-clicked the column letter button at the top of column D to exclude the data in column D from the graph. For more information about excluding data, see "Excluding Data," page 147.

The numbers along the vertical axis of the graph in Figure 6-8 are formatted with the currency style you specified earlier in the datasheet window. Other aspects of the graph's appearance are controlled by the template that formats the current presentation and by the chart type you selected. The template gives

P A R T 2: **Creating the Basic Presentation**

FIGURE 6-8.

The graph based
on the data
entered in the
sample datasheet.

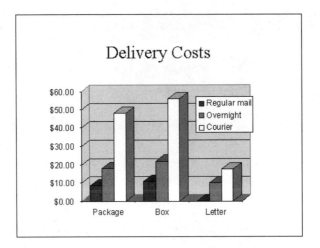

the graph its color scheme and font selections. The chart type gives the graph its overall design and special option settings. If necessary, you can now start revising the content of the graph and adjusting the appearance of the graph. To do the latter, you can select one of PowerPoint's autoformat options rather than make individual formatting choices for different parts of the graph.

Selecting an AutoFormat

An autoformat is a combination of a chart type, a subtype, and special formatting options for each part of a graph, such as the placement of the legend or the location of the data labels. Selecting an autoformat gives a graph a complete top-to-bottom design overhaul and can relieve the tedium of making detailed formatting changes to individual graph elements. Graph comes with a broad selection of autoformats for each of the 14 basic chart types. You can also create custom graph designs and save them as user-defined autoformats.

To select an autoformat for a graph, choose AutoFormat from Graph's Format menu or shortcut menu. The AutoFormat dialog box appears, as shown in Figure 6-9.

The AutoFormat dialog box contains a gallery of chart designs for each of the chart types in Graph. Select a chart type from the Galleries list, and then select a format by double-clicking one of the options in the Formats section. The graph will immediately reflect the autoformat you select. If you have created custom graph formats, you can select the User-Defined option in the Formats Used section, and then double-click the custom format you want.

144

FIGURE 6-9.
The AutoFormat
dialog box.

For information about creating custom autoformats, see Chapter 10, "Formatting Graphs," page 241.

Editing the Data

PowerPoint offers a variety of ways to edit the data displayed by the graph, including moving, copying, inserting, and deleting the data. Before you can put any of these techniques to work, however, you must activate the datasheet by clicking the View Datasheet button on Graph's Standard toolbar or by choosing the Datasheet command from Graph's View menu.

Moving and Copying Data

You might want to move the data in your datasheet to make room for new data. Or you might want to rearrange the data so that the graph becomes more meaningful. For example, by ordering the data in your datasheet from largest to smallest or vice versa, you can enhance the impression the graph makes. As in Outline view and Slide view, you can move or copy data in the datasheet window by selecting it and then using the Cut, Copy, and Paste buttons on Graph's Standard toolbar; the Cut, Copy, and Paste commands on Graph's Edit menu or shortcut menu; or the corresponding key combinations. You can also use drag and drop to drag the data to a new location.

To move data with drag and drop, select a rectangular region of cells in your datasheet, place the pointer on the border of the selected cells (the pointer changes to an arrow), hold down the mouse button, and then drag. Release the mouse button when the cells are at the correct position.

By holding down the Ctrl key as you drag, you can copy the selected cells and then drop the copy in a new location on the datasheet. A small plus sign appears next to the pointer when you hold down the Ctrl key.

NOTE: PowerPoint displays a warning if you inadvertently try to drop data on a cell that already contains data. To continue the drag-and-drop operation, just click OK in the message box.

Now try using drag and drop to rearrange the data in your sample graph:

1. Select the three columns of data you've entered by dragging across column letter buttons A, B, and C, as shown below.

Presentation - Datasheet					
		A	**B**	**C**	**D**
		Package	Box	Letter	4th Qtr
1	Regular mail	$8.60	$10.75	$0.29	20.4
2	Overnight	$17.90	$22.00	$9.95	31.6
3	Courier	$48.00	$56.00	$17.50	43.9
4					

2. Place the pointer on the outline of the selected range, and when the pointer changes to an arrow, hold down the mouse button and drag the outline to the right, until it's over columns E, F, and G. Then release the mouse button to drop the data into place. (Be careful not to over-write the contents of column D.)

3. Next, click the column G button to select the contents of column G.

4. Drag the outline of column G to the left until it's over column A, and then release the mouse button. (Is this beginning to sound like "Insert tab A into slot B?")

5. Finally, select columns E and F, and drag them to columns B and C. Now the data is arranged sequentially from least expensive to most expensive.

Presentation - Datasheet		A	B	C	D	
		Letter	Package	Box	4th Qtr	
1	Regular mail	$0.29	$8.60	$10.75	20.4	
2	Overnight	$9.95	$17.90	$22.00	31.8	
3	Courier	$17.50	$48.00	$56.00	43.9	
4						

Inserting and Deleting Data

To insert a row or column of cells in the datasheet, click a row number or column letter button, and then choose Cells from Graph's Insert menu. To remove a row or column from the datasheet, click the row number or column letter button for the row or column you want to delete, and then choose Delete from Graph's Edit menu or shortcut menu. To add or remove more than one row or column at a time, drag across the row number or column letter buttons for as many rows or columns as you want to add or remove before you choose the Cells command or the Delete command. For example, to add three columns, drag across three column letter buttons, and then choose Cells from Graph's Insert menu.

When you select only some of the cells in a row or column and choose Cells from Graph's Insert menu or shortcut menu, the Insert dialog box, shown in Figure 6-10, appears. Here you can specify whether you want to push aside (shift) the other cells in the row or column or insert an entire row or column. If you want to push the cells aside, select Shift Cells Right or Shift Cells Down. If you want to insert an entire row or column, select Entire Row or Entire Column. Then click OK.

FIGURE 6-10.
The Insert dialog box.

Excluding Data

You can temporarily exclude data from a graph without deleting the data from the datasheet. Excluding data can be helpful when you want to use the same set of data to create several graphs. In one graph, you can compare only certain sets of data, and then, in another graph, you can compare different sets of data from the same data pool.

To exclude a row or column of data, double-click the corresponding row number or column letter button. The selected data in the row or column is dimmed, and the graph adjusts immediately. To include the data once again, double-click the same row number or column letter button.

You can also exclude multiple adjacent rows or columns of data by first selecting one or more cells in the rows or columns you want to exclude. Then choose the Exclude Row/Col command from Graph's Data menu. When the Exclude Row/Col dialog box appears, as shown in Figure 6-11, select the appropriate option and click OK.

FIGURE 6-11.
The Exclude Row/Col dialog box.

To return excluded data to a graph, select the excluded row or column, and choose the Include Row/Col command from Graph's Data menu.

Data Arrangements for Special Chart Types

For each chart type, Graph expects you to follow certain rules when it comes to arranging the data in the datasheet. Otherwise, the graph may deliver a message that is different from the one you intended.

Area, Bar, Column, Line, and Surface Charts

Charts with areas, bars, columns, lines, or a surface as their markers all require the same arrangement of data in the datasheet. You enter each series of numbers in a row or column, and then let Graph create the chart. By default, Graph interprets each row of numbers as a series. If you want Graph to interpret each column of numbers as a series, you must click the By Column button on Graph's Standard toolbar or choose the Series in Columns command from Graph's Data menu.

Clicking the By Column button after you've entered numbers in rows can give you an equally legitimate view of the data when you create a bar chart or column chart. In fact, you may want to try both options to see which makes your case more clearly. For example, Figure 6-12 shows a chart plotted by row. Figure

6-13 shows the same chart plotted by column. The chart in Figure 6-12 emphasizes the comparison of results from quarter to quarter whereas the one in Figure 6-13 emphasizes the comparison of results by region.

FIGURE 6-12.
A chart plotted by row.

FIGURE 6-13.
The same chart plotted by column.

Pie Charts

A pie chart can plot only one series, with each number in the series represented by a pie slice. To plot more than one series, you must use a doughnut chart, which plots multiple series in two dimensions as concentric rings in the chart. To show multiple breakdowns in three dimensions, you might want to consider using the stacked or 100% stacked subtype of a 3-D bar or column chart. Each bar or column can show the breakdown of a different series.

If you've entered more than one series in the datasheet for a pie chart, the chart plots the first series only. To plot a different series, exclude the earlier series. For example, to plot the third series in a datasheet, exclude the first and second series. Figure 6-14 shows a pie chart that plots the data in row 3 of the datasheet. Notice that rows 1 and 2 have been excluded and that a pie chart marker appears on the row 3 button.

FIGURE 6-14.

This pie chart plots the numbers in the third series, row 3, in the datasheet.

Radar Charts

The numbers in a series are represented as data markers on different radial axes of a radar chart. All the data markers in the same series are connected by a line that forms a ring around the center of the chart.

When you enter series in rows, each column is represented by a different radial axis. (The labels at the top of the columns identify the axes.) Figure 6-15 shows a radar chart and its datasheet.

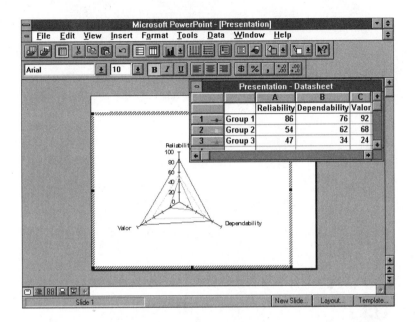

FIGURE 6-15.
A radar chart and its datasheet.

High-Low-Close and Open-High-Low-Close Charts

To create these two line chart subtypes, which are most often used to depict stock prices, you must enter all the high numbers in one series, all the low numbers in another series, and so on. The order in which you enter the numbers is important. If the chart depicts data series in rows, then follow one of these patterns:

Row	High-Low-Close Chart	Open-High-Low-Close Chart
1	High value	Opening value
2	Low value	High value
3	Closing value	Low value
4		Closing value

Figure 6-16 on the next page shows an open-high-low-close chart and the datasheet that underlies it.

FIGURE 6-16.

An open-high-low-close chart and its datasheet.

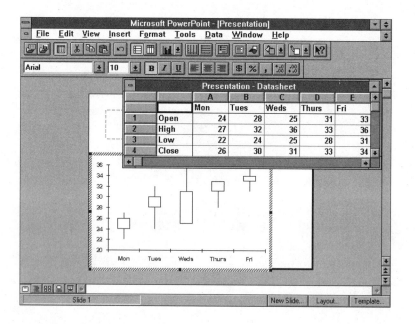

Using Data and Graphs from Microsoft Excel

If you've already typed the numbers for a chart in a Microsoft Excel worksheet, the last thing you want to do is retype the numbers in PowerPoint. Fortunately, there's an easy way to transfer your Excel data to PowerPoint. In fact, you can set up a link between the original numbers in Excel and the copies in Power-Point. Then, if you change the numbers in Excel, the numbers in PowerPoint are updated automatically. You can also import Excel charts into PowerPoint; and you can even drag a chart from an Excel window onto a PowerPoint slide.

Importing Excel Data into Graph

To perform a simple transfer of data from an Excel worksheet to Graph, you can use the Import Data command on Graph's Edit menu. You can then specify the Excel file and the range that contains the data you want to import.

> **NOTE:** Use the Import Data command when you want to copy data from an Excel worksheet. To establish a link between the Excel data and the PowerPoint graph, however, you must use a different procedure, as described in the next section.

To import data from an Excel worksheet like the one shown here, follow the steps below.

1. Switch to the Graph datasheet by clicking the View Datasheet button on Graph's Standard toolbar or by choosing Datasheet from Graph's View menu.

2. In the datasheet, click the cell located in the upper left corner of the area into which you want to import the data.

3. From Graph's Edit menu, choose the Import Data command. The Import Data dialog box appears, as shown here:

4. Use the Directories list and File Name list to navigate to the Excel file containing the data you want to import.

5. At the bottom of the dialog box, select Entire File to import all the data in the file or select Range to import only the data in the range you specify. (If you select Range, be sure to enter the range address or the range name in the Range edit box.)

6. Click OK to import the data.

7. If the destination cells in the datasheet already contain data, Graph displays a message warning you that the data will be overwritten. Click OK to proceed or click Cancel to cancel the import operation. If you click Cancel, you can then select a different destination in the datasheet and begin the procedure again. When the data is successfully imported, it appears in the Graph datasheet like this:

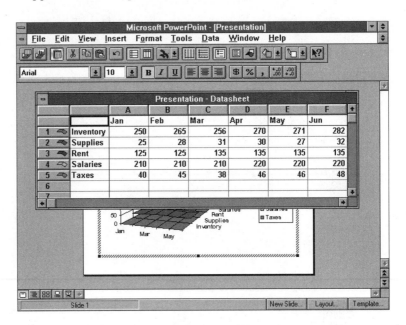

NOTE: To import data from an Excel 5 workbook, the data must reside in the first worksheet in the workbook. If it does not, you must reorder the worksheets in the workbook.

TIP You can use the Import Data command to consolidate data from several Excel worksheets into a single Graph datasheet. After you import data from the first worksheet, select another location in the datasheet, import data from the second worksheet, and so on.

Creating a Link Between Excel and Graph

Establishing a link between the data in an Excel worksheet and the data in a Graph datasheet allows you to update the numbers in Excel and then see the changes automatically reflected in PowerPoint.

To create a link, you use a special feature of Windows called object linking and embedding (OLE). Don't worry, you won't need to deal with terms that are any more technical than "link." Windows takes care of all the behind-the-scenes complexity. Simply by copying the data to the Windows Clipboard in Excel and then using the Paste Link command in Graph to paste the data from the Clipboard to the datasheet, you automatically establish the link you need. Then, after the link is created, PowerPoint's ChartWizard appears to help you complete the transfer of data.

To create a link, follow these steps:

1. In Excel, select the range of data you want to link to PowerPoint, as shown here:

2. Choose the Copy command from Excel's Edit menu to copy the data to the Windows Clipboard.

3. Switch to the datasheet window in PowerPoint, and select the cell in the upper left corner of the area into which you want to paste the data.

4. From Graph's Edit menu, choose the Paste Link command. If Graph displays a message box warning you about overwriting existing data, click OK to continue the operation or click Cancel. When you click OK, the ChartWizard dialog box opens in its own window, as shown here:

The ChartWizard has only one step, as you can see in the title bar of the dialog box, and it provides several options you can use to determine how data is arranged in the resulting graph. The Sample Chart on the left side of the dialog box displays the results of the options you select.

Use the options in the Data Series in section to specify whether the data series in the Excel worksheet are arranged by row or column. Use the other options to specify how the information in the first row and first column of the Excel worksheet should be treated. If you want to import both the labels and the data from the Excel worksheet, you select the Category (X) Axis Labels option and the Series (Y) Axis Labels option.

5. In the ChartWizard dialog box, select the options you want and then click OK. The data appears in the Graph datasheet, like this:

		A	B	C	D	E	
		Eric	Lola				
1	02-Jan	34	54				
2	09-Jan	34	45				
3	16-Jan	36	54				
4	23-Jan	37	61				
5	30-Jan	39	64				
6							
7							
8							
9							

Presentation - Datasheet

Updating the Link

After you create a link between Excel and PowerPoint, the link will be updated automatically unless you change it to a manual update link. Just for interest's sake, you can arrange the Excel and PowerPoint windows side by side to see the link in action; when you change a number in Excel, you can immediately see the number updated in PowerPoint.

To change the characteristics of the link, choose the Link command from the Graph Edit menu. The Link dialog box appears, as shown in Figure 6-17. To change the link so that it updates only when you click the Update Now button, select the Manual option at the bottom of the Link dialog box. Other options in this dialog box allow you to open the original data in Excel for editing; select a different data source—perhaps a different range in the Excel worksheet; or break the link between Excel and PowerPoint. If you break the link, the data remains in the Graph datasheet, but it is no longer updated when you make changes in the Excel worksheet.

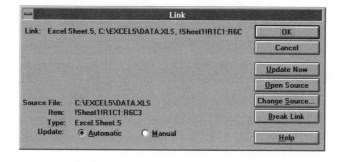

FIGURE 6-17.

The Link dialog box.

Importing an Excel Chart

If you've already created a graph in Excel, you can import the graph into PowerPoint. The graph arrives as a standard graph that you can edit in Graph as if you'd created the graph in PowerPoint rather than Excel.

 TIP Another way to bring a Microsoft Excel graph into a presentation is to drag the graph from Excel to a PowerPoint slide (press the Ctrl key while you drag to copy the graph into PowerPoint rather than move it) or copy and paste the graph from Excel to PowerPoint. However, both of these methods produce a picture of the graph rather than an actual graph that you can modify in PowerPoint.

To import a graph that you have created in Excel, follow these steps:

1. From Graph's Edit menu, choose the Import Chart command to display the Open Chart dialog box shown below.

2. In the List Files of Type drop-down list, select either Microsoft Excel 4.0 Charts (*.xlc) or Microsoft Excel 5.0 Charts (*.xls).

3. Use the Directories and File Name lists to navigate to the Excel file you want to import, and then double-click the filename.

The Excel graph data appears in the Graph datasheet, and the graph appears on the slide with the same formatting it had in Excel. You can then use Graph's features to reformat the graph.

> **NOTE:** PowerPoint imports the graph on the first chart sheet it finds in an Excel 5 workbook. You may have to rearrange the sheets to bring the chart sheet you want to the front.

Using Text and Data from Data Files

When the data you need for a graph is stored in an ASCII text file (a text file without formatting), you can import the file into Graph using the Import Data command. The columns of data in the file should be separated by tabs, semicolons, commas, or spaces.

To import an ASCII text file, follow these steps:

1. In the Graph datasheet, click the cell in the upper left corner of the destination area for the data.

2. Choose the Import Data command from Graph's Edit menu, and when the Import Data dialog box appears, select Text Files (*.prn, *.txt, *.csv) in the List Files of Type drop-down list.

3. Use the Directories and File Name lists to navigate to the file you want to import, and then double-click the filename. The Text Import Wizard opens, as shown below.

If the columns of data are separated by tabs, semicolons, or commas, the file is *delimited*, and by default the Delimited option is selected as the file type. If the columns of data are separated by spaces, the Fixed Width option is selected. A preview at the bottom of the first Text Import Wizard dialog box shows the data to be imported.

4. Click the Next button or press N to move on to step 2, shown here:

5. If the Text Import Wizard has not properly identified the delimiter used in the file (tabs or commas, for example), select the correct delimiter in the Step 2 dialog box. Vertical lines should properly separate the columns of data in the Data Preview box.

6. Click the Next button or press N to get to step 3, shown below.

7. Select each column of data in the preview by clicking anywhere in the column. Then check the Column Data Format section that appears in the upper right corner of the Step 3 dialog box. If the Text Import Wizard has selected the incorrect data format, select the correct format now.

8. Click the Finish button to complete the import procedure. The data appears in the Graph datasheet, and you can then format the resulting graph to suit your needs.

That completes your introduction to creating graphs and graph slides. In Chapter 10, "Formatting Graphs," you'll learn how to create custom graphs that you can tailor to meet even the most demanding requirements. For now, you might want to spend a little time reviewing PowerPoint's graphing features before moving on to the next chapter, where you'll learn how to add organization chart slides to your presentations.

7

Adding Organization Chart Slides

An organization chart, or *org chart*, shows the hierarchy of an organization using a series of boxes and connecting lines. A classic hierarchy is the military's structure of commanding officers, officers, and enlisted men and women. But an org chart can also depict the structure of a company, a division within a company or a government department, or even groups of organizations that are affiliated in a "top-down" arrangement.

This chapter introduces you to PowerPoint's built-in organization chart module. You'll learn how to create an org chart slide from scratch, how to add an org chart to an existing slide, and how to incorporate an existing org chart in a presentation. In addition, you'll learn how to create and modify the org chart's structure and how to format its text, boxes, and connecting lines.

Org Chart Basics

The procedure you use to add an org chart to your presentation depends on where you want the chart to appear. If you want the org chart to be on a new slide that is dedicated to the chart, you can create a new slide and then select a layout that includes an org chart placeholder. If you want the chart to be on an existing slide or if you want to use an existing org chart, you can add an org chart object to a slide.

Creating an Org Chart Slide

PowerPoint's autolayouts make it easy to create an org chart slide for a presentation. When you click the New Slide button and select the Org Chart autolayout, PowerPoint creates a new slide with an org chart placeholder.

Here are the specific steps for creating an org chart slide:

1. In Slide view, move to the slide that you want the org chart slide to follow.

2. Click the New Slide button at the bottom of the PowerPoint window.

3. In the New Slide dialog box, select the Org Chart autolayout, as shown on the facing page.

4. Click OK or double-click the Org Chart autolayout. PowerPoint creates this new slide with an org chart placeholder:

5. Double-click the org chart placeholder. The Microsoft Organization Chart module opens, as shown on the next page.

Icon bar

As you can see, the org chart contains a number of placeholders to simplify the task of entering information in the chart. All you have to do is type away.

Adding an Org Chart to an Existing Slide

If you want a slide to include both an org chart and another object, such as a group of bulleted text items or a graph, you can add an org chart to an existing slide. The bulleted text items can help explain the org chart, and a graph can depict a numeric achievement that resulted from a change in the organization's structure.

 TIP Org charts should be large enough that viewers can see the boxes and the text inside clearly. If the chart is too small, viewers won't be able to make out the detail. You might consider breaking the structure into separate charts that show divisions, or you might want to place the chart on a new slide that will give it plenty of space.

 The easiest way to add a new org chart to an existing slide is to display the slide in Slide view, and then click the Insert Org Chart button on the Standard toolbar. The Microsoft Organization Chart module opens in a window, as shown above. Note the icon bar below the menu bar.

Here's another method for adding an org chart to an existing slide:

1. In Slide view, move to the slide you want to add the org chart to.

2. Choose Object from the Insert menu to display the Insert Object dialog box shown below.

3. Make sure the Create New option is selected, and then double-click Microsoft Organization Chart 1.0 in the Object Type list. (You'll probably have to scroll down to it.)

The Microsoft Organization Chart module opens in a window so that you can create the org chart.

 See Also: For more information about entering text in org charts, see "Filling in the Boxes," page 169.

Using an Existing Org Chart

If you've already created and saved an org chart, you can pull it into a presentation by inserting the chart as an object. If you follow the procedure below, you can double-click the chart to edit it from within PowerPoint:

1. In Slide view, move to the slide you want to add the org chart to.

2. Choose Object from the Insert menu.

3. In the Insert Object dialog box, select the Create from File option.

4. Enter the org chart's pathname in the File edit box. If you can't remember the pathname, click the Browse button to display the Browse dialog box, in which you can search for the org chart file. After you find the file, simply double-click it to enter its pathname in the Insert Object dialog box.

5. Select the Display As Icon option only if you want an icon to represent the chart on the slide. During an electronic presentation, you can then "drill down" to the Microsoft Organization Chart module by double-clicking the icon. The org chart opens in the module, and you can modify it right in front of your audience.

6. Click OK to add the org chart to the current slide.

    NOTE: If you want to establish a link between the original org chart file and the picture of the org chart that will be displayed in PowerPoint, select the Link option in the Insert Object dialog box. Linking allows the chart in the presentation to reflect any subsequent changes that are made in the original org chart file. But be careful: If you select Link and then move the presentation to another computer, the chart will not come along for the ride. That's because the data for the chart is stored in the external org chart file rather than in PowerPoint. To store the data for the org chart in PowerPoint, you must leave the Link option unselected in the Insert Object dialog box.

Creating the Org Chart Structure

When the Microsoft Organization Chart window (hereafter known as the *Org Chart window*) opens, the beginning of a hierarchy (one manager and three subordinates) is displayed in four boxes. (If you see only one box in the Org Chart window, you can choose Options from the Org Chart Edit menu, select the Use standard 4-box template for new charts option, and click OK. Then close the Org Chart window, and click No when the program asks whether to update the presentation. You can then create a new org chart with four boxes.)

Before you begin entering text in the org chart's boxes, you may want to give the chart a title. Select the text *Chart Title* at the top of the chart, and type a new title, such as *Our Division*. You can press Enter at the end of the title line to add a line for a subtitle. In fact, you can create a series of subtitles, but then you'll have little room left for the chart!

Filling in the Boxes

To start entering names in the org chart's boxes, follow these steps:

1. Click the box at the highest level.

2. Type a name in the box, and press Enter. You can also press Tab or the Down arrow key. As shown below, when you begin typing, the box opens to reveal spaces for two comments in addition to the name and the title.

3. Type the title and press Enter.

4. If you want to include comments, type them in, pressing Enter after each one. If you don't want to include comments, skip to the next step.

5. Press Ctrl+Down arrow key to move to the first subordinate box.

6. Follow steps 2 through 4 above to fill in the box.

7. To move to the next box, simply press Ctrl+Right arrow key. You can also press Ctrl+Left arrow key to move to the box to the left, and you can press Ctrl+Up arrow key to move to the top box.

Editing the Text

After you enter text in an org chart box, you can edit the text by clicking the box once to select it and then clicking an insertion point in the text you want to edit. You can use all the same text selection and editing techniques you use elsewhere in PowerPoint.

TIP   After you enter text in a box, you can press Esc to complete the entry but leave the box selected. Then you can immediately edit the text if necessary.

You can also edit the text in an org chart by clicking the Text button on the icon bar and then clicking any of the text in the chart. As you'll learn later, the Text button is useful for typing text directly on the chart background as well.

For more information about text editing techniques, see "Editing Text in Ouline View," page 68.

Adding and Deleting Boxes

Chances are, your organization has more than three members, so you need to know how to add more boxes to the org chart. Fortunately, adding boxes couldn't be easier. On the icon bar, click the button for the type of box you want to add, and then click the box that you want to connect the new box to. To add several boxes at a time, click the appropriate icon bar button several times, and then click an existing box.

The boxes you can add to an org chart are shown in Table 7-1, along with their corresponding buttons and a description of each button's function.

To add a subordinate to one of the three subordinates already in the chart, follow these steps:

1. Click the Subordinate button on the icon bar.

2. Click one of the three boxes in the second row of the chart. A new box appears, ready for you to type in a name, title, and comments, as shown on the facing page.

Box	Icon Bar Button	Function
	Subordinate	Adds a box at the level below the selected box.
	Left Co-worker	Adds a box to the left of the selected box at the same level.
	Right Co-worker	Adds a box to the right of the selected box at the same level.
	Manager	Adds a box at the level of the selected box and moves the selected box down one level. The selected box is attached to the new box as a subordinate.
	Assistant	Adds a box below the selected box. The new box is attached to the line of command but is not a part of it (a staff position).

TABLE 7-1.

The org chart boxes and their corresponding icon bar buttons.

171

TIP   You may want to diagram each division of a complicated organizational structure in a separate chart to avoid
overcrowding. You can create a preliminary organization
chart that depicts the broad picture (the branches of the
organization without any of the "leaves"), and then show
each division in detail in a separate chart.

Deleting an org chart box is as easy as adding one. Simply select the box
you want to delete, and then press the Delete key or choose Clear from the Org
Chart Edit menu. To delete two or more boxes, first select the boxes by clicking
one box, holding down the Shift key, and clicking the other boxes. Then press
Delete to delete all the selected boxes.

TIP   If the org chart boxes you want to delete are adjacent
to one another, you can use the Selection button on the icon
bar to drag a selection box around the boxes. Then you can
press Delete to delete the selected boxes.

A Sample Org Chart

To try your hand at creating an org chart with an assortment of boxes, follow
this example: Imagine that you need to diagram the structure of a nonprofit
organization and its regional affiliates. If you've been following along by
creating an actual chart, choose Exit and Return to *Presentation* from the Org
Chart File menu now, and then click No when you are asked if you want to
update the chart. When you return to PowerPoint, start a new org chart by
clicking the Insert Org Chart button on the Standard toolbar, and then follow
these steps:

1. After the Org Chart window opens, select the text *Chart Title* at the top
    of the new chart, and type *League of Lefties*.

2. Click the topmost box once, type *Renee A. Gauche* as the name, press
    Enter, and type *President* as the title.

3. For the first comment, type *Wash., D.C.* You won't enter a second
    comment, so press Ctrl+Down arrow key to move to the first subordi-
    nate box. The org chart should look like this:

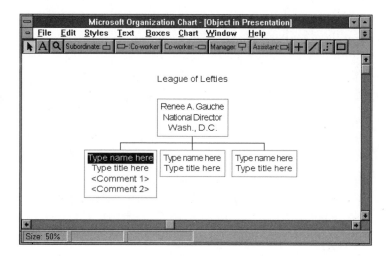

4. In the first subordinate box, type *Greta Links,* press Enter, and type *Director* as the title and *California* as the first comment. Then press Ctrl+Right arrow key to move to the second subordinate box.

5. In the second subordinate box, type *Leonora Izquierda,* press Enter, and type *Director* as the title and *New York* as the first comment.

6. The League of Lefties does not have a third individual at the Director level, so click the third subordinate box, and press Delete. The chart now looks like this:

7. Greta Links has two subordinates, so click the Subordinate button on the icon bar twice, and then click Greta's box. Two subordinates appear.

8. Leonora Izquierda has three subordinates, so click the Subordinate button three times, and then click Leonora's box.

9. Renee A. Gauche has an assistant, so click the Assistant button, and then click Renee's box. Next, type *Sylvia Southpaw* as the name, type *Assistant* as the title, and then click anywhere outside the org chart.

10. Enter the names of the subordinates under both Greta and Leonora. Click the first subordinate box under Greta, type *Tiffany*, press Ctrl+Right arrow key, and type *Brent*. Type *Sal, Howie*, and *Clarice* as the subordinates under Leonora. Here are the results:

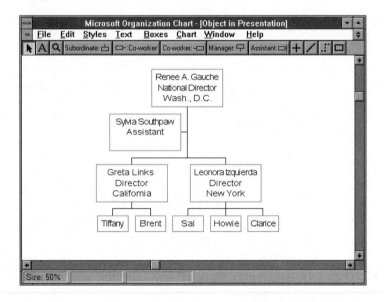

Later in this chapter, you'll modify the structure and change the formatting of the org chart you've just created. For now, return with the chart to PowerPoint by first choosing Update *Presentation* from the Org Chart File menu and then choosing Exit and Return to *Presentation* from the File menu. In a moment, the chart appears on the current PowerPoint slide. Save the PowerPoint presentation with the name SAMPLORG.PPT so that you can retrieve it later.

Moving Boxes

The ease with which you can modify the structure of an org chart suits today's dynamic organizations. But fortunately or unfortunately, depending on your place in the organization, restructuring an actual org chart in PowerPoint is far easier than restructuring an actual organization.

Restructuring an organization in real life often results in moving people from one manager to another. The counterpart in PowerPoint is dragging a box from one place in the org chart to another. You can drag boxes to other positions at the same level in the chart, or move them up or down within the organization's structure.

To move a box in an org chart, follow these steps:

1. Open the org chart in the Org Chart window.

2. Place the mouse pointer on the box you want to move.

3. Hold down the left mouse button, and drag the box's frame to another box, as shown below.

4. When the frame is in position, release the mouse button.

When you drag a box's frame near the left or right inside edge of another box and release the mouse button, the moved box appears to the left or right of the other box, at the same level. When you drag the frame near the bottom inside edge of another box, the moved box appears below the other box, as a subordinate.

When you drag the frame onto another box, an indicator appears inside the frame. As shown in Figure 7-1, the indicator is a left arrow when the moved box will appear at the left side of the existing box. The indicator is a right arrow when the moved box will appear at the right side of the existing box. The indicator is a subordinate box when the moved box will appear below the existing box, as a subordinate.

FIGURE 7-1.

The left arrow indicates that the moved box will appear to the left of the existing box.

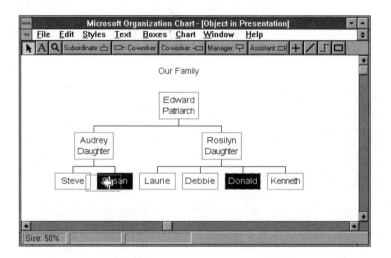

Try moving a box in the org chart you created earlier by first opening the SAMPLORG.PPT file (if necessary), double-clicking the org chart to open the Org Chart window, and then placing the mouse pointer on Sal's box. Next, hold down the left mouse button, and drag Sal's box onto Greta's box without releasing the mouse button. Then move Sal's box toward the bottom of Greta's box, and when the subordinate indicator appears inside Sal's box, release the mouse button to drop the box into place. Sal appears to the right of Brent. Now move Sal between Tiffany and Brent by clicking anywhere outside the chart to deselect Sal's box and dragging Sal's box onto Brent's box. Notice the left arrow inside Sal's box when you drag it onto Brent's box. The arrow indicates that Sal's box will drop to the left of Brent's box, just as you want. Release the mouse button to see the results shown in Figure 7-2.

Finally, return to the presentation by choosing Update SAMPLORG.PPT from the Org Chart File menu and then choosing Exit and Return to SAMPL-ORG.PPT from the File menu. Resave the presentation file with the changes by clicking the Save button on the Standard toolbar, choosing Save from the File menu, or pressing Ctrl+S.

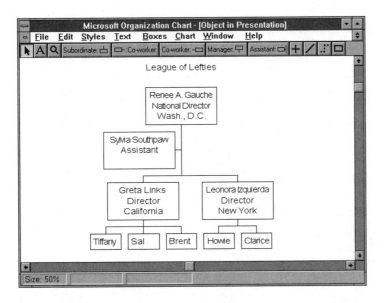

FIGURE 7-2.
The revised org chart.

Changing the Style of Groups and Branches

The subordinates under a manager are called a *group*. By default, PowerPoint displays a group in boxes that are side by side. But, from the Styles menu, you can choose several other ways to display a group. For example, the members of a group can be shown as a vertical list, or they can be depicted as leaves that emanate from a central branch.

Obviously, before you can change the style of an org chart group, you must select the group. So your first step is to double-click any member of the group, or click a member and then press Ctrl+G (*G* for *Group*) to select the entire group. You can also select a group by selecting one member of the group and choosing Select and then Group from the Org Chart Edit menu. Figure 7-3 on the next page shows the members of a group after they have been selected. Note that the group members report to the same manager.

 TIP   You can also select a group of org chart boxes by clicking the Selection button on the icon bar and dragging a selection box around the group.

FIGURE 7-3.

The members of a
selected group.

After you select a group, open the Styles menu, and click one of the six group style buttons at the top of the menu. For a group at the lowest level of a chart, a useful style is that shown on the second button in the second row of styles. Arranging a group in this style can reduce the horizontal space needed by a chart whose organizational structure is wide rather than deep.

Just as you can change the style of an org chart group, you can also change the style of an org chart *branch*. A branch consists of a manager and all the manager's subordinates. To select a branch, select the manager at the top of the branch, and then press Ctrl+B (*B* for *Branch*), or choose Select and then Branch from the Org Chart Edit menu. After you select a branch, you can choose one of the styles from the Styles menu.

TIP   You can also select an org chart branch by clicking the Selection button on the icon bar and dragging a selection box around the branch.

Two special styles at the bottom of the Styles menu let you change the rank of members of a group. The first style, Assistant, changes selected members of a group to assistants. For example, Figure 7-4 displays two org charts on a slide. The left chart shows three subordinates under a manager. The right chart shows the result after two of the subordinates are converted to assistants with the Assistant style.

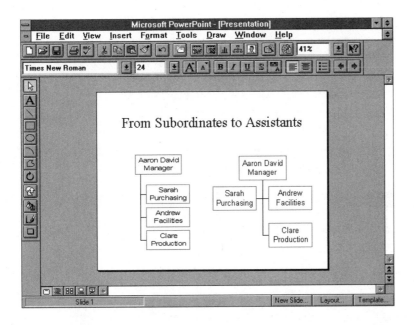

FIGURE 7-4.
Subordinates converted to assistants with the Assistant style.

The second style at the bottom of the Styles menu is the Co-manager style. You can use this style to indicate two or more members of the organization who report to the same manager and share power. After you select the members you want to make comanagers, click the Co-manager style on the Styles menu. Figure 7-5 shows two subordinates who have become comanagers.

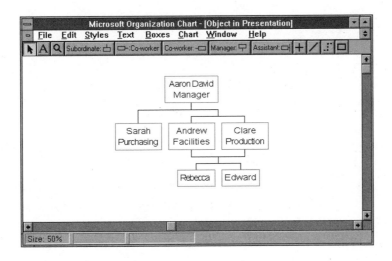

FIGURE 7-5.
Subordinates converted to comanagers with the Co-manager style.

179

Try changing the style of the groups in the org chart you created earlier, by first opening the SAMPLORG.PPT file, if necessary, and then double-clicking the org chart to open the Org Chart window. Next, click one of the subordinates under Greta, and press Ctrl+G to select the entire group of subordinates who report to Greta. Open the Styles menu, and click the second style in the second row. The three side-by-side boxes of the group change to a small ladder that lists the three subordinates. You can try other styles or choose the same style for Leonora's group of subordinates. Figure 7-6 shows Greta's group with its new style.

FIGURE 7-6.

The new style applied to the group of subordinates who report to Greta Links.

Formatting the Org Chart

An org chart inherits the design characteristics of the template that you attached to the current presentation. For example, the template determines the font of the text and the color of the boxes in the org chart. But, as you'll learn in this section, after you complete an organizational structure, you can still make changes to the appearance of the chart. For instance, you can emphasize the titles of the organization members with a special color or change the borders of the boxes.

Zooming In and Out

Before you start formatting an org chart, you should get acquainted with the Org Chart zoom feature. That way, you can see exactly what you're doing when you make changes to a chart.

To zoom in on an org chart, click the Enlarge button on the icon bar, and then click the area of the org chart you want to zoom in on. To zoom out, click the Reduce button that appears in place of the Enlarge button, and then click the org chart. You can also use the following commands to change the zoom percentage of the chart: Choose Size to Window from the Chart menu or press F9 to fit the entire chart within the Org Chart window; choose 50% of Actual or press F10 to reduce the chart to 50 percent of its actual size, which, in turn, is approximately 50 percent of its printed size; and choose 200% of Actual or press F12 to enlarge the chart so that you can focus on some of the chart detail.

TIP   As a shortcut, you can hold down the Ctrl+Shift keys and click the left mouse button to toggle between the Actual Size command and the Size to Window command.

Formatting the Text

The procedures for formatting the text in an org chart are similar to the procedures for formatting text elsewhere in PowerPoint. Rather than use commands on the Format menu, however, you use commands on the Org Chart Text menu. These commands allow you to change the font, color, and alignment of the text in org chart boxes.

Of course, before you can use the commands on the Text menu, you must select the text you want to format. To select all the text in a box, click the box. To select all the text in several boxes, hold down the Shift key as you click each box. You can also select specific boxes by using the Select commands on the Org Chart Edit menu. Table 7-2 on the next page describes each of the Select commands.

TABLE 7-2.
The Select
commands.

Command	Function
All	Selects all boxes in the org chart.
All Assistants	Selects all assistants.
All Co-Managers	Selects all members who have been made comanagers with the Co-manager style.
All Managers	Selects only members who have subordinates.
All Non-Managers	Selects only members who do not have subordinates.
Group	Selects the other members of a group. You must have one group member selected first.
Branch	Selects the other members of a branch. You must have one branch member selected first.
Lowest Level	Selects only the boxes at the lowest level of the org chart.
Connecting Lines	Selects only the connecting lines between boxes.

TIP   You can also select several adjacent boxes by clicking the Selection button on the icon bar and dragging a selection box around the boxes.

To format specific text in a box, such as the title only, click the box, and then click an insertion point in the text you want to format. Next, use any of the standard text selection techniques to select the text in the box. For example, drag across the text with the mouse, double-click a word, or hold down the Shift key as you press the Left or Right arrow key. By selecting only certain text within a box, you can change the appearance of as little or as much text as you want. You can even format a single character with a special font or color.

Unfortunately, PowerPoint provides no easy method to select all names or all titles in an org chart. You must move from box to box, selecting the name or the title, if you want to apply special formatting to only those elements.

Formatting the Boxes

By selecting an org chart box and then using the commands on the Boxes menu, you can change the box's borders, add a shadow, and modify the box's color. Before you can make any of these changes, however, you must select the box or boxes you want to format using the techniques described in the previous section. Then simply choose the desired commands from the Boxes menu. For example, to format a box with an extra-thick border and the color red, first click the box to select it, choose the Box Border command from the Boxes menu, and then click the third border option in the second column of the Box Border submenu. Next, choose Box Color from the Boxes menu, and then click the red color option in the Box Color submenu.

To change the thickness, style, and color of a selected box's border, use the Line Thickness, Line Style, and Line Color commands on the Boxes menu. Figure 7-7 shows the org chart in SAMPLORG.PPT formatted with heavier borders.

FIGURE 7-7.

The sample org chart formatted with heavier borders.

The Box Shadow options allow you to apply a shadow that extends in one or more directions behind the selected box or boxes. Shadows give boxes a three-dimensional look. Figure 7-8 on the next page shows shadows added to the boxes in the sample org chart.

FIGURE 7-8.

The sample org chart with shadows added.

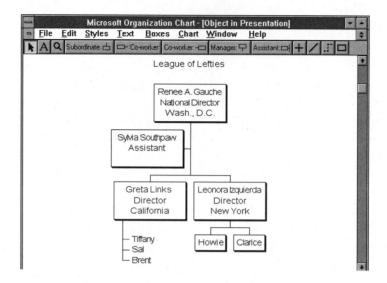

The Box Color options allow you to apply any of the colors in the current color palette to the interior of the selected box or boxes. (After you finish creating the org chart, you'll see it on the slide, against the slide background, and you'll be able to determine whether the box interior color clashes with the slide background color.)

Formatting the Lines

You can change the thickness, style, and color of the lines that connect org chart boxes just as easily as you change the formatting of the boxes. Before you can change the formatting of a line, however, you must select the line by clicking it. The line then changes to a light gray to show that it is selected. You can select multiple lines by holding down the Shift key as you click each line.

TIP   You can also select multiple lines by clicking the Selection button on the icon bar and dragging a selection box around the lines. Be careful as you drag the selection box. If you also enclose organization boxes in the selection box, the borders of the boxes will change when you change the line settings.

After you select the line or lines you want to format, choose the Line Thickness, Line Style, or Line Color command from the Boxes menu. Each command offers a set of options that are fairly self-explanatory. Figure 7-9 shows the org chart in SAMPLORG.PPT formatted with thicker connecting lines. Figure 7-10 shows the chart's connecting lines with the Dotted line style.

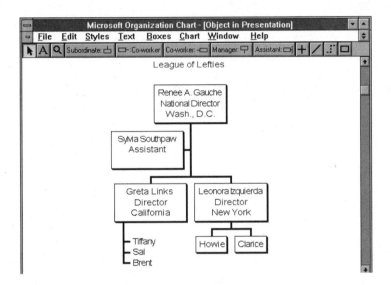

FIGURE 7-9.

The sample org chart formatted with thicker connecting lines.

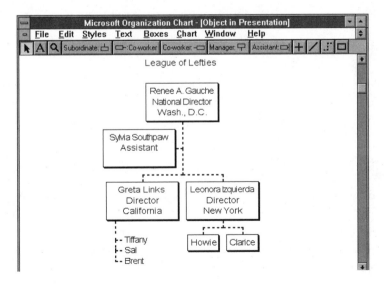

FIGURE 7-10.

The connecting lines in the sample org chart formatted with the Dotted line style.

185

Drawing Boxes and Lines with the Drawing Tools

Sometimes the built-in box arrangements (subordinates under managers, assistants below managers, and comanagers sharing power) simply cannot describe the complicated, spaghetti-like reporting structures in an organization. Fortunately, you can add new boxes and lines easily with the Microsoft Organization Chart module's drawing tools, shown below.

There's one very important caveat about the objects you draw with the org chart module's drawing tools, however: These objects appear on the chart's background and do not become part of the actual chart. Therefore, if you move or resize the chart or make changes to its structure, you must adjust the boxes and lines you've added. You may want to wait until the organization chart is otherwise complete before you add any last-minute boxes and lines.

> **NOTE:** If you don't see four drawing tools to the right of the Assistant button on the icon bar, choose Show Draw Tools from the Chart menu or press Ctrl+D.

To draw perpendicular or diagonal lines on the chart, click the appropriate tool, place the cross-hair pointer at the starting point for the line, hold down the left mouse button, and then drag to draw the line. After you add a line, you can select the line by clicking it with the mouse. You can then delete the line with the Delete key, format the line with the commands on the Boxes menu, or move the line by dragging the handles at either end.

To connect two boxes with a line, click the Connecting Line tool, place the pointer at the edge of the first box, and then drag to the edge of the second box, as shown in Figure 7-11. As you drag, you'll see the connecting line appear. If the connecting line has three segments (like the one in Figure 7-11), you can drag the middle segment to change the size or shape of the line. You may have to move the middle segment if the connecting line overlaps an existing line or box.

FIGURE 7-11.

A new connecting line has been added to the sample org chart.

To draw a new box, as shown in Figure 7-12, click the Rectangle tool, place the cross-hair pointer where you want the box to appear, and then drag to create the new box. To adjust the size or shape of the new box, drag one of the handles at the sides or corners of the box. To move the box, place the mouse

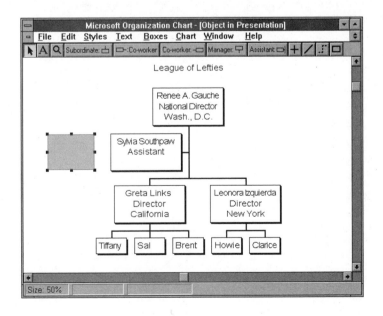

FIGURE 7-12.

A new box has been added to the sample org chart.

pointer on the border of the box, between two handles, and drag in the desired direction.

You cannot use the Connecting Line tool to connect new boxes with existing chart boxes or with other new boxes. To connect new boxes, you must draw lines with the Perpendicular Line tool or the Diagonal Line tool.

Returning to PowerPoint

When the org chart is complete, choose Update *Presentation* from the Org Chart File menu, and then choose Exit and Return to *Presentation* from the File menu. If you choose Exit and Return without choosing Update first, PowerPoint displays a dialog box asking whether you want to update the chart. Click Yes to proceed.

The new org chart appears on the current PowerPoint slide. You can move the entire chart or drag a corner handle to resize the chart, but the chart always remains the same shape.

To edit the chart, double-click it. The Microsoft Organization Chart window reopens with the chart inside, ready for editing.

In this chapter, you've learned to create another special type of object that you can place on PowerPoint slides: organization charts. You learned about graph slides in the previous chapter, and in the next chapter, you'll complete the survey of slide types by learning about table slides.

Adding Table Slides

When you want to display text paragraphs side by side—to lay out the pros and cons of an issue, for example—you can use the row-and-column format of a table. PowerPoint's table slides are quick to make and easy to modify, especially when compared to the alternative, which is to align text in columns with tab stops.

Table slides often hold text only, but they can hold numbers just as easily. When you don't need the power of a graph to illustrate a result, a table can do quite nicely. Tables are also useful as a backup to a graph, when the audience needs to see the raw data.

This chapter focuses on how to create a slide devoted entirely to a table and how to add a table to an existing slide. Because PowerPoint uses the table-making module from Microsoft Word 6 for Windows, not everyone can create a table in PowerPoint. If you do not have Word 6, you must create a table in another application and import it into PowerPoint as an object, which is a more complex process.

By borrowing Word's table-making module, PowerPoint gives you all of Word's advanced text handling and formatting capabilities as you create tables. For example, you can use Word's thesaurus to find a synonym. In fact, you gain access to all of Word's menus and tools without having to leave PowerPoint. (An in-depth discussion of Word's capabilities is beyond the scope of this book. For more information about Word's features, see the *Microsoft Word 6 User's Guide.*)

Table Basics

When you need to include a table in a presentation, you can create a new slide devoted to the table or you can add the table to an existing slide that already contains other objects, such as a group of bulleted text items.

Creating a Table Slide

Creating a table slide for a presentation is easy. Just follow these steps:

1. In Slide view, move to the slide that the table slide should follow.

2. Click the New Slide button at the bottom of the PowerPoint window.

3. In the New Slide dialog box, double-click the Table autolayout:

Table autolayout

As you can see here, the new slide contains two placeholders: one for the slide title and one for the table.

4. Double-click the table placeholder to display the dialog box shown on the next page.

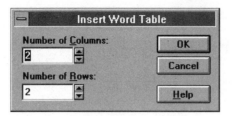

5. In the Insert Word Table dialog box, enter the number of columns and the number of rows you want to include in the table by typing new numbers in the Number of Columns and Number of Rows edit boxes or by clicking the up or down arrows next to the edit boxes. Then click OK to create the table.

Using a Microsoft Excel Table

If the data for a graph comes from Microsoft Excel, you might want to reserve a slide to display the Excel table as a backup slide. (That way, if someone asks for clarification of the table's data, you can produce the original Excel table.) When you embed an Excel table in a PowerPoint slide, the table appears just as it does in Excel, plus you gain all the advantages of Excel's data calculation powers from within PowerPoint. For example, Excel tables (actually small worksheets embedded in PowerPoint slides) can include formulas that carry out complicated calculations, and the formula results are updated automatically when any of the numbers change. For information about embedding an Excel table, see "Using PowerPoint with Microsoft Excel 5," page 416.

Adding a Table to an Existing Slide

You can use either of two methods to add a table to an existing slide. Here are the steps for the first method:

1. Click the Insert Microsoft Word Table button on the Standard toolbar to display the following 4 x 5 grid of empty cells:

2. Position the mouse pointer on the cell in the upper left corner of the grid, hold down the left mouse button, and drag across the number of columns (up to 15) and down the number of rows (up to 5) you want in the table. For example, the result of the grid selected below would be a table with five rows and three columns.

3. Release the mouse button to add the table to the current slide.

The second method you can use to add a table to an existing slide involves the following steps:

1. Choose the Microsoft Word Table command from the Insert menu.

2. When the Insert Word Table dialog box appears, as shown earlier, enter the number of columns and rows you want in the table, and click OK.

TIP If you've already created a table in Word, you can drag and drop the table onto a PowerPoint slide, as you'll learn in "Using PowerPoint with Microsoft Word 6 for Windows," page 409.

Entering Text in a Table

When you create a new table slide, an empty table appears within a gray frame on the slide. Vertical and horizontal rulers adjoin the table, and dotted lines called *gridlines* mark the boundaries of the columns and rows of cells in the table. Figure 8-1 shows a slide with a brand new table.

FIGURE 8-1.
A slide with a new table.

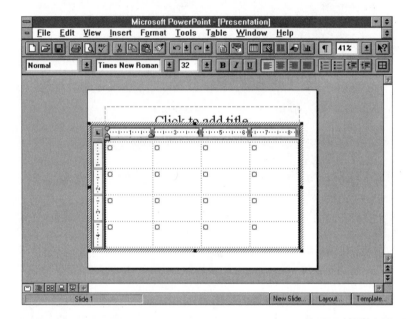

When the new table appears on the current slide, the menus and toolbars from Microsoft Word 6 for Windows replace the PowerPoint menus and toolbars. In fact, if it weren't for *PowerPoint* in the title bar, you might think you had switched to Word entirely. PowerPoint's chameleon-like ability to transform itself, provided by OLE2, lets you use all of Word's menus and tools without leaving PowerPoint.

After you finish the table, you must click outside the gray frame. Only the part of the table within the gray frame is placed on the slide, and PowerPoint's menus and toolbars reappear.

WARNING: If you move a table's gray frame before you add the table to a slide, you may not see the entire table on the slide.

If you have created a table in Word before, you know exactly what to do after you specify the dimensions of the table. The close partnership among all the Microsoft Office applications makes it easy to move from one application to another. But if you haven't used Word's table features, don't worry. This chapter leads you through everything you need to know.

The first thing you should consider is the structure of the table. For example, you'll probably want to use the cells at the tops of columns or beginnings of rows for table headings. Then, after you enter the table headings, you can enter data in the remaining cells. As you'll learn later in the chapter, it's not necessary to know exactly how many columns and rows you need from the start because you can easily add columns and rows at any time.

When you start a table, the insertion point flashes in the first cell in the upper left corner of the table. As always, you type to enter text at the location of the insertion point. To move the insertion point to another cell, press the Tab key or click the destination cell. Press Shift+Tab to move back one cell.

As you type, the text wraps within the current width of the cell. In other words, when you've typed all the way across a cell, the next word you type moves to a second line within the cell, as shown in Figure 8-2. In fact, as shown in Figure 8-3 on the next page, the entire table row grows vertically rather than horizontally to accommodate its longest text entry. Later in this chapter, you'll learn how to change the height of rows, as well as the width of columns, manually.

Name¤	Region¤	Division¤	Description¤
Audrey· Marr¤	Northeast¤	Circulation¤	Director·of· Circulation¤
Eric· Weinberger¤	Northeast¤	Sales¤	Sales· Manager¤
¤	¤	¤	¤

FIGURE 8-2.

The text in four cells of this table has wrapped to the second line.

FIGURE 8-3.

A table row grows
vertically to
accommodate its
longest text entry.

FIGURE 8-3.

A table row grows vertically to accommodate its longest text entry.

TIP   Although a cell can accommodate lengthy text entries, try to use short text entries to avoid overwhelming the screen with words. Type a word or two rather than a sentence. Keep in mind that in tables, as in charts, less is more.

You can use a variety of keys and key combinations to move around in a table. For example, to move quickly to the end of a row, press Alt+End. To move to the first cell in a column, press Alt+PgUp. Table 8-1 summarizes the keystrokes you can use to move around in a PowerPoint table.

TABLE 8-1.

The navigation keys for a PowerPoint table.

To Move...	Press...
To the next cell	Tab
To the previous cell	Shift+Tab
To the first cell in a row	Alt+Home
To the last cell in a row	Alt+End
To the first cell in a column	Alt+PgUp
To the last cell in a column	Alt+PgDown

NOTE: When you press Tab to move to a cell that contains text, the text is highlighted. You can then replace the highlighted text by simply typing new text. (Remember, any selected text is instantly replaced when you type.)

As you enter text in a cell, you can end a paragraph and start a new paragraph by pressing Enter. When you get to the end of the last cell in the last row, you can add a new row at the bottom of the table by pressing Tab.

A Sample Table

You can try your hand at creating a sample table. Imagine that you need to compare two vendors who want to supply coffee for your office kitchen. You can start by creating a new presentation, or you can use an existing presentation. Then follow the steps below.

1. Click the New Slide button to start a new slide. When the New Slide dialog box appears, double-click the Table autolayout.

2. On the new slide, double-click the table placeholder to start the table. When the Insert Word Table dialog box appears, enter *3* in the Number of Rows edit box, and then click OK to create the empty 2 x 3 table.

3. With the insertion point in the first cell of the table, type *The Coffee Pot,* press Tab to move to the next cell, and type *Roast and Brew.* Now you can begin typing the benefits provided by each service in the cells below.

4. Press Tab to move to the second cell in the first column, and type *Freshly ground beans each week.* Then press Tab to move to the second cell in the second column, and type *Free donuts on Fridays.*

5. Press Tab again to move to the third cell in the first column, and type *Daily 7 AM service.* Then press Tab one more time, and type *Jelly donuts, too.* Your table should now look something like the table shown on the next page.

6. Click anywhere outside the gray frame surrounding the table to place the table on the current slide.

As you can see, this table could use a little formatting. The text is too large, the rows are too tall, and the column headings are not distinguished in any way. Later in this chapter, you'll learn how to make these improvements, and others as well. But first, you need to learn how to make basic modifications to the structure of the table, such as adding a column if a third vendor makes a bid.

Modifying the Table

After you've created a table, you can modify its structure by adding, deleting, moving, and copying cells, columns, and rows. You can also change the widths of columns, the heights of rows, and merge and split cells to accommodate the contents of your table. All these changes are easy to accomplish. (If you've already clicked outside the gray frame to place a table on a slide, you must double-click the table to reactivate it for modifications.)

Selecting Cells, Columns, and Rows

As always, if you want to modify something in PowerPoint, you must select it first. This section discusses the various ways you can select cells, columns, and rows in a table.

Clicking the middle of a cell places an insertion point inside the cell, so the usual approach of clicking something to select it doesn't work in tables. Instead, you must carefully position the mouse pointer near the left inside edge of the cell you want to select, and when the pointer changes to a right arrow, click the cell. To select adjacent cells in the same column, click anywhere in the first cell, and drag down the column. To select adjacent cells in the same row, click anywhere in the first cell, and drag across the row. Word's Automatic Text Selection feature ensures that everything in the cells is also selected. In addition, you can click one cell, hold down the Shift key, and then click another cell to select both cells and any cells in between. Figure 8-4 shows a table with all the cells in one row selected.

FIGURE 8-4.
All the cells in the second row have been selected.

A shortcut for selecting a column of cells is to first position the mouse pointer on the top border of the column. Then, when the pointer changes to a down arrow, click the left mouse button to select the entire column, as shown in Figure 8-5.

FIGURE 8-5.
The third column in this table has been selected. (Note the down arrow at the top of the column.)

Just to make things a bit complicated, there's a difference between selecting all the cells in a row and selecting a row. You select all the cells in a row when you want to modify the contents of all the cells. You select a row when you want to add a new row or delete the current row. As shown in Figure 8-6, to select a row, you must also select the end-of-row marker that sits just to the right of the last cell in the row.

FIGURE 8-6.

The second row in this table has been selected.

If you don't see any end-of-row markers in your table, click the Show/Hide ¶ button on the Standard toolbar. (You may also need to drag the right side of the table's gray frame a little to the right.) When the end-of-row markers appear, you'll also see end-of-cell markers that mark the end of the contents of each cell.

TIP   If you have trouble selecting rows and columns with the mouse, you can use Table menu commands instead. First use the arrow keys and the Tab key to move the insertion point to a cell in the row or column you want to select, and then choose Select Row or Select Column from the Table menu. After you place the insertion point in a cell at one end of a range of cells that you want to select, you can also hold down the Shift key, and press the arrow keys to select adjacent cells.

Adding and Deleting Cells, Columns, and Rows

Depending on whether you've selected a cell, column, or row, the first command on the Table menu becomes Insert Cells, Insert Columns, or Insert Rows. When you insert new cells, the Insert Cells dialog box appears, as shown in Figure 8-7. You can then specify where the currently selected cell (or cells) should be moved in order to accommodate the new cell (or cells).

FIGURE 8-7.
The Insert Cells dialog box.

When you insert a new column, it appears to the left of the selected column. When you insert a new row, it appears above the selected row.

NOTE: If you want to add a new row to the end of a table, click the last cell in the table, and then press Tab.

Like the Insert command, the Delete command on the Table menu becomes Delete Cells, Delete Columns, or Delete Rows depending on whether you've selected a cell, column, or row. When you delete a cell, the Delete Cells dialog box appears. The options in this dialog box are similar to those in the Insert Cells dialog box. When you delete a column or row, the contents of the cells in the column or row are also deleted.

TIP   You can also use the Insert Cells and Delete Cells dialog boxes to insert and delete entire columns or rows. In addition, the Insert and Delete commands are available on the shortcut menu that appears when you select a cell, column, or row and then click the right mouse button.

Moving and Copying Cells

After you select the contents of a cell, you can move or copy the contents to another cell using the drag-and-drop techniques you learned in Chapter 4. As an alternative, you can use the Cut, Copy, and Paste buttons on the Standard toolbar or the commands on the Edit menu. The Cut, Copy, and Paste commands are also available on the shortcut menu that appears when you select the contents of a cell and then click the right mouse button.

Keep in mind that when you select only the contents of a cell without selecting the end-of-cell marker and then you move or copy the contents to a different cell, the contents of the destination cell are not overwritten. When you select both the contents of a cell and the end-of-cell marker, the contents of the destination cell are overwritten.

To move or copy a cell's contents using drag and drop, follow these steps:

1. Select the information you want to move or copy. Also select the end-of-cell marker if you want the contents of the cell to replace the contents of the destination cell. The figure on the left shows the contents of a cell selected without the end-of-cell marker selected. The figure on the right shows the contents of a cell selected with the end-of-cell marker selected, too.

2. Position the mouse pointer over the selected information, hold down the left mouse button, and drag the information to the destination point in another cell. To copy rather than move the contents of a cell, hold down the Ctrl key as you drag the contents. At the top of the next page, the figure on the left shows the result when only the contents are selected. The figure on the right shows the result when the end-of-cell marker is dragged to another cell, too—the moved or copied contents replace the contents in the destination cell.

Moving and Copying Columns and Rows

To move a column or row in a table, select the column or row, and drag it between two other columns or rows. To copy a column or row in a table, simply hold down the Ctrl key as you drag the column or row. You can also move or copy multiple columns or rows by selecting all the columns or rows that you want to move before you drag.

When you select a row (or rows) to move or copy, you must be sure to select the end-of-row marker as well; otherwise, the contents of the moved or copied row will overwrite the contents of the destination row. In addition, when you move or copy a row (or rows), you must drag the row to the beginning of the first cell in the destination row. If you don't, the contents of the moved or copied row will be added to the destination row, overwriting the contents of the destination row. Figure 8-8 shows a second set of rows created by copying the first set.

FIGURE 8-8.

The second set of rows was copied from the first set.

203

Changing Column Widths and Row Heights

To decrease or increase the width of a column in a table, drag the dotted column border at the right side of the column to the left or right, respectively. You can also drag the column markers on the table's horizontal ruler, shown in Figure 8-9, to the left or right to change the width of a column. When you reduce the width of a column so that some of the text no longer fits within the width of the column's cells, the extra text in each cell wraps to a second line.

FIGURE 8-9.

The column and row markers on the table rulers.

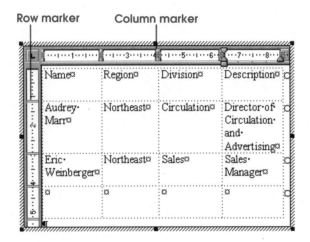

To decrease or increase the heights of rows in a table, drag the corresponding row markers on the table's vertical ruler up or down, respectively. As shown in Figure 8-9, the row marker for a row aligns with the bottom of the row. Changing the heights of rows is especially important because the default row height is determined by the number of rows in the table and the amount of space allotted for the table. Thus, the fewer the rows, the taller they must be. You may prefer shorter row heights that better fit the text height.

To change column widths and row heights in a table, you can also use the Cell Height and Width command on the Table menu. This command is also available on the shortcut menu that appears when you select a column or row and then click the right mouse button.

To change the widths of columns using the Cell Height and Width command, follow these steps:

1. Select as many columns as you want to modify.

2. Choose Cell Height and Width from the Table menu or from the short-cut menu.

3. Click the Column tab in the Cell Height and Width dialog box to display the dialog box shown below.

4. Enter a new width in the Width of Columns edit box by typing directly in the edit box or by using the up and down arrows to the right of the edit box.

You can also use the Space Between Columns option on the Column tab to add a little breathing room to a crowded table. Or click the AutoFit button to set the width of each selected column to fit the longest text entry in the column. If you want to quickly move to adjacent columns, click the Previous Column or Next Column button on the Column tab.

To change the heights of rows using the Cell Height and Width command, follow these steps:

1. Select as many rows as you want to modify.

2. Choose Cell Height and Width from the Table menu or from the short-cut menu.

3. Click the Row tab in the Cell Height and Width dialog box to display the dialog box shown on the next page.

4. Click the arrow to the right of the Height of Rows edit box to display a drop-down list of options. Select the Auto option to set the height of the row to the height of the tallest cell in the row. Select the At Least option to set a minimum row height. When you select At Least, the row becomes taller if the contents of the cells are taller than the row height. Select Exactly to set an exact row height. Any text that does not fit in the cells at the exact row height is cut off. Note that when you select the At Least or Exactly options, you can enter a point size in the At edit box to specify a particular row height.

You can also use the Indent From Left setting on the Row tab to change the distance between the text and the left edge of the cells in the row. In addition, you can select Left, Center, or Right to specify the alignment of the text within the row. The Allow Row to Break Across Pages option lets you determine whether the contents of the row are split at an automatic page break or whether the entire row is moved to the following page. To format the previous or next row, you can click the Previous Row or Next Row button.

Dragging the column and row markers to change column widths and row heights is usually the easiest way to go, but you may want to select the entire table by clicking any cell and choosing Select Table from the Table menu. Then use the Cell Height and Width dialog box to set all the columns or rows to a uniform width or height, respectively.

Merging and Splitting Cells

To create a large cell that spans two or more cells, you can merge adjacent cells. As shown in Figure 8-10, merging cells allows you to enter a column heading in one large cell that occupies the same width as several smaller cells below.

Pros vs Cons				
	Alternative 1		Alternative 2	
	Pros	Cons	Pros	Cons
Alternative X				
Alternative Y				

FIGURE 8-10.

The cells in row 1 of columns 2 and 3 and columns 4 and 5 have been merged to accommodate the column headings.

To merge two or more cells, simply select the cells, and then choose **Merge Cells** from the Table menu. Even when two or more cells have been merged, they retain their separate identities so that you can always select the merged cell and choose Split Cells from the Table menu to return to the original grouping of individual cells.

Formatting the Table

After you enter the contents of the table and make any necessary structural changes, you can turn your attention to the overall appearance of the table. By default, PowerPoint uses the current presentation template to format elements of the table such as text font and color. You can change the formatting of table text by using the same methods that you use to change the formatting of text elsewhere in PowerPoint. Simply select the text, and then use the buttons on the Formatting toolbar or the commands on the Format and shortcut menus.

In addition to the text, however, there are other elements that you should consider when you format a table, such as borders and shading. These elements are discussed in the next section.

Adding Borders and Shading with Table AutoFormats

The dotted gridlines that depict the boundaries of table cells on the screen do not appear when you view the completed table on the slide, so you must add borders to make the gridlines visible. You can also add shading to certain cells to give them a little emphasis.

PowerPoint provides both a Borders toolbar and a Borders and Shading command, but the easiest way to add borders and shading is to select one of the prefabricated table autoformats. Each table autoformat (there are a total of 34) offers its own combination of cell borders, cell shading, fonts, and color selections. In addition, while applying a table autoformat, you can automatically size the table so that its columns and rows are sized to fit the contents of the cells perfectly.

To select a table autoformat, follow these steps:

1. Click anywhere in the table.

2. From the Table menu or the shortcut menu, choose Table AutoFormat. Be careful not to choose AutoFormat from the Format menu by mistake.

3. In the Table AutoFormat dialog box, shown below, select a format from the Formats list, and view the result in the Preview box.

As you click each option, the sample table in the Preview box changes to reflect your selections.

4. To format specific elements in your table, select any or all of the options in the Formats to Apply section.

Option	Effect
Borders	Applies the cell borders shown in the preview.
Shading	Applies the shading shown in the preview.
Font	Applies the fonts shown in the preview. Leave Font unselected to use a font that matches your presentation font.
Color	Applies the colors shown in the preview. Leave Color unselected to use shades of gray.
AutoFit	Automatically sizes columns and rows to fit the largest entry.

5. To add special formatting to other table elements, select any or all of the options in the Apply Special Formats To section. Again, as you select options, the sample table in the Preview box changes to reflect your selections. Depending on the table element you select, the special formatting may be shading, a bold font, a wider column, or special cell borders.

Element	Effect
Heading Rows	Applies a special format to the heading rows of the table.
First Column	Applies a special format to the first column of the table.
Last Row	Applies a special format to the last row of the table.
Last Column	Applies a special format to the last column of the table.

6. Click OK to implement the table autoformat you selected. The table at the top of the next page is formatted using the Simple 3 table autoformat.

FIGURE 8-12.

The Borders and Shading tabs of the Cell Borders and Shading dialog box.

On the Borders tab, you can select Box from the Presets section to add a border to the outside of the selected cells, or you can select Grid to add a border around each individual cell in the selection. You can also select one or more borders in the Border section, and then select a line style from the Style list and a color from the drop-down Color list. To remove all borders from the selected cells, select None in the Presets section. To remove a specific border, simply click the border in the Border section.

When you click the Shading tab in the Cell Borders and Shading dialog box, you can select a shading percentage from the Shading list and a foreground and background color from the Foreground and Background drop-down lists. The selections you make are then displayed in the Preview box. The resulting shade is a percentage of the foreground color against the background color. For example, 50% mixes the foreground and background colors evenly. To see just the background color, select Clear from the Shading list. To see just the foreground color, select Solid. Because you can mix the foreground and background colors to any degree, you can create special colors. For example, you can create a color that is 20% dark blue against a light yellow background.

After you select a border, shading, or both, click OK to apply the border and shading to the selected cells.

Now that you've learned how to create table slides and add them to a presentation, you know how to work with all the basic presentation building blocks. In Part 3, you'll learn how to make overall changes to the presentation and how to add enhancements to strengthen its powers of communication.

Modifying
the Presentation

9

Making Overall Changes

As you've seen, PowerPoint offers a sophisticated system for creating an entire presentation's worth of slides that share a common design. This chapter focuses on the central controls behind the presentation design process: the template, the color scheme, and the slide master. You can use these controls to make overall changes to your presentation, such as redesigning the background or applying a different combination of colors to all the slides. The following list shows the elements that are managed by each of the three controls.

- The template contains a color scheme, a slide master, and a set of autolayouts that control where objects are positioned on slides.

- The color scheme contains a background color and seven other colors that are applied to particular elements in the presentation.

- The slide master contains a background design and default text formatting for the slide titles and main text items.

  ❑ The background design contains graphic objects that are placed on the background color. The background color can be shaded from light to dark or from dark to light across the slide horizontally, diagonally, or vertically.

  ❑ The default text formatting is the standard text formatting for the slide titles and bulleted text items.

What is so powerful—and potentially confusing—about these controls is the way they overlap. When you alter the slide master, for example, you can change the current color scheme, which can change the background color. To make things even more interesting, you can also change the background color directly, without changing the color scheme. To help you understand how these controls interact, this chapter is organized from macro to micro. It begins with a discussion of the controls that have the broadest influence on a presentation and then goes on to cover the controls that affect a single aspect of a slide.

Applying a Different Template

The easiest—and most sweeping—step you can take when you want to change the appearance of a presentation is to apply a different template. Changing the template makes a wholesale change to just about every aspect of the presentation's appearance. Figure 9-1 shows a basic presentation, both before (top) and after (bottom) the TRIDOTSB.PPT template is attached.

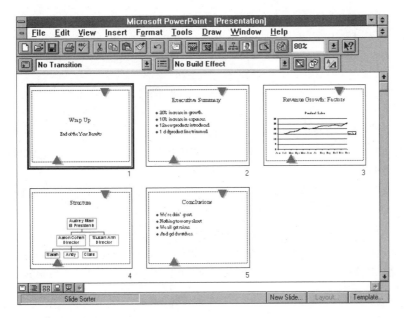

FIGURE 9-1.

A basic presentation slide before (top) and after (bottom) a new template is attached.

The Template

The template is the most powerful and far-reaching of the central controls. By changing the template, you can give your presentation an entirely new look: All the slides of the presentation get the same new background and new color scheme, and even a new selection of text fonts. But you can control each of these design aspects individually without going to the extreme of applying a new template. You can even make design changes on selected slides, leaving the other slides to conform to the template's design. Some of the overall changes you can make without changing the template are:

- Decorate the background with a company logo or project name.

- Add special text to the background that spells out the presentation's subject.

- Modify the presentation colors to match a client's corporate color scheme.

- Change the font and text formatting used in slide titles to give the presentation a more playful or more serious character.

Among other things, changing the template:

- Changes the color scheme that controls the colors used in the presentation.

- Changes the slide master, which in turn changes the background design and default text formatting.

The templates that come with PowerPoint were created by professional artists, so they produce polished, attractive presentations. As a result, you may not need to make further changes to the appearance of the presentation after you apply a template.

If someone else has created a unique new presentation design, he or she may have saved it in a template that you can use. When you apply the custom template to your presentation, you get the same special presentation design. Often, the chief PowerPoint user in an organization will create a template you can use to conform to the company look. In fact, the design guru may even have changed the characteristics of the default template so that each new presentation you create gets the standard, approved presentation design automatically.

TIP To find out which template is applied to the current presentation, you can check the Summary Info dialog box by choosing Summary Info from the File menu. The template name appears in the upper section of the dialog box.

PowerPoint templates are organized into three groups:

Template Group	Description
Black and white overheads	Black and white templates suitable for printing on black and white printers, such as laser printers.
Color overheads	Templates with a light color scheme suitable for projecting on an overhead projector.
Slide show	Templates with a dark color scheme suitable for using on 35-mm slides or in electronic presentations.

To see samples of all the PowerPoint templates (shown in black and white), turn to the Appendix , page 432.

You can create and print a presentation using one template, and then easily switch to another. For example, you can create a presentation using a black and white template, and then apply a color template so that you can also use a color printer to produce a set of color overheads.

Selecting a Template

When you create a new presentation using the AutoContent Wizard, a template is automatically attached to the presentation. When you use the Pick a Look Wizard, you select a template in the first step. If you want to select a template by name when you start a new presentation, click the Template option in the New Presentation dialog box, and then select a template from the Presentation Template dialog box.

To change the template for a presentation that you are creating or modifying, follow these steps:

1. Click the Template button at the bottom of the PowerPoint window or choose Presentation Template from the Format menu. The Presentation Template dialog box appears, as shown below.

Select a directory here

Select a template here

2. In the Directories list, check to see which of the following three directories is open under the TEMPLATE directory. (The directories appear as folders in the list.)

    ❏ The BWOVRHD directory contains templates for black and white printing.

❏ The CLROVRHD directory contains templates with light colors for overheads.

❏ The SLDSHOW directory contains templates with dark colors for 35-mm slides and electronic presentations.

To open a different directory, double-click the TEMPLATE directory, and then double-click the directory you want to open. The templates available in the directory appear in the File Name list.

3. Click any template to see its preview in the lower right corner of the Presentation Template dialog box.

4. Double-click a template name to apply it to the current presentation, or click a template name and then click Apply. The new template reformats every slide in the presentation.

NOTE: You cannot use the Undo command on the Edit menu to undo a template. To change back to an earlier design, reapply the template that contained the design.

If you've never changed a template before, you can get some practice by creating a simple presentation (you can use the AutoContent Wizard to quickly generate a multipage dummy presentation). You can then click the Template button, and select a template name from the Presentation Template dialog box. Notice the different effects created when you apply different templates.

Modifying a Template

To alter a template and create a custom look for future presentations, you can open the template and then modify the color scheme, the slide master, or both. You'll learn how to change the color scheme and slide master later in this chapter.

To open a template for editing, follow these steps:

1. Click the Open button on the Standard toolbar or choose the Open command from the File menu. The Open dialog box appears, as shown on the next page.

2. In the Directories list, open one of the three directories under the TEMPLATE directory.

3. In the File Name list, double-click the template you want to edit. The template appears in its own presentation window in PowerPoint, as shown here:

You can then make changes to the template's color scheme and slide master. When you're finished, use the Save As command, and save the template with a new name so that it doesn't overwrite the original template.

To use a modified template for a new or existing presentation, either click the Template option in the New Presentation dialog box or click the Template button at the bottom of the PowerPoint window, and then select the template in the Presentation Template dialog box.

Changing the Color Scheme

Every template contains a color scheme that provides the various parts of a presentation with a coordinated set of eight default colors. The most distinctive part of the presentation is the background, so the first color in the color scheme is the background color. The other seven colors are tastefully matched to fit the background color and are applied to text, charts, and other objects that appear against the background. Whenever you choose a command that allows you to change the color of an object, such as the Font command, you can display the default color scheme by clicking the arrow at the right end of the Color box. Figure 9-2 shows the default color scheme displayed in the Font dialog box.

The eight colors of the current scheme

FIGURE 9-2.
The default color scheme in the Font dialog box.

Changing the colors of the color scheme without making additional changes to the presentation can be enough to dramatically transform the look. When you modify the color scheme, you can apply the revised color scheme to the entire presentation or to the current slide only. If you apply the color scheme to all the slides in a presentation, the new colors are applied to every object in the presentation as well. The only exceptions are those objects to which you have assigned specific colors. For example, if you have selected a special color

TABLE 9-1.

The eight color boxes in the Slide Color Scheme dialog box.

Color Box	Description
Background	The color applied to the background of the slides. The background color may be shaded in a template from light to dark or dark to light, and, on selected slides, it can be superseded by a different background color you select.
Text & Lines	The color applied to bulleted text and to text blocks typed onto the slides with the Text Tool. Also used for lines and arrows drawn with the Line Tool and as the outline color for auto-shapes and objects drawn with the other drawing tools.
Shadows	The color applied to shadows created with the Shadow command.
Title Text	The color applied to slide titles.
Fills	The color used to fill autoshapes and objects drawn with any of the drawing tools. Also the color used to fill the first series in a graph.
Accent	The color used as a second color in graphs, org charts, and other added elements.
Accent	The color used as a third color in graphs, org charts, and other added elements.
Accent	The color used as a fourth color in graphs, org charts, and other added elements.

5. Click a color in the Text & Line Color list. The Choose Scheme dialog box now looks something like this:

Four previews in the Other Scheme Colors box show you how the first two color selections you've made might look with several variations of the third through eighth colors. If you don't like any of the color schemes shown, you can select a different Text & Line color to see a different set of possibilities. If you still can't find a combination you like, you can start over by selecting a new background color.

6. Click one of the four previews, and then click OK to return to the Slide Color Scheme dialog box.

7. Click Apply to All to apply the new color scheme to the entire presentation, or click Apply to apply the color scheme to the current slide only.

   NOTE: If you previously applied a color to a specific element in your presentation, that element will not be affected by the new color scheme.

Creating a Custom Color Scheme

You can create a custom color scheme using one of two methods. The first method involves selecting a template, revising the template's color scheme, and saving the template with a new name. Then, when you want to apply the new color scheme to a presentation, you simply select the template. Note that when you use this method you should first select a template that has a color scheme similar to the one you want to create.

The second method for creating a custom color scheme involves modifying the color scheme of an existing presentation. Then, to apply the modified color scheme to a new presentation, you simply copy the color scheme from the old presentation to the new one.

To create a custom color scheme using either method, follow these steps:

1. Click the Open button or choose Open from the File menu, open one of the three template directories, and then double-click the name of the template you want. To change the color scheme of an existing presentation, open the presentation, instead.

2. Choose Slide Color Scheme from the Format menu or the shortcut menu to display the Slide Color Scheme dialog box. Table 9-1 provides information about the eight color boxes displayed at the top of the dialog box.

3. To change one of the colors in the eight color boxes, double-click its color box, or click its color box once and then click Change Color. For example, to change the fill color, double-click the Fills box. The Fill Color dialog box appears, as shown here, displaying 90 color panes from which you can select a new color:

4. Select a color by clicking its pane, and then click OK. If you don't see the color you want, click the More Colors button to display this dialog box:

You can use the two controls in the upper half of the More Colors dialog box to select a color. The large box has a cross hair that identifies the general color (the *hue*) and intensity of the hue (the *saturation* level) when you drag it across the box. The vertical strip to the right of the box has a triangular marker that indicates how much black or white is mixed with the color (the *luminance* of the color) when you drag it up or down the strip. Two color boxes below the large box show the currently selected color and the solid color on which it is based. The remaining boxes contain numeric values for the hue, saturation, and luminance (HSL) and red, green, and blue (RGB) of the current color. You can use the HSL and RGB numbers to specify an exact color. For example, you can record the numbers of a color you like in one color scheme and then enter the numbers in another color scheme to reproduce the same color. (You can enter either the three HSL numbers or the three RGB numbers—you don't need both sets.)

5. In the More Colors dialog box, drag the cross hair in the large box to the general color you want, and then drag the marker on the vertical strip to brighten or darken the color. Check the Color box at the bottom of the dialog box to see the current color. When you're satisfied, click OK to return to the Slide Color Scheme dialog box.

6. Follow steps 3 through 5 to change any of the other colors in the eight color boxes. Then click Apply to All to apply the color scheme to the entire presentation, or click Apply to apply the color scheme to the current slide only.

After you create a custom color scheme and apply it to a single slide, you can return the slide to the template's original color scheme by choosing Slide Color Scheme from the Format menu or the shortcut menu and clicking the Follow Master button in the Slide Color Scheme dialog box.

> **NOTE:** After you change one or more colors and apply them to the entire presentation, the revised colors become the new master color scheme. The original color scheme is lost in the current presentation. When you revise colors on individual slides and then click Follow Master to return them to the master color scheme, the revised colors revert to the modified colors used by the rest of the slides in the presentation, not the colors the template started with.

> ### PowerPoint's Color System
>
> Although PowerPoint provides a broad palette of colors from which to choose, it does not follow the commonly used color matching systems for selecting and specifying colors, such as the Pantone system or the Trumatch system. To match a color, such as the dominant color in your company's logo, you must go through the trial-and-error process of selecting a color, sending it to your color output device, examining the output, and then adjusting the color in PowerPoint. The process can be time-consuming because most output devices produce colors that are lighter or darker than they appear on the screen. In addition, the number of colors you see on the screen and the precision with which they are displayed depend on the color capabilities of your hardware. Even the brightness control on your monitor affects how a color looks. When you do find the correct color, you might want to make note of its HSL or RGB number so that you can reproduce it later.

Editing the Slide Master

In addition to the color scheme, the slide master is the other element you can modify in a template. As with color schemes, slide masters are an integral part of a template and cannot be saved in separate files.

The slide master in each template contains:

- A background color that can be shaded.

- A scheme of fonts and text formatting for the slide titles and bulleted text on slides.

- An optional group of graphic objects placed on the background and arranged to form a design.

Therefore, it's the slide master that gives the presentation an overall look by providing the background and the design of the text.

This section first discusses how to open the slide master and then how to customize the slide master's background color and shading, title and text, and background design.

Opening the Slide Master

Before you can actually edit the slide master, you must display it on your screen. To display the slide master shown in Figure 9-3, use one of these methods:

■ Choose Master and then Slide Master from the View menu.

■ Hold down the Shift key, and click the Slide View button.

FIGURE 9-3.
The slide master.

As you can see, the slide master temporarily takes over the screen. Where the page number appeared in the lower left corner of the PowerPoint window, you now see *Slide Master*.

To close the slide master and return to another view, simply click one of the view buttons in the lower left corner of the presentation window.

Altering the Background Color and Shading

Although the color scheme supplies a background color for the template, you can modify the background color when you change the slide background for the slide master. Modifying the background color on the slide master is just like modifying the background color in the color scheme. In fact, if you return to the Slide Color Scheme dialog box, you'll see the new background color.

In addition to the color, you can also make other changes to the slide master's background. For instance, you can set a shading for the background color and then lighten or darken the shading.

To make changes to the slide master's background, choose the Slide Background command from the Format menu or the shortcut menu. (Remember, the slide master must be displayed on your screen before you choose the command.) The Slide Background dialog box shown in Figure 9-4 appears. You use the controls in the Color and Shading section of the Slide Background dialog box to change the appearance of the background. The current shade style is selected in the Shade Styles section, and its variations are displayed in the Variants box.

FIGURE 9-4.
The Slide Background dialog box.

To display a solid (not shaded) color in the background, click None under Shade Styles. Otherwise, click one of the other six Shade Styles options. If you want to select one of the variations, simply click it. For example, to create a background shade that runs vertically from light to dark, you click Vertical as the Shade Style and then leave the first variant selected, which shows a transition from light to dark. Figure 9-5 shows the Slide Background dialog box with these settings. Other variants allow you to shade the background from dark to light, from light to dark to light, or from dark to light to dark. You get the idea.

If you've selected a shade style other than None, you can also use the scroll bar under the Variants box to change the intensity of the shading.

FIGURE 9-5.

The Slide
Background
dialog box with
the Vertical shade
style selected.

Select a shade style,
and then click one
of the variants

To select a different background color altogether, click the Change Color button, and then select a color from the Background Color dialog box. You can also click the More Colors button in the Background Color dialog box, and specify a different color using the same techniques described earlier for changing the color scheme.

TIP   You can click the Preview button in the Slide Background dialog box to preview the new background shading. After you click Preview, you may need to drag the dialog box aside to see the background. If you're not satisfied with the background shading, the Slide Background dialog box is still on the screen, so you can select a different setting.

After you select a background color and shading, click Apply To All to apply the settings to the entire presentation, or click Apply to apply the settings to the current slide only.

Formatting the Master Title and Body Text

With the background color and shading set, you can turn your attention to the appearance of the text in the presentation.

235

Figure 9-6 shows the slide master of the TRAVELB.PPT template. As you can see, the slide master displays text in two areas marked by dashed boxes: The title area for autolayouts contains sample text for the slide titles, and the object area for autolayouts contains sample text at each of the five bulleted text levels. When you change the formatting of the sample text, the formatting of the corresponding text on every slide in the presentation changes accordingly.

FIGURE 9-6.

The slide master of the TRAVELB.PPT template.

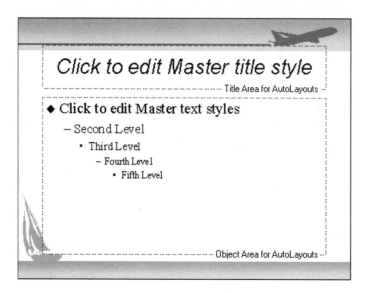

The initial colors of the text in the title and object areas are determined by the colors of the color scheme. The Title Text color of the color scheme sets the title area text color, for example. The Text & Lines color of the color scheme sets the object area text color. But changing the color of the sample text on the slide master overrides the color scheme. Even when you change the actual color scheme, the text colors on the slide master are applied rather than the color scheme's text colors.

To change the appearance of the slide titles, format the text in the title area by selecting the text and then using buttons on the Formatting toolbar or commands on the Format menu or the shortcut menu. To change the font and color of the title, for example, click the title to select it, click the right mouse button to display the shortcut menu, choose the Font command, and then select options in the Font dialog box.

If you want to make uniform changes to all the bulleted text in a presentation, click the object area of the slide master to select all the bulleted text, and then use the text formatting commands.

To change the formatting of the bulleted text at only one of the indent levels, select the text at that level, and then make a formatting change. For example, to change the font used by bulleted text lines at the second level, select the text *Second Level,* as shown in Figure 9-7, and then use the text formatting commands.

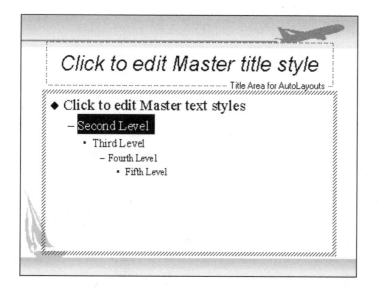

FIGURE 9-7.

To change the formatting of the bulleted text at the second level, select the level, and then use the text formatting commands.

To change the bullet used at the second level, select the second level text, choose Bullet from the Format menu, and then select a different bullet shape, color, and size from the Bullet dialog box.

TIP Although you can apply different formatting to the text at each level, you probably shouldn't deviate too much from the formatting of the first level. Otherwise, you might end up with a jumble of formatting on slides with bulleted text. You should use the same font at all levels but vary the size, for example.

Creating the Background Design

You can create your own background design by using PowerPoint's drawing tools to place graphic objects on the background of the slide master. Professional artists can do wonders with simple drawing tools, creating entire scenes like those found in the templates that come with PowerPoint. If your artistic skills are not as strong, you may prefer to add a few simple geometric shapes to the background. A line or two, or a row of small shapes that you create with the AutoShape tool, can be quite nice.

Rather than compose a background design of your own, you can make minor modifications to the background objects in one of the templates. Simply by moving some of the existing objects, duplicating objects, or changing the objects' positions, you can create a new background design with a unique look.

> **NOTE:** Any graphic objects that are already a part of the slide master have been grouped into a single object. Therefore, you must select the group of objects and then use the Ungroup command on the Draw menu before you can work with the individual objects. You'll learn more about grouping and ungrouping objects in "Grouping Objects," page 349.

Text annotations, clip art, and scanned pictures saved as bitmapped files are other elements you can add to the background of the slide master so that they appear on every slide. When you read about adding text annotations, clip art, and bitmaps to slides in Chapters 12 and 14, bear in mind that these elements can be added to the slide master background, too.

For more information about using PowerPoint's drawing tools to create and modify graphic objects, see Chapter 13, "Drawing Graphic Objects," page 329.

Adding the Date, Time, and Slide Number to the Background

PowerPoint makes it easy to add three special text elements to the background of every slide: the date, the time, and the slide number. These elements appear when you display the presentation in a slide show or print the presentation as slides, handouts, or notes pages. They do not appear while you are creating or editing the presentation. The format of the date and time is determined by the Short Date format you have selected in the International Settings dialog box. You can get to this dialog box by using the Windows Control Panel.

To add the date while editing the slide master background, choose Date from the Insert menu. As shown in Figure 9-8, the date appears in a frame as two slashes.

FIGURE 9-8.
The date appears as two slashes in a frame on the slide master.

You can position the date anywhere on the slide master by selecting its frame and then dragging it to a new location. You can also add the date outside the title and object areas of the slide master by selecting the Text Tool on the Drawing toolbar, clicking an insertion point on the slide master, and typing two forward slashes.

To add the time while editing the slide master background, choose Time from the Insert menu. The time appears as two colons in a frame. You can then drag the frame to any location on the slide master. You can also use the Text Tool and type two colons to add the time outside the title and object areas of the slide master.

To add the slide number, select Page Number from the Insert menu, or use the Text Tool and type two number signs (##) outside the title and object areas of the slide master. You can start slide numbering at a number other than 1 by choosing Slide Setup from the File menu and then altering the number in the Number Slides From edit box. Changing the starting slide number is helpful when the presentation you're creating is a continuation of an earlier presentation.

TIP   You may want to use the date and time to keep track of versions while the presentation is in the draft stage, and then remove them when you're ready to display or print the final presentation. To remove the date and time, simply select the symbols on the slide master, and press the Delete key.

The changes you have learned about in this chapter are broad in scope and affect an entire presentation. They allow you to govern the overall appearance of a presentation and customize its look. In the next two chapters, you'll learn to make further modifications to a presentation by formatting graphs you've added and using Slide Sorter view to rearrange the presentation's slides.

10

Formatting Graphs

When all you need is a standard-issue graph to get your message across, the basic steps of entering data and selecting a graph type or autoformat—covered in Chapter 6—are as far as you need to go. Graph 5, the graphing module used by PowerPoint, creates a professional-quality graph that accurately portrays your data and matches the design of your presentation.

But in many cases, simple accuracy is not sufficient. You want the graph to *communicate*—to accentuate a trend, de-emphasize an outcome, or call attention to a result. At times like these, creating the basic graph is only the first step. Formatting the graph to make it truly expressive is an equally important part of the process.

In this chapter, you'll learn how to emphasize patterns or trends in your graphs in a variety of ways, such as changing the appearance of the markers that represent numbers and changing the structure and design of the graph axes. You'll also learn how to format the titles, legend, gridlines, and other parts of the graph to communicate your data more effectively.

Activating a Graph for Formatting

After you create a basic graph by following the steps in Chapter 6, the graph appears on a slide with the default formatting prescribed by its particular chart type. For example, a new pie graph has the default formatting for pie graphs.

To activate the graph so that you can modify any aspect of its formatting, use one of these methods:

- Double-click the graph.

- Select the graph and press Enter. (Remember, you can cycle through the objects on a slide by pressing Tab.)

- Select the graph, choose Chart Object from the Edit menu, and then choose Edit from the submenu.

When you activate a graph, Graph's menus and Standard toolbar replace PowerPoint's menus and toolbars. The graph appears on a slide within a gray frame surrounded by black handles, as shown in Figure 10-1 on the next page. You haven't left PowerPoint, but you can now use any of Graph's Standard toolbar buttons to make changes to the entire graph. You learned about these buttons in Chapter 6, but they are shown on the next page for review.

FIGURE 10-1.

An active graph on a slide.

NOTE: You can open the Graph module so that its menus and toolbar appear within a separate Graph window that overlays the PowerPoint window. (This is how Graph worked in previous versions of PowerPoint.) First select the graph, and choose Chart Object and then Open from the Edit menu. When you finish editing in Graph, choose Update from Graph's File menu, and then choose Exit and Return to *Presentation* from the File menu.

After you finish formatting the graph, click outside the gray frame to exit Graph and redisplay PowerPoint's menus and toolbars.

TIP To use the Zoom command on Graph's View menu, you must first select the graph in the PowerPoint window. Next, choose Chart Object and then Open from PowerPoint's Edit menu. The Graph module is loaded, and the Zoom command on Graph's View menu becomes available. You can also quickly zoom in on a graph in the PowerPoint window by using PowerPoint's Zoom Control box or Zoom command.

Selecting a Graph Object to Format

In addition to changing the entire graph, you can change individual components, called *graph objects*. To understand which graph objects you can change, you need to know a little about the anatomy of a graph. Figure 10-2 shows a typical graph and its graph objects. Don't worry if you can't remember the names of all the graph objects right now. You'll get plenty of opportunity to become familiar with them as you read the sections of this chapter, which cover each graph object in depth.

NOTE: The words *graph* and *chart* are used interchangeably throughout this chapter.

FIGURE 10-2.

A typical graph and its graph objects.

To change a graph object, double-click the object after you've activated the graph. A dialog box opens with formatting options for the selected object. You can double-click each object in the graph in succession, and make formatting changes in a dialog box. You can double-click and format the bars in a bar graph, for example, and then double-click and format the legend.

To use the keyboard to select a graph object, first press the Up or Down arrow key to move from one group of graph objects to the next. Then to select an individual graph object from the group, such as one of the columns of a column series or one of the legend entries of the legend, press the Right or Left arrow key. After you select an object in this way, you can choose the first command on the Format menu to display a dialog box with formatting options for the selected object. The name of the command changes depending on which graph object is selected. If you select an axis, for example, the command is Selected Axis. If you select a legend, the command is Selected Legend, and so on.

A third method of indicating which graph object you want to format is to click the object and then open the shortcut menu by clicking the right mouse button. Select the Format command halfway down the shortcut menu to open a dialog box with formatting options for the corresponding object. Like the Selected command on the Format menu, the name of the Format command on the shortcut menu reflects the graph object you've selected, such as Format Legend or Format Data Series.

TIP When you have formatted as many graph objects as necessary to create a graph with the look you want, you can save the combination of formatted graph objects as an autoformat. Then you can select the custom autoformat to quickly apply its settings to all the graph objects in any new graph. For more information about saving a formatted graph as an autoformat, see "Saving Graph Formatting as an AutoFormat," page 296.

2-D Graph Formatting

Each graph object has its own special formatting options. This section, which covers these special options, assumes that you have already activated the graph and are ready to select a graph object for formatting.

Changing the Color of a Data Series

In a graph, a data series is represented by one or more markers: an area, a group of bars, a group of columns, a line, the slices of a pie, the rings of a doughnut graph, the lines of a radar graph, or the groups of points in an XY (scatter) graph. The color of a data series is the color displayed by the markers of that series. These markers can also contain a pattern of another color.

The easiest way to change the color of a data series is to click the series and then use the Color button and Pattern button on Graph's Standard toolbar. On the face of these buttons, small boxes display the current color and pattern settings—white is the default. To select a different color, click the down arrow to the right of the Color button, and then click a color in the palette of colors, which looks like this:

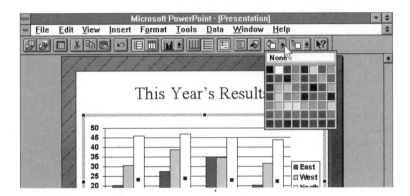

To select a different pattern, click the down arrow to the right of the Pattern button, and then click a pattern at the top and a pattern color at the bottom of the palette of patterns, which looks like this:

To select a color or pattern for the markers of a data series as well as a color for the border of the markers, you must use the Format Data Series dialog box instead. Follow these steps:

1. Double-click any of the markers in a data series to open the Format Data Series dialog box, as shown below.

The Format Data Series dialog box contains at least two tabs. The Patterns tab gives you options that change the patterns and colors of the series. The Data Labels tab lets you add numbers that show the numeric values of the data points. Other tabs in the dialog box provide advanced formatting options for certain types of graphs that are covered later in this chapter.

2. If you want to change the currently selected markers, click the Patterns tab. Then in the Border section, select a Style, Color, and Weight option from each of the Custom lists to change the appearance of the marker borders. (The Custom button is selected as soon as you change any of the default settings.) To remove the borders around the markers, click None. To reset the borders to the default setting, click Automatic.

NOTE: If the series is represented by a line, the options in the Border section control the appearance of the line.

3. In the Area section, change the look of the markers themselves by clicking a color in the Color palette and selecting a pattern from the Pattern

drop-down list. From the Pattern list, you can select a pattern color, as well.

4. Click OK to close the Format Data Series dialog box.

For example, to surround an area marker in an area graph with a white line and fill the area marker with dark blue, first double-click the marker. In the Format Data Series dialog box, select white as the Color option in the Border section and dark blue as the Color option in the Area section, and click OK.

 TIP   When you change the color of a data series, be careful to select a color that properly contrasts with the background of the graph and with the other data series.

Adding and Formatting Titles

After you enter your data, the basic graph that PowerPoint draws displays no text other than the labels that mark increments along the axes and the text in the legend. Figure 10-3 shows a graph at this earliest stage. You may want to enter a title for each of the graph axes to identify what they measure. You may also want to add a title above the graph to describe the graph's purpose, especially if you've used the slide title to describe the slide in general rather than the graph in particular.

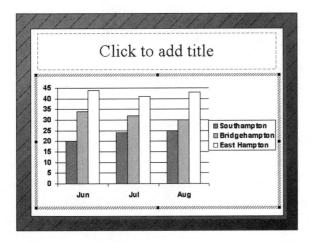

FIGURE 10-3.

A basic graph without titles.

Adding the Titles

To add titles for the graph and its axes, follow these steps:

1. With the graph activated, choose Titles from the Insert menu or shortcut menu. Graph displays the Titles dialog box, as shown here:

2. Click the check boxes to select the titles you want to add, and then click OK to display sample titles on the graph, as shown here:

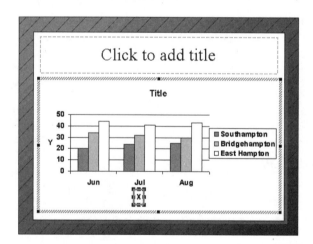

One of the titles, in this case the category (X) axis title, is selected—it appears in a text box surrounded by handles.

3. Click each title and type the actual text you want. The titles can be two or more lines; simply press Enter to start a new line.

To remove a title, select it, choose Titles from the Insert menu, and deselect the title's check box. Alternatively, you can select the title and press Delete, or click the right mouse button and choose Clear from the shortcut menu.

To replace a title, you simply click the title, and then type the replacement text. To edit a title, click the title once and then click an insertion point in the text. Edit the text as you would edit any text in PowerPoint. Press Esc or click elsewhere on the graph to complete the editing process.

After you add a title, you can reposition it on the graph by following the steps below.

1. Click the title. Graph displays the title's text box surrounded by handles, as shown here:

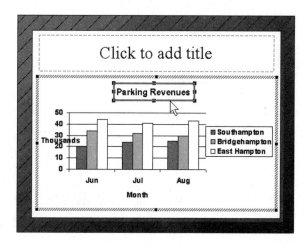

2. Place the pointer on the outline of the text box or on one of the handles, and drag to move the box.

    NOTE: Dragging the handles does not stretch the box, as you might expect. Instead, the entire box moves.

Don't worry about the value (Y) axis title, *Thousands*. You'll learn how to rotate titles later in the chapter.

Formatting the Titles

The default formatting of the graph determines the formatting of the titles. However, you can select and format each title separately—making the chart title larger and the axis titles smaller, for example. You can format both the text of the title and the rectangle that contains the text. Unfortunately, you cannot select multiple titles for formatting; you must select and format each title in turn.

To format both a title and its box, double-click the title. A Format dialog box for the selected object appears, as shown in Figure 10-4. (If the title is already selected, be sure to click elsewhere first, and then double-click the title outline, or you will end up clicking an insertion point in the text.)

FIGURE 10-4.

The Format Chart Title dialog box that appears when you double-click the chart title.

Alternatively, you can click the title and display the Format dialog box by choosing the first command from the Format menu, which is either Selected Chart Title or Selected Axis Title; by pressing Ctrl+1; or by clicking the right mouse button and choosing the Format command from the shortcut menu.

To format only the text of a title or a selected part of a title, click the title and select the text you want to format. Then display the Format dialog box by choosing Selected Chart Title or Selected Axis Title from the Format menu; by pressing Ctrl+1; or by choosing the Format command from the shortcut menu. (The Format dialog box consists of only the Font tab when you select part of the title and choose either of the Format menu commands.)

To format the title's text box rather than its text, you use the options on the Patterns tab in the Format dialog box. The Border settings control the appearance of the border of the text box. The Area settings control the color and pattern of the interior of the text box. A sample in the lower right corner shows the results of the Border and Area settings. You can select the appropriate None option if you want the text box to have no border or a clear interior. To restore the defaults for the Border or Area settings, select the Automatic option.

TIP When you select an Area color for the text box, be careful to select a color that properly contrasts with both the plot area of the graph and the text of the title. You may have to change the text color to contrast with the text box color, as described below.

To add a border, select a Style, Color, and Weight option from the drop-down lists under Custom in the Border section. To add a shadow, click the Shadows check box. The color of the shadow is determined by the Shadows color of the color scheme.

To change the appearance of the title's text, select the title and then click the Font tab in the Format dialog box. Figure 10-5 shows the Font tab options. Use the Font, Font Style, Size, Underline, and Color options to change the look of the text. Leaving the Color option set to Automatic applies the Window Text Color specified by the color option of the Windows Control Panel. This color is probably black, but you can select any other text color.

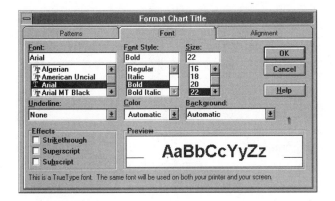

FIGURE 10-5.

The Font tab options in the Format Chart Title dialog box.

 TIP You can also format the text of a title by selecting the text and then using the text formatting buttons on Graph's Formatting toolbar. Display this toolbar by choosing Toolbars from Graph's View menu, selecting the Formatting option in the Toolbars dialog box, and then clicking OK.

The Background option on the Font tab of the Format Chart Title dialog box is a fine-tuning control. Leave it set to Automatic to let Graph select a background that contrasts properly with the foreground text color. If the text and text box are the same color, the Automatic setting fills the area behind the letters of the text with a contrasting color to ensure that the text is readable. You can select Transparent to make the area behind the letters transparent so that the text box color shows through, or you can select Opaque to make this area a solid color. When you select Opaque, any pattern is removed from the area behind the letters of the text.

The Effects options on the Font tab let you turn on Strikethrough (a horizontal line through the text), Superscript, or Subscript. Figure 10-6 shows an axis title with a subscripted character.

FIGURE 10-6.

An axis title with a subscripted character.

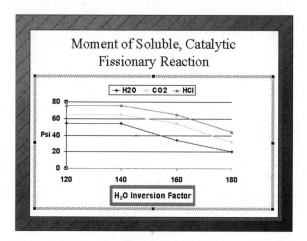

To change the alignment of the text in the text box, click the Alignment tab in the Format dialog box. Figure 10-7 shows the Alignment tab options in the Format Axis Title dialog box. You can then position the text within the text box by selecting options in the Horizontal Text Alignment and Vertical Text Alignment sections. For example, selecting Left for Horizontal and Center for Vertical aligns the text against the center-left interior edge of the text box.

The Orientation option is especially useful for rotating the value (Y) axis title of the graph, as shown in Figure 10-8.

FIGURE 10-7.
The Alignment tab options in the Format Axis Title dialog box.

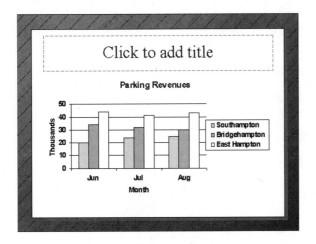

FIGURE 10-8.
The value (Y) axis title, *Thousands,* rotated 90 degrees. (Compare this graph with the one on page 251.)

Formatting All the Graph Text

By double-clicking the chart area, you can display the Format Chart Area dialog box. You can then use the Font tab of this dialog box to make changes to all the text in the graph. This is an efficient way to set the font, for example, for all the graph text.

Adding and Formatting a Legend

If the graph you've created does not already have a legend, you can add one by clicking the Legend button on Graph's Standard toolbar or by choosing Legend from the Insert menu. The plot area of the graph shrinks, moving in from the right to allow space for the legend. If you change your mind, you can quickly remove the legend by clicking the Legend button again or by selecting the legend and pressing the Delete key.

Repositioning the Legend

If you want the legend to appear above, below, or to the left of the graph instead of to the right, you can select a preset legend location by choosing a menu command, or you can drag the legend into position. The advantage of using the menu command is that Graph adjusts the plot area to make room for the legend and adjusts the shape of the legend to fit its new location. The advantage of dragging the legend is that you can place it anywhere you want—even within the graph, if you can find a position that won't obscure the graph's data. Placing the legend within the graph allows you to recover the space formerly occupied by the legend. You can then stretch the plot area of the graph to make the graph larger and easier to see.

To reposition a legend using a menu command, follow these steps:

1. Select the legend, and then choose Selected Legend from the Format menu, press Ctrl+1, or choose Format Legend from the shortcut menu.

2. When the Format Legend dialog box appears, click the Placement tab, as shown below.

3. Click one of the Type options to select a placement, and then click OK. The legend jumps to the new placement, and its shape adjusts to fit the space.

4. If you want to recover the space that is now empty, select the plot area of the graph, and drag its right handle to the right.

When you drag a legend above, below, or to the left of the graph, the plot area of the graph does not adjust to make space. Also, the legend does not automatically change shape to fit its new location. You must perform these steps by dragging the handles of the plot area and the legend. You can reshape a legend by dragging one of its corner handles. As the boundaries of the legend move, dotted boxes in the legend show the new arrangement of the legend entries. For example, when you stretch the legend horizontally, the boxes indicate that the legend entries will be arranged side by side, as shown in Figure 10-9.

FIGURE 10-9.
Stretching a vertical legend horizontally.

TIP When you move a legend from the right or left of the graph to the top or bottom, you can widen the graph to reclaim the legend's space. But when you widen an area, bar, column, or line graph, you decrease the impression of change over time. The lines of a line graph, for example, do not appear to climb or fall as rapidly. You can use this fact to your advantage. To dramatize positive change, place the legend on the left or right side of the graph, and to de-emphasize negative change, place the legend above or below the graph.

Formatting the Legend Entries

You can format the legend box, the text within the legend, and even an individual legend text entry or legend key (the small box within the legend that shows the identifying color or pattern). To format the legend box and all the text within it, double-click the legend to display the Format legend dialog box. To format a legend entry or legend key, double-click the legend entry or legend key to display the corresponding dialog box. You can also select the legend, legend entry, or legend key and then choose the corresponding Selected command from the Format menu, press Ctrl+1, or choose the Format command from the shortcut menu.

> NOTE: When you change the color or pattern of a legend key,
> the color or pattern of the corresponding data series changes, too.

In the Format Legend dialog box, you use the options on the Patterns tab to format the legend box and legend key and you use the options on the Font tab to format the legend text. Both tabs work the same way with legends as they do with chart titles.

See Also: For more information about using the Patterns tab and the Font tab, see "Formatting the Titles," page 251.

Formatting the Axes and Tick Marks

The axes of an area, bar, column, line, XY (scatter), or radar graph are the scales against which the values of the markers in the graph are measured. Pie and doughnut graphs do not have axes. By scaling the axes (changing the minimum or maximum values), you can dramatize or de-emphasize the graph's data. By adding, removing, and formatting tick marks and tick mark labels, you can make the graph easier to interpret—or harder, if that's your goal.

Showing or Hiding the Axes

By default, axes are displayed on the basic graph that Graph creates, but you can turn off one or both axes if you need to display only the markers of the graph. For example, you may not need to give your audience a scale against which to measure the actual values in the graph. Or you may prefer to omit the axes and instead display data point labels, which specify the exact value of each data point.

To turn off an axis, follow these steps:

1. Choose Axes from the Insert menu. The Axes dialog box appears, as shown below.

2. Deselect one or both of the Primary Axis check boxes, and click OK. For example, deselecting the Value (Y) Axis option and adding data point labels (you'll learn how later in this chapter) produces the graph shown here:

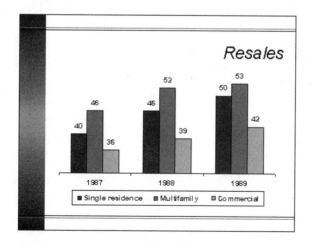

To remove an axis, you can select the axis, and then press the Delete key or choose Clear from the shortcut menu. (The Insert Axes command, which opens the Axes dialog box, is also available on the shortcut menu.)

Formatting the Axes

To change the color or line style of an axis, start by double-clicking the axis. Alternatively, select the axis and then choose Selected Axis from the Format menu, press Ctrl+1, or choose Format Axis from the shortcut menu. When the Format Axis dialog box appears, click the Patterns tab, shown in Figure 10-10.

 TIP   If you have trouble double-clicking the axis, you can double-click any of the labels along the axis to open the Format Axis dialog box.

You can select a line style, line color, and line weight from the three drop-down lists under Custom in the Axis section. The Sample box shows the result of your changes. Click OK to return to the graph, or click a different tab to make other changes to the axis.

Scaling the Axes

Graph automatically determines appropriate axis scaling for the numbers you entered in the datasheet. The maximum value of the value axis is set to the next major interval above the largest value in the data. However, you might want to change the automatic settings to achieve specific effects. To accentuate change in a line graph, for example, you can reduce the maximum value and increase the minimum value.

To change the scale of an axis, start by double-clicking the axis. Alternatively, select the axis and then choose Selected Axis from the Format menu, press Ctrl+1, or choose Format Axis from the shortcut menu. When the Format Axis dialog box appears, click the Scale tab. Figure 10-11 shows the Scale tab for a value (Y) axis. Figure 10-12 shows the Scale tab for a category (X) axis. If the graph is an XY (scatter) type, it has two value axes.

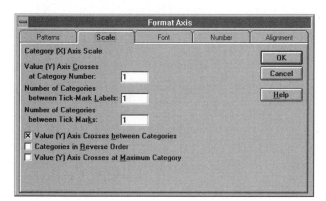

FIGURE 10-11.

The Scale tab options in the Format Axis dialog box when a value (Y) axis is selected.

FIGURE 10-12.

The Scale tab options in the Format Axis dialog box when a category (X) axis is selected.

If you've selected a value axis, the Scale tab shows the current settings for the Minimum, Maximum, Major Unit, Minor Unit, and Category (X) Axis Crosses at options, which are described in Table 10-1 on the next page. The Auto check box to the left of each option is checked to show that Graph has automatically supplied a standard setting. When you change a setting, Graph clears the Auto check box.

TABLE 10-1.

The Value (Y) Axis
Scale options.

Option	Description
Minimum	The minimum value along the axis.
Maximum	The maximum value along the axis.
Major Unit	The increment between the major units along the axis.
Minor Unit	The increment between the minor units that appear between the major units along the axis.
Category (X) Axis Crosses at	The point on the value axis at which the category axis intersects. This setting might be less than 0 if your data includes negative values.

NOTE: The minimum value of a bar or column graph must always be 0. Anything other than 0 hides the full lengths of the bars or columns. If you can't see the full bars or columns, you can't gauge their relative lengths, and the graph is truly misleading.

The other three options on the Scale tab for a value axis serve special purposes. To use a logarithmic scale along the value axis when your data has vast variations, click the Logarithmic Scale option. Then each successive interval along the axis is 10 times the previous interval. To invert an entire graph, click the Values in Reverse Order option. Figure 10-13 shows an inverted graph.

FIGURE 10-13.

An inverted graph created by selecting the Values in Reverse Order option on the Scale tab of the Format Axis dialog box.

To invert a graph without inverting the value axis, click the Category (X) Axis Crosses at Maximum Value option. You can use such a graph to show the amount of progress still needed to reach a goal by setting the Maximum option to the value of the goal and entering the progress so far on the datasheet. Figure 10-14 shows such a graph.

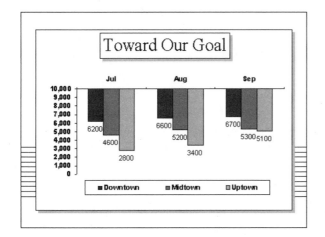

FIGURE 10-14.
An inverted graph created by selecting the Category (X) Axis Crosses at Maximum Value option on the Scale tab of the Format Axis dialog box.

If you've selected the category axis, the Scale tab shows the three edit boxes described in Table 10-2.

Option	Description
Value (Y) Axis Crosses at Category Number	Moves the value axis to the right along the category axis to the category number in the edit box.
Number of Categories between Tick-Mark Labels	Determines the number of labels along the category axis. Enter 2, for example, to show every other label.
Number of Categories between Tick Marks	Determines the number of tick marks along the category axis. Enter 2, for example, to show every other tick mark.

TABLE 10-2.
The Category (X) Axis Scale options.

Deselecting the Value (Y) Axis Crosses between Categories option draws the value axis in the middle of a category rather than between categories. Selecting the Categories in Reverse Order option reverses the order of the

P A R T 3: **Modifying the Presentation**

categories along the category axis. For example, if the categories are chronological, they appear in reverse chronological order. Selecting the Value (Y) Axis Crosses at Maximum Category option moves the value axis to the right side of the graph (or the left side if the categories are reversed).

Formatting the Tick Marks Along the Axes

Major and minor tick marks are the tiny notches that appear along the value axis of a graph to indicate the major and minor units specified on the Scale tab of the Format Axis dialog box. Tick marks also appear between categories on the category axis.

An axis can have major and minor tick marks inside, outside, or crossing the line of the axis. These tick marks automatically have the same color and pattern as the axis to which they are attached. You can change the position of the tick marks by changing the Tick Mark Type options on the Patterns tab of the Format Axis dialog box, shown in Figure 10-15. Figure 10-16 shows a graph with major tick marks that appear outside the value axis and minor tick marks that appear inside the axis.

FIGURE 10-15.
The Tick Mark Type options on the Patterns tab of the Format Axis dialog box.

Formatting the Labels Along the Axes

Tick mark labels appear at the major tick marks of the value axis and between tick marks on the category axis. You control the formatting of these labels using options on the Patterns, Font, Number, and Alignment tabs of the Format Axis dialog box.

To change the location of the tick mark labels, use the Tick-Mark Labels options on the Patterns tab of the Format Axis dialog box, shown in Figure

264

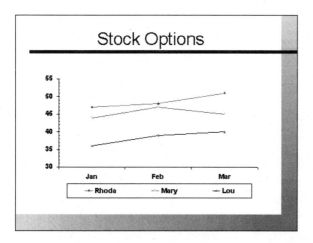

FIGURE 10-16.
An axis with major tick marks outside and minor tick marks inside.

10-15. The default setting, Next to Axis, places the labels near their own axis. To place them near the maximum or minimum values of the other axis, select High or Low, respectively. For example, selecting High moves the tick mark labels to the opposite side of the graph, adjacent to the maximum value on the other axis, as shown in Figure 10-17.

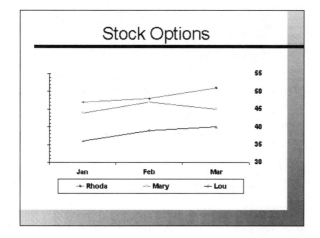

FIGURE 10-17.
A graph for which the Tick-Mark Labels option is set to High.

To remove tick mark labels, click None, but unless you want to show only relative values in a graph, be sure to use data point labels to specify the absolute values.

NOTE: The Font tab options for formatting the text of tick mark labels work just like the Font tab options for formatting titles. For more information about the Font tab options, see "Formatting the Titles," page 251.

The options on the Number tab, shown in Figure 10-18, let you modify the formatting of the numbers along a numeric axis. If the Linked to Source option is selected, these numbers have the same formatting as the numbers in the datasheet. To change the formatting, select a category from the Category list, and then select an option from the Format Codes list. The Sample number in the dialog box reflects the selected formatting.

FIGURE 10-18.
The Number tab options in the Format Axis dialog box.

The options on the Alignment tab let you change the orientation of the tick mark labels. The Automatic setting (horizontal) usually works best for the value tick mark labels, but you may want to select one of the vertical orientations for the category tick mark labels if the labels are long. Figure 10-19 shows a graph with vertical tick mark labels along the category axis.

TIP Be aware that setting the tick mark label orientation to vertical leaves less vertical space for the graph, so the graph becomes shorter without a corresponding change in its width. Changing a graph only vertically or only horizontally increases or decreases the impression of change in the graph.

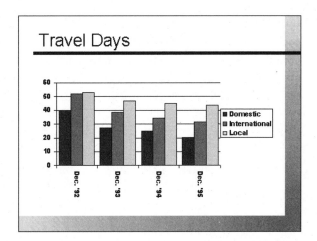

FIGURE 10-19.

A graph with vertical tick mark labels along the category axis.

Showing or Hiding Gridlines

Gridlines extend from major unit tick marks and help you gauge the heights of areas and lines, the lengths of bars and columns, and the position of data points. The easiest way to turn gridlines on or off is to click the Vertical Gridlines and Horizontal Gridlines buttons on Graph's Standard toolbar. Click once to turn on gridlines, and click again to turn them off. You can also choose Gridlines from the Insert menu or choose Insert Gridlines from the shortcut menu to turn gridlines on or off.

Formatting the Gridlines

After you turn on gridlines, you can format them by double-clicking any gridline to display the Format Gridlines dialog box. Then use the options on the Patterns tab to set the style, color, and weight of the gridlines. You can click Automatic to return to the default settings.

> **NOTE:** The options on the Scale tab in the Format Gridlines dialog box allow you to set the scaling of the axis from which the gridlines emanate.

Modifying the Graph Background

A graph has two background areas you can format: the plot area immediately behind the markers, axes, and axis tick mark labels; and the chart area within the heavy border surrounding the graph, including the area occupied by the legend and chart title.

Formatting the Plot Area

To format the plot area, first double-click within the graph but away from the axes or markers. If the graph is three-dimensional, you must double-click just outside the graph, but away from the axes or axis labels. You can also click once to select the plot area and, when you see a border appear around the plot area, choose Selected Plot Area from the Format menu, press Ctrl+1, or choose Format Plot Area from the shortcut menu. The Format Plot Area dialog box contains only the Patterns tab. Use the options in the Border and Area sections to change the look of the plot area. Figure 10-20 shows the plot area of a graph filled with a medium gray.

FIGURE 10-20.

The plot area of a graph filled with a medium gray.

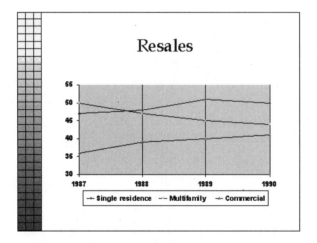

Formatting the Chart Area

To format the chart area, double-click within the heavy border of the graph but outside the plot area, or click once to select the chart area and then choose Select Chart Area from the Format menu, press Ctrl+1, or choose Format Chart Area from the shortcut menu. (Be careful not to click the legend or the chart title.) The Format Chart Area dialog box appears, as shown in Figure 10-21.

Use the options in the Border and Area sections of the Patterns tab to change the look of the border and the interior of the chart area. You can select a border style, color, and weight, and you can fill the chart area with a background color and pattern. Use the Font tab options to change the look of

FIGURE 10-21.

The Format Chart Area dialog box.

all the text in the graph. Figure 10-22 shows a line graph with contrasting formatting in the plot and chart areas.

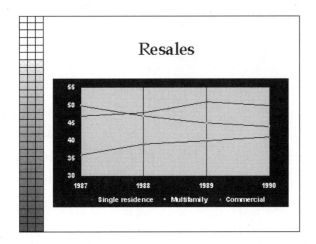

FIGURE 10-22.

A line graph with contrasting chart and plot area formatting.

NOTE: The Replace Fonts command on the Tools menu, which changes the fonts used throughout a presentation, does not affect the fonts used by the text in graphs. After changing the presentation font, you can quickly change a graph's font to match by using the options on the Font tab of the Format Chart Area dialog box. That way, you don't have to select and format each graph text object individually.

Adding and Formatting Data Labels

The markers of a data series provide only an approximate representation of the numbers in the datasheet. To show the actual numbers, you must provide a table of numbers or place the numbers directly on the markers as data labels.

To add data labels to a data series, start by double-clicking the series. When the Format Data Series dialog box appears, click the Data Labels tab, which is shown in Figure 10-23.

FIGURE 10-23.
The Data Labels tab options in the Format Data Series dialog box.

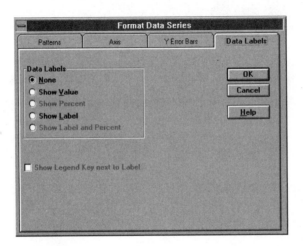

To add data labels to all the markers in the graph, you can select the graph and then choose Data Labels from the Insert menu or choose Insert Data Labels from the shortcut menu. The Data Labels dialog box shows the same options as the Data Labels tab of the Format Data Series dialog box.

When you have displayed the dialog box, click Show Value to display the numeric value of each data point in the series. Click Show Percent if the graph is a stacked bar, stacked column, pie, or doughnut graph and you want to show the percentages represented by the segments or slices. Click Show Label to display the category assigned to the data point. (In an area graph, clicking Show Label displays the series names.) Click Show Label and Percent to display both the category or series names and the percentages.

If an Automatic Text check box appears on the Data Labels tab, the data labels of the datasheet are being used. Click this check box to synchronize the data labels with those on the datasheet. If the Show Legend Key next to Label check box is available, you can check it to place the legend key, which displays the color of the series, next to the data label.

TIP   You can add a data label to a single marker—perhaps an outstanding result—by clicking the marker to select it and then double-clicking the marker to open the Format Data Point dialog box, which contains the same Data Labels and Patterns tabs as the Format Data Series dialog box. Alternatively, you can select a single marker and choose Data Labels from either the Insert menu or the shortcut menu. Then select one of the Show options in the Data Labels dialog box, and click OK.

To format the data labels on a graph, double-click any data label in a series. The Format Data Labels dialog box appears. The options on the four tabs of the dialog box (Patterns, Font, Number, and Alignment) work just as they do when you format any other text in a graph. For example, you can use the Patterns options to create a filled box around each data label and the Number options to change the number of decimal places shown in the data labels.

To format a single data label, select the data labels for the series, and click the data label you want. Then double-click the same data label, and use the options in the Format Data Labels dialog box as usual. You can also select a single data label, click an insertion point in it, and then edit or add text. For example, you might want to delete the number and enter a note about the data point, as shown in Figure 10-24.

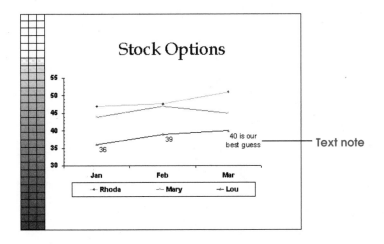

FIGURE 10-24.
A text note attached to a data point.

> **TIP**   Don't try to crowd too many data labels on a graph. You might prefer to add a table to the slide or to the following slide showing the numbers.

Moving and Resizing Graph Objects

You've already seen that you can move a graph's title or legend by dragging its border. You can also drag the border of the entire graph to move it on the slide and drag the plot area to move or resize the area of the graph bounded by the axes and axis labels. (Enlarging the plot area of a graph can make interpreting the markers easier, but changing the shape of the plot area alters the impression of change in the graph.) You can even drag each data label to reposition it relative to its data point or marker.

To move or resize a graph object, click the object and then drag the object's border. To drag a data label, for example, first click the data label to select it, and then drag the border surrounding the data label.

After you finish formatting the graph, click outside the graph's border to redisplay PowerPoint's menus and toolbars. Later, if you want to make additional changes to the graph, you can open the Graph module by simply double-clicking the graph.

3-D Graph Formatting

PowerPoint's 3-D chart types are almost always worthy replacements for their 2-D equivalents. They portray the same data with the added touch of depth and, if you want, perspective. The third dimension also adds more formatting possibilities, which are the subject of this section.

Adjusting the 3-D View

PowerPoint provides 3-D versions of area, bar, column, line, and pie graphs, in addition to 3-D surface graphs which are by definition three-dimensional. You can slant, rotate, and change the height of 3-D graphs by changing their 3-D view. For all types other than 3-D bar and 3-D pie graphs, you can also increase the illusion of depth by adding perspective.

To change both the elevation (the forward slant) and the rotation of a 3-D graph, you don't even have to use a dialog box. You can simply drag the corners of the graph by following these steps:

1. Click one of the corners of the graph. A handle appears at every corner of an imaginary box that encloses the graph. (If you see handles only at the corners of the back wall, try clicking the corner again or click a different corner.)

2. Place the mouse pointer on one of the corner handles, hold down the mouse button, and drag the mouse slightly. The outlines of the imaginary box appear. If you hold down the Ctrl key as you drag, you see outlines of the markers, too, as shown below:

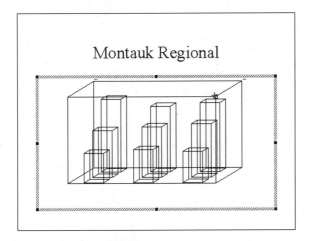

3. Still holding down the mouse button, drag the corner up or down to change the elevation, or drag the corner left or right to rotate the graph.

4. Release the mouse button to redraw the graph at its new elevation and rotation.

You can also use the options in the Format 3-D View dialog box to accomplish the same task. Select the graph and then choose 3-D View from the Format menu or the shortcut menu to open the dialog box shown in Figure 10-25 on the next page. As you can see, additional options in the dialog box let you change the height of 3-D graphs and add perspective to those graphs that can show perspective.

FIGURE 10-25.

The Format 3-D View dialog box.

In the Format 3-D View dialog box, a model of the 3-D graph shows the current option settings. By viewing the model as you change the options, you can determine how the actual graph will look when you click OK.

To change the elevation of the graph, enter a number in the Elevation edit box or click the Increase Elevation or Decrease Elevation button to the left of the model. Each click changes the elevation by 5 degrees. To change the rotation, enter a number in the Rotation edit box or click the Rotate Left or Rotate Right button below the model. Each click changes the rotation by 10 degrees.

To change the height of the graph, deselect the Auto Scaling option, and then edit the number in the Height edit box. (You cannot change the height of 3-D pie graphs.) The height of the graph is specified as a percentage of the length of the base. To let PowerPoint select a height that is appropriate for the graph, turn on Auto Scaling by clicking the option again.

To add perspective, deselect the Right Angle Axes option. (You cannot add perspective to 3-D bar graphs or 3-D pie graphs.) Then edit the number in the Perspective edit box or click the Decrease Perspective or Increase Perspective button to the right of the model. Each click changes the perspective by 5 units. Valid perspective numbers are 0 to 100. The default perspective setting of 30 is just enough to give the graph a true sense of depth without the kind of distortion shown in Figure 10-26.

After you change the options in the Format 3-D View dialog box, click Apply to apply the new settings without removing the dialog box, or click OK to return to the graph. If you click Apply, you can drag the dialog box aside to see the revised graph. You can also click Default to return the graph to its default 3-D view settings.

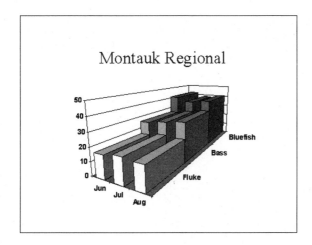

FIGURE 10-26.
A rotated, 3-D column graph distorted by a Perspective setting of 60.

To change the depth of a 3-D graph, select the graph and then choose either the 3-D Group command from the bottom of the Format menu or the Format 3-D Group command from the bottom of the shortcut menu. Figure 10-27 shows the Options tab of the dialog box that appears when a 3-D column graph is selected. Then change the Chart Depth option and click OK. The minimum and maximum chart depths are 20 and 2000, respectively.

FIGURE 10-27.
The Options tab options in the Format 3-D Column Group dialog box.

Formatting 3-D Graph Objects

3-D graphs have unique graph objects that 2-D graphs do not have, such as walls and a floor. Figure 10-28 identifies the graph objects that are unique to 3-D graphs.

FIGURE 10-28.

The unique graph objects of a 3-D column chart.

Formatting the Axes

When the series in 3-D graphs appear behind one another at various depths in the graph, a third axis—the series (Y) axis—extends along the floor of the graph from front to back. The category axis remains the X axis, but the value axis rises from the floor and is called the Z axis. The graph shown in Figure 10-28 shows all three axes.

Formatting the value axis of a 3-D graph is just like formatting the value axis of a 2-D graph. You double-click the value axis or select the axis and then choose Selected Axis from the Format menu, press Ctrl+1, or choose Format Axis from the shortcut menu. All three methods display the Format Axis dialog box. The options on the Patterns, Font, Number, and Alignment tabs of this dialog box are the same as those for 2-D graphs. However, the Scale tab has a new option, Floor (XY Plane) Crosses At, that lets you change the position of the floor within a 3-D area, bar, column, line, or surface graph.

When you change the vertical position of the floor, markers in 3-D area and column graphs extend either above the floor or below the floor, but do not cross the floor to reach their proper length along the value axis. Figure 10-29 shows a graph with the floor set at 35. Such a graph can show an excess above or deficiency below a budget or target value. In 3-D bar graphs, the floor runs vertically, so markers extend to the left or right of the floor. In 3-D line and 3-D surface graphs, the floor appears as a transparent panel within the graph and has no effect on the display of the lines or surface.

FIGURE 10-29.

A graph in which the floor (XY plane) crosses at 35.

You can click the Floor (XY Plane) Crosses at Minimum Value option to place the floor at the minimum value of the value axis.

Formatting the Walls and Floor

All 3-D chart types, except 3-D pie graphs, have walls and a floor. The walls are behind and to the side of the markers, and the markers rest on the floor.

By double-clicking the walls of a 3-D graph, you can open the Format Walls dialog box shown in Figure 10-30 on the next page, which displays only Patterns options. Use the options in the Border and Area sections to change the border and surface color and pattern of the walls. Figure 10-31, also on the next page, shows a 3-D area graph with black walls. The floor must be formatted separately. Double-click the floor to open the Format Floor dialog box, which contains the same options as the Format Walls dialog box.

FIGURE 10-30.
The Format Walls
dialog box.

FIGURE 10-31.
The walls of a 3-D
area graph with the
Area section's
Color option set
to black.

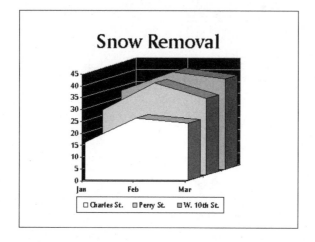

Formatting the Gridlines

When a graph has three axes, you can add major and minor gridlines to all three axes. When you choose Gridlines from the Insert menu, the Gridlines dialog box appears, as shown in Figure 10-32. The options in this dialog box let you turn on major and minor gridlines for the category, series, and value axes.

NOTE: When 3-D graphs contain markers that look three-dimensional but are not at planes of different depths, you can display 2-D walls and gridlines by clicking the 2-D Walls and Gridlines option at the bottom of the Gridlines dialog box.

278

FIGURE 10-32.
The Gridlines dialog box for a 3-D graph.

Advanced Area, Bar, Column, and Line Graph Formatting

In Chapter 6, where you created basic graphs, you learned about selecting a chart type and subtype. Each subtype has a unique style and arrangement of markers that convey a different message; changing the subtype is the quickest way to dramatically change the look of a graph.

To change the subtype of a graph, select the graph, choose Group from the bottom of the Format menu or choose Format Group from the bottom of the shortcut menu, and then select one of the subtypes from the dialog box that appears.

> **NOTE:** If you select the 2-D stacked bar or 2-D stacked column subtype, you can click Series Lines on the Options tab of the Format Column Group dialog box to connect the series in the columns with lines.

Creating Combination Graphs

PowerPoint allows you to mix 2-D chart types, selecting the best chart type for each series or group of series in the graph. You might use a line for one series and columns for another to compare the fluctuating change of a series (for example, sales volume) in response to incremental adjustments in another series (for example, price). Figure 10-33 on the next page shows such a graph.

FIGURE 10-33.

A graph that
compares sales
volume (shown as
a line) and price
(shown as
columns).

NOTE: You can't mix chart types in a 3-D graph.

The easiest way to change the chart type of one or more series is to select the series, click the down arrow to the right of the Chart Type button on Graph's Standard toolbar, and then select a different 2-D chart type from the palette of chart types. You can also choose Chart Type from the Format menu or the shortcut menu, and then double-click one of the 2-D chart types in the Chart Type dialog box. After you change the chart type of one or more series, you can use the Group command at the bottom of the Format menu to apply different formatting to each chart type.

If you want to change one of the chart types in a combination graph, choose Chart Type from the Format menu. Each chart type group is listed in the Chart Type dialog box's Group list. You can select a group and then change its appearance by selecting a different chart type. To change all the groups back to the same type, click the Entire Chart option in the Apply To section of the Chart Type dialog box, and then double-click the chart type you want.

When a graph has two or more series or groups of series with different chart types, you can add a secondary category or value axis against which you can plot one or more of the chart type groups. A secondary axis appears on the opposite side of the graph and is scaled according to the chart type group assigned to it. As a result, the same graph can show two chart type groups that have very different ranges of values. For example, you might plot the price of a product over time against the primary axis, which ranges from 39 to 49 cents, and plot the units sold against the secondary axis, which ranges from 250,000 to 350,000.

To add a secondary axis, select one of the groups in the graph, and choose Axes from the Insert menu. The Axes dialog box appears, with two Secondary Axis options: Category (X) Axis and Value (Y) Axis. Select one or both options to add one or two axes to the graph.

To assign a group to a secondary axis, first select the group and choose the Group command from the bottom of the Format menu or shortcut menu. Then click the Axis tab in the Format Group dialog box to display the options shown in Figure 10-34, click either the Primary Axis or Secondary Axis option, and click OK.

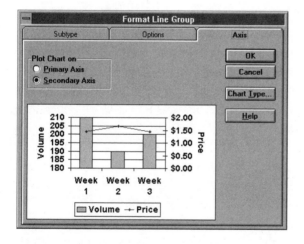

FIGURE 10-34.

The Axis tab options in the Format Line Group dialog box.

Adjusting the Spacing of Areas, Bars, Columns, and Lines

With the Gap Width and Gap Depth settings on the Options tab of the Format Group dialog box, you can modify the spacing between 2-D and 3-D areas, bars, and columns, and between 3-D lines. Figure 10-35 on the next page shows these

FIGURE 10-35.

The Options tab options in the Format 3-D Bar Group dialog box.

options for a 3-D bar graph. For 2-D bar and column graphs, you can also use the Overlap option, which is not available for 3-D graphs.

The bars or columns of a default graph are arranged in clusters along the category axis. To change the spacing between clusters, change the Gap Width setting, which can range from 0 to 500 percent of the width of a single bar or column. A setting of 0 percent creates a step graph or histogram. The default setting of 150 percent leaves 1.5 times the width of a bar or column between each cluster. As you increase the gap width, the width of the bars or columns decreases.

To separate the areas, bars, columns, or lines along the Y axis of a 3-D graph, change the Gap Depth setting on the Options tab. The gap depth, like the gap width, is a percentage of the depth of a single marker.

To change the spacing of 2-D bars or columns within a cluster, rather than between clusters, change the Overlap setting. At 0 percent, the bars or columns are side by side without overlapping. At 100 percent, they overlap completely. Figure 10-36 shows a column graph with a 50-percent overlap and a 100-percent gap width.

TIP To separate the bars or columns within a cluster, you can enter a negative overlap percentage. An overlap setting of −50 percent, for example, separates the columns within a cluster by half the width of a single column.

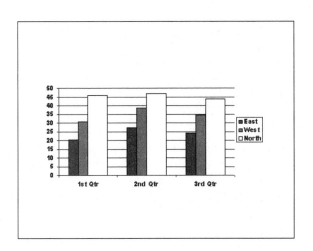

FIGURE 10-36.
A column graph with a 50-percent overlap and 100-percent gap width.

Adding Drop Lines to Area and Line Graphs

Drop lines are vertical lines that help identify the data points of 2-D and 3-D area and line graphs. They run from the data points of the areas or lines to the category axis of the graph. Figure 10-37 shows a 3-D line graph with drop lines.

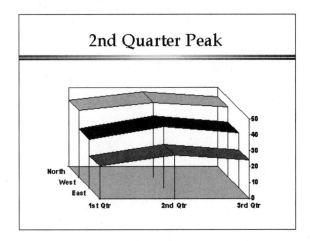

FIGURE 10-37.
A 3-D line graph with drop lines.

To turn on drop lines, choose the Group command from the bottom of the Format menu or shortcut menu, click the Drop Lines option on the Options tab of the Format Group dialog box, and click OK.

Adding High-Low Lines to Line Graphs

High-low lines can be added to individual lines or to all lines in a 2-D line graph to depict the range over which a measurement varies, such as the high and low temperature of the day or the high and low test scores of different groups of people. Figure 10-38 shows high-low lines added to all the data series in a temperature fluctuation graph.

FIGURE 10-38.

High-low lines added to a temperature fluctuation graph.

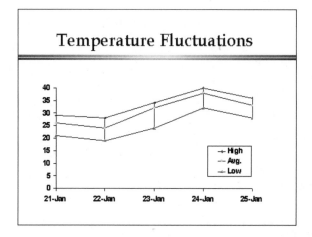

To create a graph that shows discrete ranges of measurements instead of connected series, you can set the Line option on the Patterns tab of the Format Data Series dialog box to None. Figure 10-39 shows the temperature fluctuations graph with this setting.

To change the style, color, and weight of drop lines and high-low lines, first double-click a line. Or select a line and choose the Selected command from the Format menu, choose the Format command from the shortcut menu, or press Ctrl+1. Then change the Line options in the dialog box that appears.

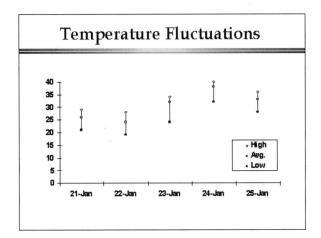

FIGURE 10-39.

A 2-D line graph with high-low lines, and with the Line option on the Patterns tab of the Format Data Series dialog box set to None.

A Sample Stock Tracking Graph

To create an open-high-low-close graph with up-down bars, like those used by stock watchers, follow these steps:

1. Enter four series of stock data in the datasheet in this order: the opening values, the high values, the low values, and the closing values.

2. Plot the data as a 2-D line graph.

3. To form the familiar stock chart, add up-down bars and high-low lines to the graph by first choosing the Line Group command from the bottom of the Format menu or by choosing the Format Line Group command from the shortcut menu. Then click the Up-Down Bars and High-Low Lines options on the Options tab of the Format Line Group dialog box, and click OK.

4. Next, remove the lines connecting the data points by selecting each line (or data series) in turn and setting the Line option to None on the Patterns tab of the Format Data Series dialog box.

Figure 10-40 on the next page shows a sample open-high-low-close graph. Up bars (when the stock's closing value is greater than the opening value) are filled with white. Down bars are filled with black, as is the case in the bar for Wednesday.

FIGURE 10-40.

A typical stock
tracking graph
created with
up-down bars and
high-low lines.

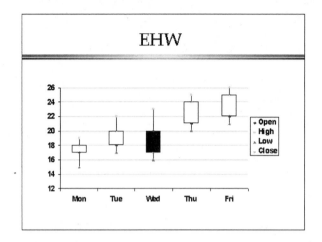

To change the appearance of the up-down bars in the graph, select one of them and then choose the Selected Up Bars command from the Format menu, press Ctrl+1, or choose the Format command from the shortcut menu. If the graph contains both up bars and down bars, you must select and format the up bars and down bars separately.

Showing and Predicting Trends with Trendlines

When working with area, bar, column, line, and XY (scatter) graphs, you can add an automatic regression line that depicts the general trend of the numbers in a data series and allows you to predict approximate future data points based on the existing data. The regression line, called a *trendline*, overlays the series markers. The default trendline is a linear regression that depicts a "best fit" straight line passing nearest to all the data points. You can select one of five other regression types, each based on a different mathematical regression formula. You can also format the trendline to set the intercept; change the number of forecast periods; or display the trendline name, the R-squared value, or the regression equation on the graph. (If terms like "intercept" and "R-squared value" puzzle you, you might want to stick with a simple linear regression trendline and leave the higher math to the statisticians.) Figure 10-41 shows standard linear regression lines on a column graph.

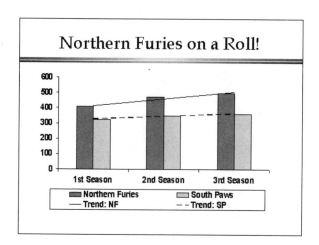

FIGURE 10-41.
Linear regression lines on a column chart.

To add a trendline to a graph, select a data series and then choose Trendline from the Insert menu or choose Insert Trendline from the shortcut menu. On the Type tab, shown in Figure 10-42, select an option in the Trend/ Regression Type section and click OK.

FIGURE 10-42.
The Type tab options in the Format Trendline dialog box.

To delete a trendline quickly, select the line and then press the Delete key or choose Clear from the shortcut menu.

To format a trendline, first double-click it or select it, and then choose the Selected Trendline command from the Format menu, press Ctrl+1, or choose

287

the Format Trendline command from the shortcut menu. When the Format Trendline dialog box appears, click the Options tab, shown in Figure 10-43.

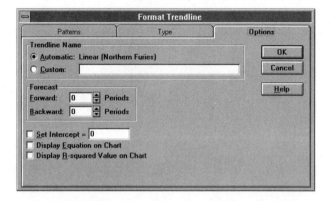

In the Custom edit box in the Trendline Name section, you can enter a custom trendline name that will replace the default name in the legend. The options in the Forecast section allow you to extend the trendline beyond the actual data by adding a number of forecast periods forward and backward. If regressions are the stuff of your daily life, you will want to vary the intercept by entering values in the Set Intercept edit box and display the math behind the trendline by clicking the Display Equation on Chart and Display R-squared Value on Chart options.

To change the line style, color, and weight of the regression line, use the options on the Patterns tab of the Format Trendline dialog box.

Allowing for Error with Error Bars

Error bars in a graph allow you to depict the minor deviations that you expect in your data. You can enter this "margin of error" as a fixed number, a percentage, the number of standard deviations from the mean of plotted values, or the standard error. You can also add a custom plus and minus error value. 2-D area, bar, column, and line graphs have Y error bars that apply to the Y axis only. XY (scatter) graphs can have both X error bars and Y error bars. Figure 10-44 shows a column graph with Y error bars.

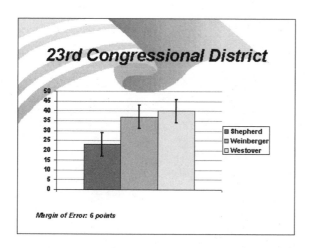

FIGURE 10-44.

A column graph
with Y error bars.

To add error bars that extend from each data point in a series, select each series in turn and then choose Error Bars from the Insert menu or choose Insert Error Bars from the shortcut menu. On the Y Error Bars tab of the Format Error Bars dialog box, shown in Figure 10-45, select a display type by clicking the Both, Plus, Minus, or None option in the Display section, and select an error type and amount in the Error Amount section. If the graph is an XY graph, the Format Error Bars dialog box has two tabs; one to set the X error bars and another to set the Y error bars.

FIGURE 10-45.

The Y Error Bars
tab options in the
Format Error Bars
dialog box.

To format the error bars, double-click one of the error bars, and click the Patterns tab of the Format Error Bars dialog box. You can then select the style, color, and weight of the bars, and you can select one of two marker styles: a T or a straight line extending from the data point.

Varying the Colors of a Single Series Graph

When a graph displays only one series, you can have each marker in the series display a different color rather than the same color. Double-click the series, and in the Format Data Series dialog box, select Vary Colors by Point on the Options tab. The Vary Colors by Point option is not available for 2-D area, 3-D area, or 3-D surface graphs.

> **NOTE:** A related option, Vary Colors by Slice, applies a different color to each slice in a pie or doughnut graph. This option is turned on by default.

Formatting Pie and Doughnut Graphs

Pie and doughnut graphs offer special formatting options that are unique to their chart types. You can select and format the entire pie or doughnut group, or you can select and format a pie slice, a doughnut ring, or a segment of a doughnut ring.

Separating Slices

To call attention to certain pie slices, you can separate them from the rest of the pie by dragging them away from the center one by one. You can also separate segments of the outermost doughnut ring by dragging them.

Labeling Slices

The easiest way to label the slices of a pie is to apply an autoformat with the type of labels you want. To apply an autoformat, select the pie, choose Auto-Format from the Format menu or the shortcut menu, and then select one of the seven autoformats shown in Figure 10-46. Autoformats 2 and 5 show slice labels, autoformat 6 shows percentages, and autoformat 7 shows both labels and percentages.

FIGURE 10-46.
The autoformats
available for pie
graphs.

You can also label the slices by selecting the pie and choosing Data Labels from either the Insert menu or shortcut menu. (To label a single slice, select that slice before choosing Data Labels.) Selecting Show Value in the Data Labels dialog box places the value of each slice next to the slice. Selecting Show Percent shows the calculated percentage of each slice. Selecting Show Label shows the name of the slice. (You may prefer to show slice names rather than a legend so that the viewer can see what each slice represents without having to match up the legend key with the slice colors.) Selecting Show Label and Percent shows both the name and percentage next to each slice, as shown in the example in Figure 10-47.

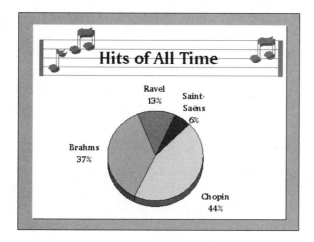

FIGURE 10-47.
A pie with data
labels created by
turning on the
Label and Percent
option in the Data
Labels dialog box.

TIP   You can drag the values, percentages, or labels onto their corresponding pie slices. But if you have turned on the Label and Percent option, you cannot drag the percentages onto the slices and leave the labels off to the side unless you convert the pie to graphic objects. For more information, see "Converting a Graph to Graphic Objects," page 300.

Varying Colors by Slice

By default, the Vary Colors by Slice option on the Options tab of the Format Pie Group dialog box is turned on. When you turn off Vary Colors by Slice, all slices get the same color, and the legend is no longer helpful unless the slices are filled with different patterns.

Changing the Angle of the First Slice

On the Options tab of the Format Pie Group dialog box or the Format Doughnut Group dialog box, you can set the Angle of First Slice option to rotate the entire pie or doughnut. Slices or segments start in the location specified by the Angle of First Slice option and are plotted clockwise to the pie. The default setting is 45 degrees. To rotate the pie 90 degrees to the right, for example, you would change the Angle of First Slice setting to 135 degrees.

> **NOTE:** You can also rotate a 3-D pie graph by changing the Rotation setting in the Format 3-D View dialog box. For more information about rotating a 3-D graph, see "Adjusting the 3-D View," page 272.

Changing the Hole Size of a Doughnut Graph

Reducing the hole size of a doughnut graph enlarges the segments so that they are easier to see. The default hole size, specified as a percentage of the width of the graph, is 50 percent. To change the hole size, simply modify the Doughnut Hole Size percentage setting on the Options tab of the Format Doughnut Group dialog box.

Formatting Radar and 3-D Surface Graphs

The size of the ring of each data series in a radar graph shows the aggregate of the values in the series. Where the ring bulges from the center, the series shows the greatest measurements. For example, Figure 10-48 shows a radar graph in which each ring represents the yearly sales, by month, of a store in a three-store chain. As you can see, the sales of all three stores swelled during the months before Christmas. The store with the largest ring, E. 23rd St., had the greatest overall sales.

FIGURE 10-48.

A radar chart showing the monthly sales of three stores.

In a radar graph, value (Y) axes extend from the center of the graph, evenly spaced, in different directions. Each data point in the series has its own value axis. Double-clicking any axis and changing a setting in the Format dialog box formats all of the axes, except that changing the tick mark label options affects only the axis that rises vertically from the center of the graph.

Most of the formatting options for radar graphs are available as auto-formats, and you are likely to find an autoformat that suits your need. If you don't, double-click the graph and then change the settings in the Format Radar Group dialog box. To label the axes of the radar graph, click the Category Labels option on the Options tab. To display markers at each data point, select the first subtype on the Subtype tab. To display each series as a filled ring, select the second subtype.

To change the formatting of a data series, double-click the data series and then change the options in the Format Data Series dialog box.

Formatting 3-D Surface Graph Intervals

In a 3-D surface graph, each height interval along the vertical (Z) axis—the 3-D axis—has its own color, as shown in the graph's legend. The color of a 3-D surface graph region indicates the height interval along the Z axis that the region has reached. If you want to change the colors of the Z axis intervals, you cannot select the surface or the intervals themselves. Instead, you must double-click the legend keys and then change the Color and Pattern options in the Area section of the Patterns tab in the Format Legend Key dialog box. (Remember, the legend keys are the small boxes that show colors within the legend.)

Creating Picture Graphs

By replacing the markers of a graph with pictures, you can create a picture graph, also called a *pictograph*. The pictures can identify the series and communicate more information at a glance, as shown in Figure 10-49.

FIGURE 10-49.

A picture graph.

To turn a regular graph into a picture graph, select a picture in another application, and copy it to the Windows Clipboard using the Copy command. When you return to PowerPoint, activate the graph and then select one of the series of markers you want to replace with pictures. Click the Paste button or choose Paste from the Edit menu to replace all the markers of that data series with the picture.

To change the appearance of the pictures, double-click a picture and then change the options on the Patterns tab of the Format Data Point dialog box, shown in Figure 10-50.

FIGURE 10-50.
The Patterns tab options for a picture graph in the Format Data Point dialog box.

When you replace bar or column markers with pictures, the pictures stretch to fill the markers. You can tell PowerPoint to stack the pictures instead, using as many copies of the picture at its original size as necessary to fill the marker. You can also tell PowerPoint to stack the pictures at a size you specify.

When you replace the markers of a line, XY, or radar graph with pictures, the pictures always appear at their original size. They cannot be stretched, stacked, or scaled.

Saving Graph Formatting as an AutoFormat

After you've created a special combination of graph formatting, you can save the combination as an autoformat that you can then apply to other graphs. To create a new autoformat, follow these steps:

1. Activate a completed graph and then choose AutoFormat from the Format menu or shortcut menu. The AutoFormat dialog box appears.

2. Click the User-Defined option in the Formats Used section. The dialog box changes to look like this:

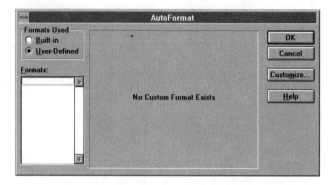

3. Click the Customize button, and in the User-Defined AutoFormats dialog box, click the Add button. The Add Custom AutoFormat dialog box appears, as shown here:

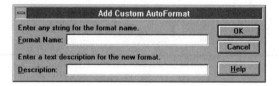

4. In the Format Name edit box, enter a name of up to 31 characters. (You can include spaces.) If you want, enter a description of up to 32 characters by pressing Tab and then typing in the Description edit box.

5. Click OK. The selected graph appears in the Format Sample dialog box.

6. Click Close to close the dialog box and return to the graph.

To delete an autoformat, display the User-Defined AutoFormats dialog box, select the autoformat, click the Delete button, and then click OK.

Adding and Formatting Text Boxes

You can add a free-floating text box to contain a note that describes or highlights some aspect of a graph. The text box becomes an intrinsic part of the graph. If you resize or move the graph, or copy it between slides or presentations, the text box goes along for the ride.

Adding a Text Box

To add a text box to a graph, follow these steps:

1. Click the Text Box button on Graph's Standard toolbar.

2. Position the mouse pointer approximately where you want the upper left corner of the text box to be, hold down the mouse button, and drag down and to the right to create a text box approximately the correct shape and size. When you release the mouse button, an insertion point appears within the text box.

3. Enter the text. The text will wrap within the boundaries of the invisible text box, as shown below.

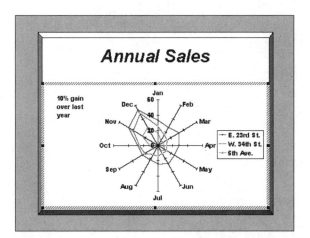

To reposition the text box, click the edge of the text, and drag the box to a new position. To resize the text box, click the edge of the text, and drag one of the handles.

Formatting a Text Box

To format the text box and the text within it, start by double-clicking the border of the text box. The Format Object dialog box appears, as shown in Figure 10-51. You can also select the text box, and then choose Font from the Format menu or choose Format Object from the shortcut menu to display this dialog box.

FIGURE 10-51.
The Format Object
dialog box.

Use the options on the Patterns tab of the dialog box to change the formatting of the text box containing the text. Use the options on the Font tab and Alignment tab to change the formatting of the text.

The Properties tab of the dialog box holds a single option you can use to set whether text should resize when the graph resizes. The default Don't size with chart option prevents the text from becoming too small to read when you reduce the size of the graph.

TIP   To change the formatting of selected words or characters within a text box, click an insertion point in the text box, select the text you want to format, and then choose Font from the Format menu or choose Format Object from the shortcut menu.

Adding and Formatting Arrows

After you add a text box containing a note about an item in the graph, you can connect the text box to the item with an arrow, as shown in Figure 10-52.

FIGURE 10-52.

An arrow points to the item described by the text in the text box.

To add an arrow, follow these steps:

1. Click the Drawing button on Graph's Standard toolbar to display Graph's Drawing toolbar.

2. Click the Arrow button on the Drawing toolbar.

3. Position the mouse pointer near the text box, hold down the mouse button, and drag to the item in the graph to which you want the arrow to point. When you release the mouse button, an arrow appears.

To format the arrow, start by double-clicking it. The Format Object dialog box appears, as shown in Figure 10-53 on the next page.

On the Patterns tab of the dialog box, use the Line options to change the appearance of the arrow's line. Use the Arrowhead options to change the appearance of the arrowhead. On the Properties tab, select the Object Positioning option if you want the arrow to be resized with the graph.

See Also: For more information about using the tools on Graph's Drawing toolbar, see Chapter 13, "Drawing Graphic Objects," page 329.

FIGURE 10-53.
The arrow
formatting options.

Converting a Graph to Graphic Objects

PowerPoint offers a wealth of choices that allow you to change the appearance of a graph, but for the ultimate in flexibility, you can convert the graph to a collection of graphic objects, each of which can be modified individually. You can convert the columns of a column graph to a collection of rectangles, for example, and then revise them with PowerPoint's comprehensive drawing and editing commands.

When you convert a graph to a set of graphic objects, it loses its identification as a graph object that represents an underlying set of data. You can no longer use Graph's commands and controls, and the datasheet is no longer available. The result of the conversion is a picture of what was once a graph. And the conversion process is a one-way street: You cannot convert the collection of graphic objects back to a graph.

Before you convert a graph to a set of graphic objects, you might want to copy the graph to another presentation slide. Then you can convert the copy of the graph to graphic objects, knowing that you can always return to the original, unchanged graph. You can even hide the slide containing the original graph so that you can access it even though it does not appear when you display the presentation.

To convert a graph to a collection of graphic objects, follow these steps:

1. Click the graph once to select it without activating it.

2. Choose the Ungroup command from PowerPoint's Draw menu. Power-Point warns you that proceeding will permanently discard any embedded data and asks *Convert to PowerPoint objects?*

3. Click OK to convert the graph. After a moment, the graph reappears as a collection of graphic objects, each of which is selected.

4. Click outside any of the objects to deselect all of them.

Now you can select the objects one by one and make any necessary modifications.

 For more information about editing graphic objects, see "Editing Objects," page 342.

In this chapter, you learned how to modify the appearance of the graphs in your presentation. In the next chapter, you'll learn how to use Slide Sorter view to make broad changes to the presentation's design.

Using Slide Sorter View

By displaying the slides of a presentation as miniatures arranged side by side on the screen, Slide Sorter view, the third of Power-Point's views, gives you a working view of the presentation as a whole. But Slide Sorter view allows you to do more than just view the presentation. You can also do real work on the presentation before switching to another view.

Some of the tasks you can accomplish in Slide Sorter view are:

- Checking the overall presentation for flaws and design consistency
- Rearranging slides
- Changing the template, color scheme, and background of all slides or only selected slides
- Duplicating slides
- Moving and copying slides between two presentations
- Setting up and previewing the transition effects that will appear in Slide Show view

All of these tasks except the last one are covered in this chapter. Creating slide shows while in Slide Sorter view is the subject of Chapter 16, "Creating Slide Shows."

Switching to Slide Sorter View

Switching to Slide Sorter view is as easy as clicking the Slide Sorter View button in the lower left corner of the presentation window. You can also choose Slide Sorter from the View menu.

Slide Sorter View

When you switch to Slide Sorter view, the current presentation is displayed as a set of miniature slides, and the Slide Sorter toolbar appears below the Standard toolbar, replacing the Formatting toolbar. Figure 11-1 shows a presentation in Slide Sorter view.

Slide Sorter toolbar

FIGURE 11-1.

A presentation in Slide Sorter view.

To leave Slide Sorter view and view a single slide in Slide view, double-click a slide. You can also use the arrow keys to move the highlighted border to a slide, and then press Enter.

Zooming In and Out

To zoom in and out on the slide miniatures in Slide Sorter view, use the Zoom Control box on the Standard toolbar or the Zoom command on the View menu. Zooming in allows you to inspect slides more closely to check for errors. Zooming out allows you to view more of the presentation as a whole so that you can check its design consistency. To change the zoom percentage, click the Zoom Control box, type a new zoom percentage, and press Enter. You can also click the arrow next to the Zoom Control box, and select a zoom percentage from the drop-down list.

If you prefer to use menu commands, choose the Zoom command from the View menu. Then, when the Zoom dialog box appears, select one of the preset zoom percentages or enter a new percentage in the Percent edit box.

Changing the Content in Slide Sorter View

In Slide Sorter view, as in most other views, you can change both the content of the presentation and the appearance. You can rearrange slides, add and delete slides, duplicate existing slides, and move and copy slides between presentations. You cannot change the content of individual slides, however; creating and editing individual slides is a task that you must perform in Slide view or Outline view.

TIP   By clicking the Show Formatting button on the Slide Sorter toolbar, you can temporarily display only the slide titles. Then, as you work with the slides, you don't have to wait for them to redraw. To redisplay the slide contents, click the Show Formatting button again.

Rearranging Slides

The most common use of Slide Sorter view is to move slides to new positions in the presentation, the same way you'd sort 35-mm slides on a light table before placing them in a slide projector. The simplest way to move a slide is to use the good old drag-and-drop technique. However, you can also move a slide by using the Cut and Paste buttons on the Standard toolbar, the Cut and Paste commands on the Edit menu, or the Cut and Paste commands on the shortcut menu that appears when you select a slide and click the right mouse button.

To rearrange the order of slides using drag and drop, follow these steps:

1. Position the mouse pointer on the slide you want to move.

2. Hold down the left mouse button, and drag the slide icon that appears to a position between two other slides. As shown on the facing page, a vertical marker is displayed to indicate where the slide will drop when you release the mouse button.

The slide will
drop here

3. Release the mouse button to drop the slide into place.

   Here are the steps for moving a slide using the Cut and Paste commands:

1. Click the slide you want to move.

2. Click the Cut button on the Standard toolbar or choose Cut from the Edit menu or the shortcut menu.

3. Click an insertion point to indicate the slide's new position (a blinking vertical line appears), and click the Paste button or choose Paste from the Edit menu or the shortcut menu.

TIP To copy a slide rather than move it, hold down the Ctrl key as you drag the slide, or choose Copy instead of Cut from the Edit menu or the shortcut menu. The slide appears both at the destination and at the original location.

Rearranging a group of slides is just as easy as rearranging a single slide. After you select the group, you can use the same techniques described above for moving a single slide.

To select a group of slides, hold down the Shift key and click each slide. Each selected slide is surrounded by a highlighted border. You can use this method to select nonadjacent slides—that is, slides located in different parts of the presentation. When a group of nonadjacent slides is moved to a new location, the slides appear in the same relative order. A slide from the first part of the presentation appears first, followed by a slide from the next part of the presentation, and so on.

To select a group of adjacent slides, you can draw a selection box across the group, like this:

1. Position the mouse pointer just outside the first slide you want to select.

2. Hold down the left mouse button, and drag the selection box across the slides, as shown below.

NOTE: You don't need to enclose entire slides to select them. As long as any part of a slide is within the selection box, the slide will be selected.

After you select a group of slides, place the mouse pointer on one of the slides, and drag the group to its new location in the presentation. As with single slides, you can also use the Cut and Paste buttons on the Standard toolbar or the Cut and Paste commands on the Edit menu or the shortcut menu.

Adding and Deleting Slides

In addition to rearranging slides, you can also change the content of a presentation by adding and deleting slides. Slide Sorter view is a good place to be when you want to make these changes, because you can quickly see their effect on the entire presentation.

To add a slide, follow these steps:

1. In the presentation, click the slide that you want the new slide to follow.

2. Click the New Slide button at the bottom of the PowerPoint window, choose New Slide from the Insert menu, or press Ctrl+M.

3. When the New Slide dialog box appears, select an autolayout, and click OK to add a slide to the presentation.

Deleting a slide is even easier than adding one. Simply click the slide you want to delete, and press Delete. You can also delete a group of slides by using the methods described earlier for selecting a group, and then pressing Delete.

Duplicating Slides

Another handy use for Slide Sorter view is to duplicate slides that have some feature you want to reproduce. Let's say you need to create the same pie graph for each salon in a chain of six beauty salons. You can create the first graph on a slide, switch to Slide Sorter view, and duplicate the slide five times. Then you can switch back to Slide view, and edit the data in each of the duplicate slides. The design of the first graph and any special formatting you've applied are carried over to the other slides, as in Figure 11-2 on the next page.

> **NOTE:** If you often need to use the same graph design, you can save the formatting of the graph as an autoformat that you can apply to a new graph. For more information about autoformats, see "Saving Graph Formatting as an AutoFormat," page 296.

To duplicate a slide in Slide Sorter view, follow these steps:

1. Click the slide.

2. Choose Duplicate from the Edit menu or press Ctrl+D. The duplicate appears to the right of the original slide.

FIGURE 11-2.

Duplicating a slide lets you carry special formatting throughout a presentation.

> **TIP**   You can also duplicate a slide by selecting the slide, holding down the Ctrl key, and dragging a copy of the slide to the left or right.

Moving and Copying Slides Between Presentations

Just as you can move and copy slides within a presentation, you can also move and copy slides between presentations. Copying slides between presentations lets you transfer an intricate, existing slide to a new presentation rather than recreate its design.

Before you can actually move or copy slides between two presentations, you must arrange the presentations side by side in Slide Sorter view. Follow the steps below.

1. Open two presentations.

2. Switch to Slide Sorter view in each presentation.

3. Choose Arrange All from the Window menu to arrange the two presentations side by side, as shown on the facing page.

NOTE: You may want to use the same zoom percentage for both presentations. You can select a presentation by clicking it, and then change its zoom percentage independently. For more information about changing the zoom percentage, see "Zooming In and Out," page 305.

After the presentations are arranged side by side, you can move a slide from one presentation to another by clicking a slide in one presentation and dragging it to the other presentation. The moved slide takes on the design of the destination presentation's template. To copy a slide rather than move it, hold down the Ctrl key as you drag the slide to the destination presentation. In Figure 11-3 on the next page, the bottom slide has been copied from one presentation to the other. Note its appearance in each presentation.

You can also transfer slides between presentations by first selecting a slide in one presentation and using the Cut or Copy button on the Standard toolbar or the Cut or Copy command on the Edit menu or the shortcut menu. Then you can click an insertion point in the other presentation, and click the Paste button on the Standard toolbar or choose the Paste command from the Edit menu or the shortcut menu. Again, the slide takes on the template design of the destination presentation.

FIGURE 11-3.

A slide copied to another presentation takes on the design of the destination presentation.

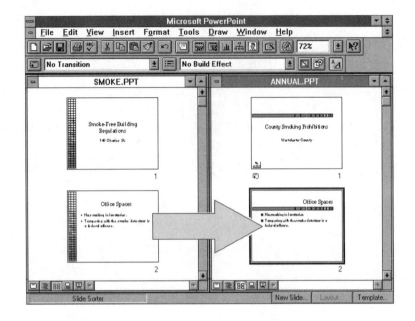

NOTE: You can move or copy a group of slides between presentations by selecting the group before you use the drag-and-drop technique, the toolbar buttons, or the menu commands. To select a group of slides, hold down the Shift key as you click each slide or drag a selection box around the group. For more information about selecting a group of slides, see "Rearranging Slides," page 306.

Changing the Design in Slide Sorter View

In Chapter 9, you learned about changing the template, color scheme, and background of a slide. Slide Sorter view is an ideal place to make these changes because you can see their effects ripple through the presentation.

Changing the Template and Color Scheme of the Presentation

In Slide Sorter view, you use the same techniques to change the template and color scheme of the presentation that you use in Slide view. For example, to change the presentation template, you click the Template button in the lower right corner of the PowerPoint window or choose Presentation Template from the Format menu, and then select a different template in the Presentation Template dialog box.

As mentioned earlier, when you change the template and color scheme in Slide Sorter view, you can see the effect of the redesign on all the slides. Only the slides that you've formatted directly—the slides whose color scheme or background you've changed individually—aren't affected by the new template.

> For more information about changing the template and color scheme of a presentation, see Chapter 9, "Making Overall Changes," page 217.

Changing the Color Scheme of Selected Slides

In Slide Sorter view, you can select specific slides and change their color scheme. For example, you can select all the slides that cover a general topic, and modify their color scheme. You can even give each segment of the presentation a different color scheme to differentiate it from the other segments.

To modify the color scheme for specific slides, first select the slides using one of the techniques described earlier. Then choose Slide Color Scheme from the Format menu, and make changes to the color scheme. Only the slides that you selected will display the revised color scheme.

> For more information about changing the color scheme, see "Changing the Color Scheme," page 225.

Copying Color Schemes Among Slides

After you change the color scheme for selected slides, you can copy the color scheme to other slides in the presentation. Copying the color scheme can be a real time-saver because you don't have to go through the process of choosing commands and selecting options. You simply select a slide that has already been formatted with the color scheme you want and copy the scheme to one or more other slides.

To copy a color scheme from one slide to another, first select the slide with the color scheme you want to copy, and then click the Format Painter button on the Standard toolbar. Next, click the slide to which you want to copy the color scheme. It's that simple!

To copy a color scheme from one slide to several other slides, select the slide with the color scheme you want to copy, and then choose the Pick Up Color Scheme command from the Format menu or the shortcut menu. Next, select one or more other slides, and choose the Apply Color Scheme command from the Format menu or the shortcut menu. After you apply a color scheme with this technique, the color scheme remains available in temporary storage so that you can use the Apply Color Scheme command again later to apply the same scheme to additional slides. The copied color scheme remains available until you use the Pick Up Color Scheme command to pick up a different color scheme.

TIP   You can also use the Format Painter button and the Pick Up Color Scheme and Apply Color Scheme commands to copy a color scheme from a slide in one presentation to one or more slides in a different presentation.

Changing the Background

Just as you can change the color scheme of selected slides, you can also change the background color of selected slides by using the Slide Background command on the Format menu. The Slide Background command works as it does in Slide view. By changing only the background, you can change only the background color without affecting the other colors in the presentation. You can also change only the background shading of selected slides for a more subtle effect.

When you select slides in Slide Sorter view and then choose the Slide Background command, you can also click the Display Objects on Selected Slides option to turn the background design on or off on the selected slides. You might want to select slides and turn off their background objects when you need a simple background on which to draw diagrams or create complicated foreground images. Figure 11-4 shows a presentation with two slides that have had their display of background objects turned off.

FIGURE 11-4.
The background objects have been turned off on two slides in this presentation.

Slides with background
objects turned off

  For more information about changing the background scheme of a presentation, see "Altering the Background Color and Shading," page 233.

In this chapter, you've learned how useful Slide Sorter view can be when you want to make overall changes to a presentation. In Part 4, you'll learn how to refine individual slides of the presentation by adding text annotations, drawings, clip art, and bitmapped images.

Adding Annotations and Graphics

Working with Text Annotations and Speaker's Notes

uring the presentation, you'll want to direct your energy and persuasive charm toward delivering your grand vision rather than detailing the minor technicalities in your graphs. Fortunately, you can leave the wherefores and the gotchas to helpful little notes that appear in text boxes alongside the other text and graphic objects on the slides. Figure 12-1 shows a typical, useful text annotation.

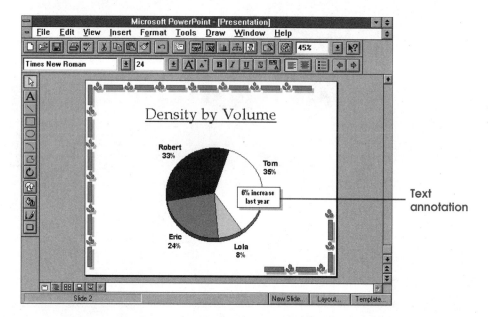

In this chapter, you'll learn how to add text annotations, as well as how to add speaker's notes to slides in Notes Pages view. While text annotations are designed to be seen by the audience, speaker's notes are seen only by the individual delivering the presentation. On the top half of a speaker's note page, the presenter sees a reduced version of the current slide. On the bottom half of the page, the presenter sees typed notes about the slide—points to make while the slide is on the screen and supporting information to bring up, if necessary.

Text annotations and speaker's notes are only two of the special additions you'll learn about in this part of the book. In Chapter 13, you'll learn how to add graphic objects that you can form into logos and diagrams, and in Chapter 14, you'll learn how to add clip art and bitmapped images to enhance your slides.

Adding a Text Annotation

The main difference between entering text in a text placeholder and adding text as a text annotation is in how you get started. To enter the main body text of a slide, such as bulleted text lines, you can simply click a *Click to add text* placeholder and begin typing. To create a text annotation, you must use the Text Tool button on the Drawing toolbar, which is shown below, and draw your own text box into which you type the annotation.

- Selection Tool
- Text Tool
- Line Tool
- Rectangle Tool
- Ellipse Tool
- Arc Tool
- Freeform Tool
- Free Rotate Tool
- AutoShapes
- Fill On/Off
- Line On/Off
- Shadow On/Off

To comment on the contents of a slide, you can add as many text boxes as you see fit, and you can move and copy them just like any other objects. But you might want to limit your use of text boxes to one every few slides to avoid cluttering the presentation or giving the impression that the exceptions to the rule are the rule. Rather than use text boxes, you can group comments, restrictions, exemptions, exclusions, and other technicalities on a subsequent slide, so they won't seem ubiquitous. The subsequent slide can even be hidden so that you can display it only if necessary during a slide show.

To add a text box and enter a text annotation, follow these steps:

1. In Slide view, move to the slide to which you want to add the text box.

2. Click the Text Tool button on the Drawing toolbar.

3. Position the mouse pointer where you want the text box to appear, hold down the left mouse button, and drag out a rectangle. If you plan to type a short one- or two-word label, you can simply click the slide to add a small text box. The text box shown below was created by dragging.

4. Type the text of the annotation. As shown below, the box grows vertically, if necessary, to accommodate the text you enter.

5. Click elsewhere on the slide to complete the text annotation or click the Text Tool button again to add another text box.

Formatting a Text Annotation

You can format a text annotation by adding formatting to the text box either before or after you actually enter the text. As with elsewhere in PowerPoint, you use the buttons on the Formatting toolbar or the commands on the Format or shortcut menu to format the text in a text box. As you know by now, before you can format existing text, you must select it. To select part of the text in a text box, drag across it with the mouse. To select the entire text box, click the border of the text box.

In addition to changing the appearance of the text in a text box, you can also change its position within the text box. To change the position of the text, choose Text Anchor from the Format menu, and select the appropriate options in the Text Anchor dialog box, shown in Figure 12-2. These options let you change the box margins, fit the boundaries of the text box to the text, and turn word wrap on or off.

FIGURE 12-2.
The Text Anchor dialog box.

See Also: For more information about formatting text, see Chapter 5, "Working with Text in Slide View," page 93.

For more information about the Text Anchor dialog box options, see "Turning Word Wrap On or Off," page 121; "Changing the Box Margins," page 122; and "Fitting Text Objects to the Text," page 122.

Moving, Resizing, and Formatting a Text Box

PowerPoint is very flexible when it comes to moving, resizing, and formatting text boxes. For example, you can move a text box to any location on a slide, even if it obscures other text or objects on the slide. You can also increase or decrease the size of the text box to accommodate more or less text. And if you're interested in changing the text box's border or fill, PowerPoint offers a variety of options to choose from.

To move a text box, position the mouse pointer on the border of the text box between two handles, and drag the box to a new location on the slide. To resize a text box, simply drag one of its handles in the desired direction. (If word wrap is turned off, it is automatically turned back on so that the text re-wraps within the resized text box.)

 TIP When you finish typing text in a text box, you can press Esc and then press the arrow keys to adjust the position of the text box incrementally.

Whether you create printed output or 35-mm slides or present an electronic slide show, by default, only the text of a text box is displayed. The box itself does not appear because its fill and border are turned off. To display the fill and border, you can select the text box, and then click the Fill On/Off button and the Line On/Off button on the Drawing toolbar. (You can also click the Shadow On/Off button to add a shadow and give the box some depth.)

To modify the text box's fill and border, select the box and then choose the Colors and Lines command from the Format menu or the shortcut menu. In the Colors and Lines dialog box, shown in Figure 12-3, use the Fill drop-down list to select a fill color, shading, and pattern. Use the Line drop-down list to select a line color, and then use the Line Styles and Dashed Lines options to select a line style.

FIGURE 12-3.
The Colors and
Lines dialog box.

TIP   To create a text annotation with a more interesting shape, you can place an autoshape on a slide, and then enter text in the autoshape. (When you double-click an autoshape, an insertion point appears within it so that you can enter the text.) To get really fancy, you can also add a text annotation to a clip art selection. For more information about auto-shapes, see "AutoShapes," page 339. For more information about using clip art, see Chapter 14, "Adding Clip Art Pictures and Bitmapped Images," page 359.

Duplicating a Text Box

Duplicating a text box creates a second text box with the same formatting as the original. After you format both the original text box and its text, select the original text box and choose Duplicate from the Edit menu or press Ctrl+D. Next drag the duplicate text box to a new position, select the text inside by dragging across it, and type replacement text.

You can also use the Copy and Paste buttons on the Standard toolbar or the Copy and Paste commands on the Edit menu or the shortcut menu to duplicate text boxes in Slide view.

Adding Speaker's Notes

Every slide in the presentation can have a special type of output called speaker's notes or *notes pages*. On a notes page, which always has a portrait orientation even if the slide is landscape, you see two objects: the slide on the top half of the page and a text placeholder on the bottom half. The notes page for each slide is an integral part of the presentation, and is stored in the same file. To switch to Notes Pages view, click the Notes Pages View button in the lower left corner of the presentation window or choose Notes Pages from the View menu. As shown in Figure 12-4, when you switch to Notes Pages view, you see only the notes pages of the presentation.

Notes Pages View

FIGURE 12-4.

The current slide shown on a notes page in Notes Pages view.

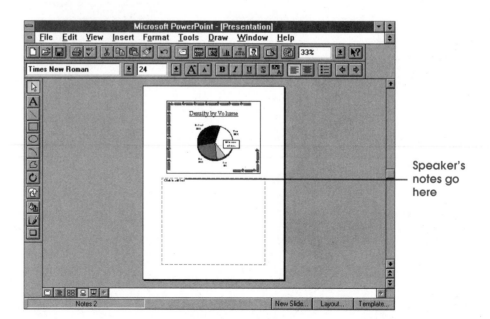

Speaker's notes go here

326

The notes page text, or any indication that notes page text exists, does not appear in any view other than Notes Pages view. But when you print the presentation, you can choose to print only the notes pages.

Your initial view of the notes page is reduced so that you can see the entire page, but you may want to zoom in to see the text you type in the text placeholder below the slide image. To zoom in, edit the zoom percentage in the Zoom Control box on the Standard toolbar or use the Zoom command on the View menu. A zoom percentage of 100 allows you to view the lower half of the notes page.

To enter a note, click the *Click to add text* placeholder below the slide image. Then begin typing in the placeholder as if you were typing text in a word processing program. The text will automatically wrap at the right edge of the text box. If you want to start a new paragraph on the notes page, press Enter.

As with text annotations, you can use the buttons on the Formatting toolbar or the commands on the Format menu or the shortcut menu to format the notes page text before or after you type it. Again, if you want to format existing text, you must select the text first. You can also use the Line Spacing command on the Format menu to add line spacing within paragraphs or to add space before or after each paragraph. Figure 12-5 shows a completed notes page.

FIGURE 12-5.
A completed notes page.

To enter speaker's notes for the next slide in the presentation, click the Next Slide button or press the PgDn key. To return to the previous slide, click the Previous Slide button or press the PgUp key.

After you enter text on the notes pages of a presentation, you should re-save the presentation to be sure the text is stored as part of the presentation file.

See Also: For more information about printing notes pages, see Chapter 15, "Creating Printed Output and 35-mm Slides," page 377.

In this chapter, you learned how to add text that can enhance the slides of a presentation. In the following two chapters, you'll learn how to draw graphic shapes and add ready-made or scanned images to slides.

13

Drawing Graphic Objects

You don't have to be an artist to create professional-looking graphics in PowerPoint. No matter what your artistic ability, you can use the program's drawing tools to add simple graphic shapes to slides. You can enclose an area within a rectangle, for example, or add a sunburst shape that contains a message like "Special!" or "New!" You can even combine individual shapes to create a more elaborate diagram or map. PowerPoint's commands for editing shapes are also easy to use. You can resize, rotate, and flip graphic objects, combine individual objects into a grouped object, and much more.

In this chapter, you'll learn how to use the drawing tools on the three drawing toolbars to add graphic objects to a slide, and you'll learn how to modify individual objects or groups of objects. In the next chapter, you'll learn how to add ready-made images to your presentation.

> **NOTE:** If you're blessed with artistic skill, you'll naturally want to take PowerPoint's drawing capabilities even further. But the program's commands for adding and editing graphic shapes aren't sophisticated enough to please everyone. Professional-level artists might prefer to use a dedicated drawing application to create special graphics for a presentation and then transfer the graphics to a PowerPoint slide. For example, with Visio, a popular application that lets you create complex drawings by combining ready-made shapes, you can create an embedded drawing using Visio tools from within a PowerPoint presentation. For more information about using the tools of other applications from within PowerPoint, see Chapter 17, "Using PowerPoint with Other Applications," page 407.

Setting Up the Drawing Area

In Slide view, you can turn on two built-in PowerPoint features that help you position items with accuracy. PowerPoint's rulers, which run along the top and down the side of the presentation window, measure distances from the horizontal and vertical centers of the slide. Two movable guides—dashed lines that cross the slide horizontally and vertically—allow you to line up objects with great precision against measurements on the rulers or against each other. Figure 13-1 shows both the rulers and the guides.

NEW!

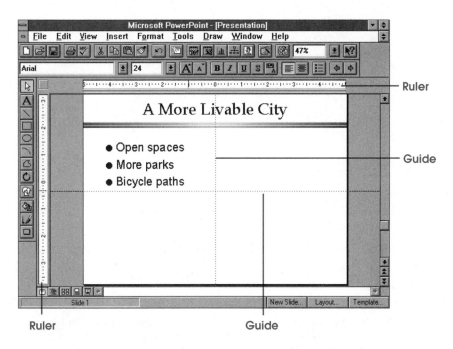

FIGURE 13-1.
The rulers and
the guides.

To turn on the rulers, choose Ruler from the View menu. To turn on the guides, choose Guides from the View menu, too. You can also choose both Ruler and Guides from the shortcut menu that appears when you position the mouse pointer on the slide background and click the right mouse button.

Dashed markers on the rulers move when you move the mouse pointer to help you "eyeball" the position of the pointer as you draw and edit objects. The fixed, unchangeable zero point of the rulers is the exact center of the slide. To more accurately position objects on a slide, move the guides by dragging them. As you drag a guide, an indicator on the guide shows the guide's horizontal or vertical distance from the ruler's zero point. For example, to precisely place an object that must extend one inch to the left of the slide's center and two inches to the right, you can drag the vertical guide one inch to the left of the slide's center, as measured by the ruler. Next, you can draw the object from the guide to approximately two inches to the right of the slide's center, and then drag the guide to the exact two-inch mark. Finally, you can adjust the right edge of the object to align with the guide.

TIP To measure distances across the slide, hold down the Ctrl key as you move a guide. While the Ctrl key is pressed, the guide displays the distance it has been moved. When you release the Ctrl key, the guide once again displays its position on the page.

The Drawing Toolbars

The basic set of drawing and editing tools is located on the Drawing toolbar that runs vertically near the left border of the PowerPoint window in Slide view. A second set of tools for editing objects is on the Drawing+ toolbar that you can turn on by choosing Toolbars from the View menu, selecting the Drawing+ option in the Toolbars dialog box, and then clicking OK or pressing Enter. A third set of drawing tools is located on the AutoShapes toolbar that you can display by clicking the AutoShapes button on the Drawing toolbar or by selecting the AutoShapes option in the Toolbars dialog box. Figure 13-2 identifies the three drawing toolbars.

FIGURE 13-2.
The drawing toolbars.

Drawing+ toolbar

Drawing toolbar

AutoShapes toolbar

Drawing the Basic Shapes

On the Drawing toolbar, you'll find a button for each of the basic shapes you can add to a slide. Each shape becomes an *object* after it is drawn. Objects have an outline and an interior area whose default colors are determined by the current color scheme. The color scheme's Text & Lines color sets the outline color and the Fill color governs the interior color. Because the color scheme controls these colors, any change to the color scheme also changes the colors in graphic objects you've drawn, unless you have directly formatted the color of an object by clicking the object and changing its line or fill color. Any object that has been directly formatted retains its own colors no matter what the color scheme dictates.

Lines and Arrows

A line or arrow is the easiest drawing you can create. A straight line simply connects two end points and becomes an arrow when you add an arrowhead.

To add a straight line or arrow to a slide, follow these steps:

1. Click the Line Tool button on the Drawing toolbar.

2. Position the mouse pointer at one end point for the line.

3. Hold down the Shift key if you want to constrain the line to exactly horizontal, vertical, or diagonal.

4. Hold down the left mouse button, and drag to the second end point.

5. Release the mouse button. A line appears between the first and second end points.

When you hold down the Ctrl key as you drag, the first end point becomes the center of the line, and the line grows in opposite directions from the first end point as you drag.

To change the appearance of the line and add an arrowhead, first select the line, and choose Colors and Lines from the Format menu or the shortcut menu. The Colors and Lines dialog box shown in Figure 13-3 on the next page appears. In the Colors and Lines dialog box, select a line color from the Line drop-down list and a line style from the Line Styles section. When you open the Line drop-down list, you see the eight colors of the color scheme in small panels. If you don't like any of the eight colors, you can click the Other Color option in the list, and then select one of the 90 colors in the Other Color dialog box.

FIGURE 13-3.
The Colors and
Lines dialog box.

In the Line Styles section, you can select from six preset line weights or four double- and triple-line combinations. In the Dashed Lines section, you can leave the first option, a solid line, or select one of the dashed or dotted lines displayed. In the Arrowheads section, you can leave the first setting selected to produce a line without arrowheads, or you can select the second or third setting, which places an arrowhead at the beginning or the end of the line, respectively. The fourth setting places an arrowhead at both ends of the line. After you select the changes, click OK to return to the slide.

You can also click the Line Color, Line Style, Dashed Lines, and Arrowheads buttons on the Drawing+ toolbar to change the corresponding attributes of a line.

TIP   To copy the formatting of an existing object to a new object, click the object with the formatting you want to copy, click the Format Painter button on the Standard toolbar, and then click the new object.

Rectangles and Squares

You can use the Rectangle Tool button on the Drawing toolbar to draw a rectangle or a square in PowerPoint. As you'll see, drawing a rectangle is almost as easy as drawing a line.

To draw a rectangle or a square, follow these steps:

1.   Click the Rectangle Tool button on the Drawing toolbar.

2. Position the mouse pointer at the location for one corner of the rectangle or square.

3. If you want to draw a perfect square rather than a rectangle, hold down the Shift key.

4. Hold down the left mouse button, and drag to the opposite corner of the rectangle or square.

5. Release the mouse button. A rectangle or square appears, displaying the line and fill colors of the current color scheme.

To have a rectangle grow outward from the first point you click, hold down the Ctrl key as you drag. To have a square grow outward from the first point you click, hold down both the Shift and Ctrl keys as you drag.

To change the colors and border style of the rectangle or square, select the rectangle or square, and then choose the Colors and Lines command from the Format menu or the shortcut menu. In the Colors and Lines dialog box, select a fill and line color from the appropriate drop-down lists. Then select a line style, dashed line style, or both for the border of the rectangle or square. As with lines, you can also click the corresponding buttons on the Drawing+ toolbar to change these options individually.

To add a more interesting fill to the rectangle or square, you can select one of the special fills from the Fill drop-down list in the Colors and Lines dialog box. These special fills, which allow you to add a background color, shading, and pattern, are covered in "Applying Special Fills to Objects," page 344.

 TIP To draw a rectangle or square with rounded corners, use the Rounded Rectangle Tool button on the AutoShapes toolbar. You'll learn about autoshapes on page 339 of this chapter.

Ellipses and Circles

Like the Rectangle Tool button, which allows you to draw rectangles or squares, the Ellipse Tool button on the Drawing toolbar allows you to draw ellipses or circles.

To draw an ellipse or a circle, follow these steps:

1. Click the Ellipse Tool button on the Drawing toolbar.

2. Position the mouse pointer at the location of one corner of an imaginary rectangle that would enclose the ellipse or circle.

3. If you want to draw a perfect circle rather than an ellipse, hold down the Shift key.

4. Hold down the left mouse button, and drag to the opposite corner of the imaginary rectangle.

5. Release the mouse button. An ellipse or circle appears, displaying the line and fill colors of the current color scheme.

To have an ellipse grow outward from the first point you click, hold down the Ctrl key as you drag. To have a circle grow outward from the first point you click, hold down both the Shift and Ctrl keys as you drag.

To change the colors and border style of the ellipse or circle, select the ellipse or circle, and then choose Colors and Lines from the Format menu or the shortcut menu. In the Colors and Lines dialog box, select a fill and line color from the appropriate drop-down lists. Then select a line style, dashed line style, or both for the border of the ellipse or circle. You can also click the corresponding buttons on the Drawing+ toolbar to change these options individually.

Arcs

An arc is a segment between two points along the curve of an ellipse or circle. PowerPoint supplies the Arc Tool button so that you can easily add arcs to your slides.

To draw an arc, follow these steps:

1. Click the Arc Tool button on the Drawing toolbar.

2. Position the mouse pointer at the first point for the arc.

3. If you want to draw a segment of a circle rather than an ellipse, hold down the Shift key.

4. Hold down the left mouse button, drag to the second point for the arc, and release the mouse button. An arc appears, displaying the line color of the current color scheme.

To center an elliptical arc at the starting point, hold down the Ctrl key as you drag. To center a circular arc at the starting point, hold down the Shift and Ctrl keys as you drag.

You can change the color and style of an arc. To do so, select the arc, and choose the Colors and Lines command from the Format menu or the shortcut menu, or use the Line Color, Line Style, and Dashed Lines buttons on the Drawing+ toolbar.

Free-Form Shapes

You might be relieved to discover that you're not confined to drawing only lines, rectangles, and circles in PowerPoint. The Freeform Tool button on the Drawing toolbar gives you the freedom to draw a combination of curved and straight line segments to create complex objects.

To draw a free-form shape, follow these steps:

1. Click the Freeform Tool button on the Drawing toolbar.

2. Position the mouse pointer at the beginning of the shape.

3. Hold down the left mouse button, and drag to draw a freehand shape, or click and move the mouse to draw a straight line segment.

4. Repeat step 3 until you have completed the entire shape.

5. Click once near the starting point of the shape to close the shape or double-click at any point to end the shape as it is and leave it open.

To constrain a straight line segment to exactly horizontal, vertical, or diagonal, hold down the Shift key as you drag.

Each point where two segments meet is called a *vertex.* (The free-form segments that look like curves are actually composed of many short, straight lines that connect vertexes.) While drawing a free-form shape in PowerPoint, you can remove the last vertex you created by pressing the Backspace key.

To modify the shape of an existing free-form figure, first double-click the figure. Every vertex in the shape becomes selected. (Notice that the status bar at the bottom of the PowerPoint window gives you advice about your options.) Then reshape the figure by dragging individual vertexes. If you want to add a new vertex, hold down the Ctrl key, and click between two existing vertexes. To remove a vertex, hold down Ctrl, and click the vertex you want to remove.

Note that when you add a vertex, the mouse pointer takes the shape of a cross hair, and when you remove a vertex, the pointer takes the shape of a large X.

To try drawing and reshaping a single figure, first click the Freeform Tool button on the Drawing toolbar, and then click three points in the shape of a V. Double-click the third point to end the shape. Next, select the shape, hold down the Ctrl key, and drag down to create a duplicate of the free-form shape. Then double-click the duplicate. Now place the mouse pointer on the vertex at the bottom of the duplicate V. When the mouse pointer becomes a small cross hair, hold down the left mouse button, and drag the vertex down an inch or so. Then release the mouse button. Figure 13-4 shows approximately how your screen should look.

FIGURE 13-4.

Dragging a vertex to reshape a free-form figure.

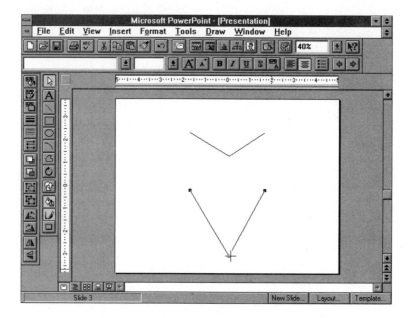

Finally, hold down the Ctrl key, and click anywhere along the duplicate V to add a vertex. Then, hold down Ctrl again, and click the vertex at the bottom of the V. When you remove a vertex, PowerPoint connects the two vertexes on either side with a straight line.

To change the colors and border style of a closed free-form shape, select the shape, and then choose Colors and Lines from the Format menu or the shortcut menu. In the Colors and Lines dialog box, select a fill and line color from the appropriate drop-down lists. Then select a line style, dashed line style, or both for the border of the shape. When the free-form shape is not closed, the Fill options are unavailable, but you can select one of the arrowhead options. You can also click the buttons on the Drawing+ toolbar to change these options individually.

AutoShapes

PowerPoint's autoshapes are familiar shapes that you are likely to use frequently, such as arrows and stars. They are generally more complex than those on the Drawing toolbar, and many of them have an *adjustment handle*, which allows you to adjust their most salient feature. For example, a cube autoshape has an adjustment handle that you can drag to adjust the depth of the cube. An arrow autoshape's adjustment handle changes the size of the arrowhead.

To draw an autoshape, follow these steps:

1. If the AutoShapes toolbar is not already displayed on your screen, click the AutoShapes button on the Drawing toolbar; or choose Toolbars from the View menu, select the AutoShapes option, and click OK or press Enter.

2. Click an autoshape on the AutoShapes toolbar.

3. On the slide, position the mouse pointer where you want the autoshape to begin, hold down the left mouse button, and then drag the autoshape into place.

4. If the autoshape has an adjustment handle, as shown below, drag the adjustment handle to adjust the autoshape.

Adjustment handle

TIP   If you want the AutoShapes toolbar to remain on your screen but out of the way, drag the toolbar to any edge of the PowerPoint window.

An autoshape can be filled and outlined, just like any other drawing object. You can also move, resize, copy and paste, and duplicate an autoshape.

Adding Text to an Object

By clicking any drawn object and then typing, you can add text to the interior of the object. Because the text becomes an integral part of the object, when you move the object, the text moves too.

If you try to enter more than a few words, however, the text may overrun the borders of the object, as shown in Figure 13-5. To wrap the text within the object, choose Text Anchor from the Format menu, select the Word-wrap Text in Object option, and click OK. Be sure not to select the Adjust Object Size to Fit Text option, because the object will adjust to the text rather than the other way around. After you turn on word wrapping and click OK, you'll see the newly wrapped text, which fits within the left and right borders of the object, but may still overrun the top and bottom, as shown in Figure 13-6.

FIGURE 13-5.

The text in this object has overrun the object's borders.

FIGURE 13-6.

The text in this object wraps between the object's left and right borders.

To keep the text from overrunning the top and bottom borders of the object, you can either return to the Text Anchor dialog box and select the Adjust Object Size to Fit Text option or reduce the text size. To make minor adjustments to the size of the text in the object, select the text, and then click the Increase Font Size button or the Decrease Font Size button on the Formatting toolbar. You can also press Ctrl+Shift+> to increase the font size or Ctrl+Shift+< to decrease the font size. Figure 13-7 shows the final object.

FIGURE 13-7.

After final adjustments, the text fits neatly inside the object.

Switching Shapes

A special command on the Draw menu, Change AutoShape, lets you replace a shape you've drawn with a different shape. You simply select the shape you want to replace, choose Change AutoShape from the Draw menu, and then select a new shape from the AutoShapes palette. Figure 13-8 shows the Auto-Shapes palette. You can convert a star to a sunburst, for example, or a thin arrow to a thick arrow.

FIGURE 13-8.
The AutoShapes palette.

The new object occupies the same size and positioning of the original shape and retains all of the original shape's formatting.

Editing Objects

You've already learned how to change the fill and border color and the border style of objects. PowerPoint provides other editing options as well, such as adding a shadow or embossing an object. These are discussed in the following section. But first you must learn how to select single objects and multiple objects.

Selecting Objects

As with most everything else in PowerPoint, before you can make changes to a graphic object, you must select the object. If you want to make changes to more than one object, you can select multiple objects.

To select a single object, simply click the object. To select more than one object, do one of the following:

- Hold down the Shift key as you click each object. To deselect one of the selected objects, click the object again while holding down the Shift key.

- Click the Selection Tool button on the Drawing toolbar, and drag a selection box around the objects. Only objects that are completely enclosed by the selection box are selected. For example, Figure 13-9 shows a selection box that will select three out of four objects on a slide.

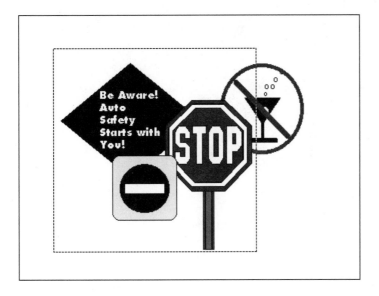

FIGURE 13-9.

Three of the four objects on this slide will be selected.

To select all the objects on a slide, choose the Select All command from the Edit menu or press Ctrl+A. All objects, including titles, bulleted text, and graphs, are selected.

After you select multiple objects, any changes you make will affect all the objects in the selection.

Applying Special Fills to Objects

When you learned how to add basic shapes earlier in this chapter, you also learned how to use options in the Colors and Lines dialog box to change the fill and border colors and styles of a selected object. Special options in the dialog box also let you create windows to the background, objects filled with a color shading, and objects filled with patterns.

Displaying the Slide Background Within an Object

You can pile up as many objects as you want. But then if you add an object to the top of the pile and fill it with the background, the background appears within the top object, despite all the other objects below. It's like creating a hole in the shape of the top object that bores all the way down to the background. Figure 13-10 demonstrates this effect.

FIGURE 13-10.

A vertical rectangle that is filled with the background overlays several other objects.

To fill an object with the background, follow these steps:

1. Select the object.

2. Click the Fill Color button on the Drawing+ toolbar, or choose Colors and Lines from the Format menu or the shortcut menu and open the Fill drop-down list.

344

3. Select Background from the drop-down list.

Filling an Object with Shading

Shadings in objects add richness and depth and can give the appearance that the objects have been illuminated from the side, top, or corner. Combined with shadows, shadings can create an impressive three-dimensional effect.

To add shading to an object, follow these steps:

1. Select the object.

2. Click the Fill Color button on the Drawing+ toolbar, or choose Colors and Lines from the Format menu or the shortcut menu and open the Fill drop-down list.

3. Select Shaded from the drop-down list to display the Shaded Fill dialog box shown here:

4. In the Shaded Fill dialog box, select a shade style and one of the four variants, which depict how the shading progresses to black.

5. To change the color of the shading, select a color from the Color drop-down list at the bottom of the dialog box.

6. To make the shading darker or lighter, use the scroll bar at the bottom of the dialog box. (To create a subtle shading, make the shading lighter.)

Filling an Object with a Pattern

Rather than fill an object with a solid or shaded color, you can fill it with a pattern made up of two colors. PowerPoint offers a number of patterns and a wide variety of foreground and background colors to choose from.

To fill an object with a pattern, follow the steps in the previous section, "Filling an Object with Shading," but select Pattern rather than Shading from the Fill drop-down list in the Color and Lines dialog box. The Pattern Fill dialog box, shown in Figure 13-11, appears.

FIGURE 13-11.

The Pattern Fill dialog box.

In the Pattern Fill dialog box, the patterns shown are composed of the foreground and background colors displayed in the Foreground and Background boxes. You can select a different pattern and different foreground and background colors to create the combination you want.

Adding Shadows to Objects

PowerPoint lets you add a shadow behind objects and determine the shadow's color, direction, and size. You can add a shadow to any object you've drawn and to any text you've added to a slide.

To add a shadow, select the object, and click the Shadow On/Off button on the Drawing toolbar. A shadow appears with the shadow color specified by the current color scheme. To alter the color of the shadow, click the Shadow Color button on the Drawing+ toolbar. To alter the color, direction, and size of the shadow, choose Shadow from the Format menu. Figure 13-12 shows the Shadow dialog box that appears.

FIGURE 13-12.

The Shadow
dialog box.

In the Shadow dialog box, open the Color drop-down list to select a shadow color. One of the options on the list, No Shadow, removes any shadow that is already present. The Other Color option lets you select a color other than the eight colors of the color scheme. To vary the direction and degree to which the shadow extends behind an object, change the direction and Points settings in the Offset section of the dialog box.

TIP To create a slide that makes visual sense, apply the same shadow to every object on the slide, even the title of the slide.

Embossing Objects

In the Shadow dialog box, the Embossed option on the Color drop-down list gives objects a raised, three-dimensional look. It also fills the objects with the background color, so you can place them directly on the background for an impressive visual effect. Figure 13-13 on the next page shows a slide with an embossed text box.

FIGURE 13-13.

The text box on this slide has been embossed.

Transferring Object Styles

After you finish modifying the appearance of an object, you can transfer the object's style to another object by using the Format Painter button on the Standard toolbar. Simply select the object whose style you want to transfer, click the Format Painter button, and then select the object you want to transfer the style to. The Format Painter button only allows you to transfer an object's style to one other object.

If you want to transfer the style to more than one object, use the Pick Up Object Style and Apply Object Style commands on the Format menu or the shortcut menu. Select the object whose style you want to transfer, choose the Pick Up Object Style command from the Format menu or the shortcut menu, select another object, and choose the Apply Object Style command from the Format menu or the shortcut menu. You can use this procedure to format as many other objects as you want (that is, until you select a different style or begin a new PowerPoint session).

TIP   Earlier versions of PowerPoint offered Pick Up Style and Apply Style buttons on the toolbar. Although the single Format Painter button has officially replaced the pair, these buttons are still available in PowerPoint 4, so you can install them on any toolbar, as you'll learn in Chapter 18, "Customizing PowerPoint," page 421.

Saving an Object's Style as the Default

After you spend time formatting an object with special attributes, you may want to save the object's style as a default. Then, when you draw new objects, they will automatically be formatted with the line style, line weight, and other attributes of the default style.

To save an object's style as the default, follow these steps:

1. Select the formatted object.

2. Choose Pick Up Object Style from the Format menu.

3. Deselect the object by clicking away from the object.

4. Choose Apply To Object Defaults from the Format menu or the shortcut menu.

The next time you draw an object, the default style will be applied.

Arranging Objects

In addition to tools and commands that change the appearance of one or more objects, PowerPoint provides several features that allow you to arrange objects on slides.

Grouping Objects

If you frequently make changes to more than one object at a time, you might want to combine the objects in a group. The objects are then treated as a unit, and any changes you make affect the entire group. For example, you can select the group and then move all the objects as a unit or modify the fill color so that all the objects in the group change simultaneously.

To group objects, use either of the selection techniques described on page 343, and then click the Group button on the Drawing+ toolbar. You can also choose the Group command from the Draw menu. When the objects are grouped, one set of handles surrounds the group, as shown in Figure 13-14.

FIGURE 13-14.

A group of objects has one set of handles.

After you group objects, you can ungroup them by clicking the Ungroup button on the Drawing+ toolbar or by choosing the Ungroup command from the Draw menu. The Regroup command, available on the Draw menu and the shortcut menu, regroups an ungrouped group, just as you'd think.

Cutting, Copying, and Duplicating Objects

You can cut, copy, and paste graphic objects as you would any object on a PowerPoint slide by using the Cut, Copy, and Paste buttons on the Standard toolbar; the Cut, Copy, and Paste commands on the Edit menu or the shortcut menu; or the keyboard equivalents (shown on the Edit menu). Not only can you cut and copy objects from one slide to another, but you can cut and copy objects from one presentation to another. By opening two presentations side by side in Slide view, you can cut or copy an object in one presentation and then paste it in another.

The fastest way to duplicate an object and position the duplicate is to hold down the Ctrl key and drag a copy of the object to its proper destination. But you can also select the object, and choose Duplicate from the Edit menu or press Ctrl+D. Then drag the duplicate into position.

 TIP Remember, you can undo any of the commands discussed in this chapter by clicking the Undo button on the Standard toolbar or by choosing Undo from the Edit menu.

Moving, Resizing, and Scaling Objects

To move an object, place the mouse pointer on the object, hold down the left mouse button, and then drag the object to a new location. To move an object horizontally or vertically, hold down the Shift key while you drag. To resize an object, drag one of the object's handles in the desired direction. If you want to maintain the proportions of the object, hold down the Shift key while you drag a corner handle. If you want the object to grow out from its center, hold down the Ctrl key while you drag a corner handle.

 TIP To use the keyboard to move an object, press Tab until the object you want to move is selected, and then press the Left, Right, Up, or Down arrow key to move the object in small increments.

To help you position an object, you can choose Snap to Grid from the Draw menu. Then, as you drag the object, it will automatically jump to the nearest horizontal and vertical ruler marking. To temporarily turn off Snap to Grid and drag an object freely on a slide, hold down the Alt key as you drag. The object will move smoothly without little jerks as it jumps from ruler marking to ruler marking.

To resize an object to a precise degree, select the object and then choose Scale from the Draw menu. In the Scale dialog box, shown in Figure 13-15 on the next page, enter a percentage in the Scale To edit box or click the up or down arrow to increase or decrease the current percentage. For example, to double the size of an object, enter 200 as the Scale To percentage. Keep in mind that objects can be scaled no larger than the size of the slide.

> For more information about the Scale dialog box, see Chapter
> 14, "Adding Clip Art Pictures and Bitmapped Images," page 359.

Rotating and Flipping Objects

You can rotate a single object or a group of objects around its center, and you
can rotate multiple selected objects, each around its own center.

To rotate a single object or group of objects, follow these steps:

1. Select the object or group, as shown below.

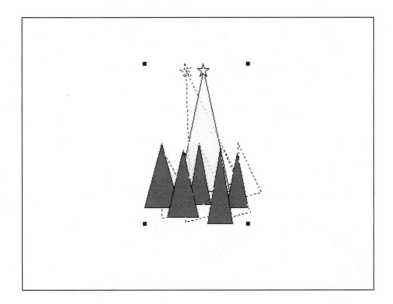

2. Click the Free Rotate Tool button on the Drawing toolbar, or choose Rotate/Flip from the Draw menu and then choose Free Rotate from the submenu.

3. Place the mouse pointer on a corner handle of the object or group, and then drag the handle left or right around the center of the object or group. The group of objects shown below is being rotated to the left.

TIP   For more precision while rotating, click a handle and drag the pointer away from the object before dragging in a circle around the object.

If you select multiple objects, each object rotates around its center when you rotate any one of the objects. In Figure 13-16 on the next page, the objects on the left were not grouped before being rotated, and each object has rotated around its own center. The group of objects on the right has rotated around its collective center.

On the Draw menu, you'll find two commands that rotate objects exactly 90 degrees to the left or right. To use these commands, follow the steps below.

1. Select the object, objects, or group you want to rotate.

FIGURE 13-16.
Rotating ungrouped objects (left) and grouped objects (right).

2. Click the Rotate Left button or the Rotate Right button on the Drawing+ toolbar, or choose Rotate/Flip from the Draw menu and then choose Rotate Left or Rotate Right from the submenu.

To create a mirror image of one or more objects, use the Flip command by following these steps:

1. Select the object or objects you want to flip, as shown here:

2. Click the Flip Horizontal button or the Flip Vertical button on the Drawing+ toolbar, or choose Rotate/Flip from the Draw menu and then choose Flip Horizontal or Flip Vertical from the submenu. The object shown below was flipped horizontally.

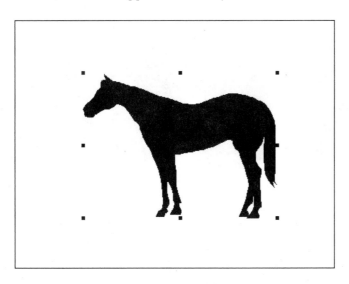

Stacking Objects

When objects overlap, you can change their order in the stack. You can move an object one level higher or lower in the stack or send an object to the top or bottom of the stack.

To move an object one level higher or lower in a stack, select the object, and then click the Bring Forward button or the Send Backward button on the Drawing+ toolbar. You can also choose the Bring Forward command or the Send Backward command from the Draw menu. If you want to move an object to the top or bottom of a stack, select the object, and choose Bring to Front or Send to Back from the Draw menu.

Figure 13-17 on the next page shows two versions of a simple scene. On the left, the pine tree is in the back. On the right, the pine tree has been moved forward one level using the Bring Forward command.

In this chapter, you learned how to create pictures by drawing them. In the next chapter, you'll learn how to import pictures that have already been created and stored in files or in PowerPoint's ClipArt Gallery.

Adding Clip Art Pictures and Bitmapped Images

Your words and graphs can tickle the brain and invoke powerful mental images, but a picture settles deep in long-term memory, where it has an effect far into the future. But if you're not an artist, where do you get the pictures you need?

The ClipArt Gallery is your first stop. Built right into PowerPoint, it contains more than a thousand pictures drawn by professional artists and grouped into categories. You can easily place any of the pictures on your presentation slides. If none of the clip art images is right, you can import an image from another program. Drawings and paintings from other Windows-based applications are especially easy to transfer over to a presentation. And if the image you need is a photo, you can insert a scanned picture into PowerPoint just as easily.

In this chapter, you'll learn how to browse and borrow images from the ClipArt Gallery and how to import drawings, paintings, and scanned pictures into PowerPoint. You'll also learn how to work with the images, separating them into individual components, if it's possible, or cropping out portions that are unnecessary. You'll even learn how to transfer your favorite and most frequently used images to the ClipArt Gallery, so you can pull them up for future presentations.

Using the ClipArt Gallery

The ClipArt Gallery is one of PowerPoint's optional components. If you installed the Gallery when you initially ran PowerPoint Setup, it is always available from within Slide view or Notes Pages view to dress up your pages with pictures. If, as you follow the instructions in this chapter, you find that the ClipArt Gallery was not installed, you can install it by running PowerPoint Setup and selecting Clip Art Files as the component you want to install.

Adding Clip Art to a Slide

You can add clip art to any existing slide while in Slide view, or you can select one of the two autolayouts that come with clip art placeholders when you start a new slide. Figure 14-1 shows the two autolayouts that have clip art placeholders.

When you select an autolayout that has a clip art placeholder, you can double-click the placeholder to open the ClipArt Gallery.

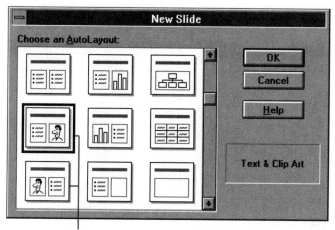

Clip art autolayouts

FIGURE 14-1.
The autolayouts with clip art placeholders.

NOTE: The first time you open the ClipArt Gallery, you may have to let the Gallery build its library of pictures by clicking Yes when you're asked if you want to add clip art now. If you don't see this prompt, the Gallery has already built its library and is ready for use.

To add clip art to a slide that does not have a clip art placeholder, turn to the slide in Slide view and then do one of the following:

- Click the Insert Clip Art button on the Standard toolbar.

- Choose the Clip Art command from the Insert menu.

The Microsoft ClipArt Gallery dialog box opens, as shown in Figure 14-2 on the next page.

An alphabetized list of clip art categories appears at the top of the dialog box, and clip art pictures from the currently selected category appear in panes below the category list. By default, All Categories is selected in the category list so that you can scroll through all the pictures in the Gallery. If you want to see only the clip art in a specific category, click the category in the list and then scroll through the pictures below.

Select the clip art image you want by clicking it. A dark border surrounds your clip art selection, and its category and name appear on buttons near the

FIGURE 14-2.

The Microsoft
ClipArt Gallery
dialog box.

bottom of the dialog box. To add the clip art selection to a slide, click OK. (You can also double-click a clip art picture in the dialog box to add it to a slide.)

When you add a clip art image to a slide, the image appears in the placeholder you double-clicked to open the ClipArt Gallery, or it appears centered on a slide without a clip art placeholder. You can then move it into position.

Figure 14-3 shows a clip art image that has been moved to the bottom of the slide. After a clip art picture appears on a slide, you can drag the picture to move it. You can also drag one of the picture's handles to resize it. Drag a corner handle to maintain the clip art's proportions while you resize it, or hold down the Ctrl key and drag a corner handle to stretch or shrink the clip art picture without moving it. You can also hold down the Ctrl key and drag a copy of the clip art picture to a new location on the slide. (Before you modify a picture, it's a good idea to create a copy of it so that you have a backup should you make a mistake. You can always delete the backup if it's not needed.)

Adding Clip Art to the Background of a Presentation

To add a clip art picture to the background of every slide in a presentation, you can add the picture to the slide master background. First choose Master and then

FIGURE 14-3.
A clip art picture on
a slide.

Slide Master from the View menu. Then open the ClipArt Gallery, and select the image you want. After the clip art picture has been added to the background of the presentation, you can place the picture behind the text of the presentation by selecting the clip art and choosing Send to Back from the Draw menu.

 TIP   The Backgrounds category in the ClipArt Gallery has a number of abstract and landscape backgrounds that you can stretch to fill the background of the slide master.

Finding Clip Art with the Find Picture Dialog Box

Each picture in the ClipArt Gallery has a text description you can use to search for a particular image. To search for a picture, first click the Find button in the Microsoft ClipArt Gallery dialog box. The Find Picture dialog box opens, as shown in Figure 14-4 on the next page.

FIGURE 14-4.

The Find Picture
dialog box.

The Find Picture dialog box allows you to narrow down the list of images displayed in the ClipArt Gallery by selecting one of four search methods: by category, by description, by filename, or by picture type.

To search by category, select the category you want from the With the Category drop-down list. To search for a keyword in the clip art picture's description, enter the keyword in the With a Description containing edit box. To search for a picture filename that contains specific characters, enter the characters in the With a Filename containing edit box. To search by picture file type, select one of the file types from the Of this Type of File drop-down list.

For example, to find a clip art image of a key, you can enter *key* in the With a Description containing edit box and click OK. Figure 14-5 shows the results of the search in the ClipArt Gallery. Along with pictures of keys, you also see pictures of items that have *key* as part of their name, such as a donkey, a keyboard, and the flag of Turkey. Unfortunately, the ClipArt Gallery does not provide a method to search for whole words only. If your first attempt at a search results in "inappropriate" pictures, click Find again and try a different keyword or search method.

FIGURE 14-5.
The Microsoft
ClipArt Gallery
dialog box after
a search for
descriptions
containing the
letters *key*.

Replacing a Clip Art Selection on a Slide

After you add a picture from the ClipArt Gallery to a slide, you can replace the
picture by first double-clicking it. (You can also select the picture, click the right
mouse button, and choose Edit Microsoft ClipArt Gallery Object from the shortcut menu.) Then, when the Microsoft ClipArt Gallery dialog box reopens, you
can select a replacement picture.

Recoloring Clip Art to Match the Current Color Scheme

The clip art from the ClipArt Gallery has a preset combination of colors that may
clash with the color scheme of your presentation. To recolor a clip art picture
so that it displays colors from the current color scheme, select the clip art, and
then choose Recolor from the Tools menu or the shortcut menu.

In the Recolor Picture dialog box, shown in Figure 14-6 on the next page,
find the original color that you want to change in the picture, and select a new
color from the adjacent drop-down list of colors. To change only the background and fill colors in the picture without changing the colors of the lines,
select the Fills option before you start changing colors.

FIGURE 14-6.

The Recolor
Picture dialog box.

When you open a color drop-down list, you can select one of the eight color scheme colors, or you can select Other Color to make the full palette of colors available. Keep in mind that when you select a color scheme color, you gain two advantages: The colors in the picture match the colors used throughout the presentation, and the color scheme attached to the presentation controls the colors in the picture, so if you change color schemes, the picture will recolor accordingly. If you select a color from the Other Color dialog box instead, the color remains fixed even when you change the color scheme. As a result, the color might clash with the new color scheme's colors.

You can recolor as many of the colors in the picture as you want, and click Preview to see the results. When the new colors of the picture are satisfactory, click OK.

Adding Clip Art to the Gallery

The ClipArt Gallery comes with a substantial number of images, but you may have additional clip art pictures on your system that were installed as part of other software or were purchased separately. Many word processing applications come with small libraries of clip art, for example. By adding the clip art that is already on your system to PowerPoint's ClipArt Gallery, you can view and gain access to all your clip art in one central place.

To add a clip art image to the Gallery, click Options in the Microsoft ClipArt Gallery dialog box. Then, in the Options dialog box, click Add to add a file to the Gallery. (The Refresh option allows you to refresh the Gallery, removing pictures whose files you have deleted, rereading pictures whose files you have changed, and adding new pictures that you have added to your system. The

Change a Category option and the Edit Picture Information option allow you to rename or delete a category of clip art and edit the description of a picture, respectively.)

After you click Add, the first of two Add Clipart dialog boxes appears, as shown in Figure 14-7. You use this dialog box to select the clip art file you want to import. To find clip art files of a certain type, select the file type from the List Type of Files drop-down list. Use the Drives, Directories, and Picture Name lists to select a picture file. Click Picture Preview to see the picture before you click OK to open the second Add Clipart dialog box.

FIGURE 14-7.
The first Add Clipart dialog box.

In the second Add Clipart dialog box, shown in Figure 14-8, select a category name from the corresponding drop-down list or enter a new category name in the edit box. You may want to enter the name *CUSTOM*, for example, to place all new clip art in a special category. You may also want to create categories for projects or clients. Then enter a description in the Description edit box. (Enter meaningful keywords that you can use later to help you find the file.) Finally, click Add to add the picture to the ClipArt Gallery category you've specified.

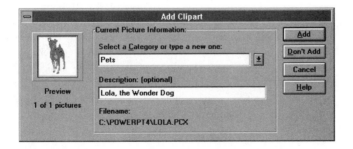

FIGURE 14-8.
The second Add Clipart dialog box.

367

Importing a Picture from Another Application

You may want to add a particular graphic to a presentation but not maintain it in the ClipArt Gallery. Perhaps the graphic is customized for a special presentation and will never be used again. To directly import a graphic from a graphic file, choose Picture from the Insert menu while you are in Slide view. Then, in the Insert Picture dialog box shown in Figure 14-9, use the Drives and Directories lists to navigate to the appropriate directory. Select the graphic file you want in the File Name list, and then click OK to place the graphic on the current slide.

FIGURE 14-9.
The Insert Picture
dialog box.

PowerPoint can import graphic files of two types: vector and bitmap. Vector files are produced by drawing and graphing programs, and contain an arrangement of individual objects—circles, rectangles, lines, filled areas, and text characters, for example. Bitmapped files contain a picture that is composed of a pattern of dots, much as newspaper photos are composed of tiny dots.

Because vector files contain objects, they can be easily edited. You can remove or resize an object to change the picture and leave other objects that are underneath untouched. Most clip art is provided in vector format so that it can be easily edited and resized to fit any need. Bitmapped files can be edited, too, but not as easily as vector files. To erase part of a bitmap, you must erase the dots, leaving a hole in the picture. Parts of objects that appeared to be behind the object you've erased are erased, too. But with their many dots, bitmaps can represent a photographic picture accurately, which is why software that you use with a scanner generates a bitmapped version of a photograph rather than a vector file. Therefore, if you intend to place a scanned image in a presentation— a photograph of a person or a scanned logo, for example—you must always import a bitmapped file.

NOTE: You can only import file types for which you've installed a graphic filter. The Microsoft Office applications share the same graphic filters, so if you installed a graphic filter when you installed Word or Excel, for example, you can use the same graphic filter in PowerPoint.

Table 14-1 identifies the graphic file types you can import.

File Format	Type
Windows Metafile (.WMF)	Vector
Computer Graphics Metafile (.CGM)	Vector
Encapsulated PostScript (.EPS)	Vector
Tagged Image Format (.TIF)	Bitmap
PC Paintbrush (.PCX)	Bitmap
Macintosh PICT (.PCT)	Bitmap
Micrografx Designer/Draw (.DRW)	Vector
CompuServe GIF (.GIF)	Bitmap
AutoCAD Plot File (.ADI)	Vector
AutoCAD Format 2-D (.DXF)	Vector
CorelDRAW! (.CDR)	Vector
DrawPerfect (.WPG)	Vector
HP Plotter Print File (.PLT)	Vector
Kodak Photo CD (.PCD)	Bitmap
Lotus 1-2-3 Graphics (.PIC)	Vector
Targa (.TGA)	Bitmap
Windows DIB (.DIB)	Bitmap
HP Graphics Language (.HGL)	Vector

TABLE 14-1.
The graphic file types.

Adding a Bitmapped Image to a Slide

To add a bitmapped image to a slide, choose Picture from the Insert menu while
you are in Slide view. When the Insert Picture dialog box appears, as shown
earlier, select the type of file you want to import from the List Files of Type
drop-down list. Next, use the Drives and Directories lists to navigate to the
appropriate directory. Then select the name of the file you want in the File Name
list, and click OK to import the file.

Placing a Bitmap on the Background

By switching to the slide master before you insert a bitmap, you can
place the bitmap on the background of every slide in a presentation.
First, choose Master and then Slide Master from the View menu. Then
use the Insert Picture dialog box to place the bitmap on the slide
master. If you want to place the bitmap behind the presentation text,
select the bitmap, and choose Send to Back from the Draw menu.
The figure below shows a bitmapped image on every slide in a presentation.

The imported bitmap appears on the current slide, ready to be moved and resized to suit your needs. To move the bitmap, drag it to a new location on the slide. To resize the bitmap, drag one of its handles in the desired direction. To maintain the bitmap's proportions, drag a corner handle. To stretch the bitmap, drag a handle in the middle of one of the bitmap's sides.

NOTE: If you added a bitmapped file to the ClipArt Gallery, you can borrow the bitmap from the Gallery by following the instructions in "Using the ClipArt Gallery," page 360.

After you stretch a bitmap out of shape, you can return the picture to its original proportions by choosing Scale from the Draw menu, selecting the Relative to Original Picture Size option in the Scale dialog box, and clicking OK. Then you can resize the picture with its proper proportions by dragging a corner handle or by entering a Scale To percentage in the Scale dialog box.

TIP   Bitmaps take somewhat longer to draw than other objects on a slide. Therefore, you might want to draw a box on the slide to use as a temporary placeholder for a bitmap while you create and format other elements of the presentation. When the presentation is otherwise complete, you can import the bitmap.

Cropping a Bitmap

To display only a rectangular portion of a bitmap, you can crop the bitmap, moving in the sides or corners to create a small window through which you see only the section of the picture you want displayed. Cropping a bitmap is like using a pair of scissors to cut away the parts of a photo you want to remove.

To crop a bitmap, first select the bitmap, and choose Crop Picture from the Tools menu or the shortcut menu. Then place the mouse pointer, which looks like the cropping icon shown in Figure 14-10 on the next page, on one of the handles surrounding the bitmap, and drag the handle toward the center of the picture. To display only the left half of a picture, for example, drag the right side handle halfway across the bitmap to the left. You can drag other handles to close in on the part of the picture you want to display. When you're finished, click anywhere outside the bitmap.

FIGURE 14-10.

Cropping a photo.

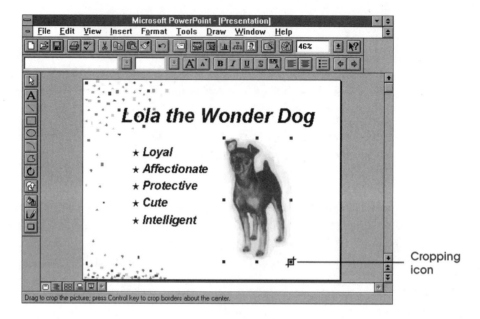

Cropping
icon

You can restore parts of a bitmap that have been cropped, by choosing Crop Picture from the Tools menu or the shortcut menu and then dragging the handles back out to the edges of the bitmap with the cropping icon.

Recoloring a Bitmap

You can replace selected colors in a bitmap the same way you replace colors in a clip art picture, using the Recolor command on the Tools menu or the shortcut menu.

 For more information about recoloring a picture, see "Recoloring Clip Art to Match the Current Color Scheme," page 365.

In this part of the book, you learned how to apply the finishing touches to a presentation by adding text, drawings, and pictures. In the next section, you'll learn how to turn your work into something tangible: a printed page, a 35-mm slide, or an electronic presentation called a slide show.

Performing
with PowerPoint

Creating Printed Output and 35-mm Slides

Somehow, printing always seems to be the most difficult part of working with a computer. You work so hard to create a look on the screen, but when you print, the darks are too dark or the lights are too light. And once you print overhead transparencies in landscape orientation, you can't get audience handouts in portrait orientation without jumping through hoops and murmuring incantations over the system.

Well, PowerPoint solves these problems, as you knew it would. It takes care of all the portrait-to-landscape, overhead-to-slide, and screen-to-paper conversions behind the scenes so that you can concentrate on expressing yourself creatively.

In this chapter, you'll learn how to tell PowerPoint exactly what type of output you want to generate. You can print overheads from your slides, or you can print audience handouts with up to six slide miniatures on each page. You can also print the speaker's notes you created in Notes Pages view, or print the presentation to a PostScript file, which you can then take to a service bureau that converts the file to 35-mm slides.

Setting Up the Slides

The first step in creating printed output or 35-mm slides is to check the current slide setup. The slide setup determines the size and orientation of the slides you've created. You may be wondering why you don't have to change the slide setup before starting a presentation. The answer is that you can, but you don't have to. You can leave the default setting, which displays the presentation properly in a slide show and on landscape overheads printed on 8½-by-11-inch pages, and change the slide setup only if you need to print 35-mm slides or custom pages with odd heights and widths.

When you change the slide setup, PowerPoint does all the work to resize and reorient the material on your slides to fit the new page size and orientation. For example, you can create landscape slides, which have a horizontal orientation, and then switch to portrait slides if you need a vertical orientation. In most cases, PowerPoint adjusts everything on your slides so well that you'll think you've been creating portrait slides all along.

To check the slide setup, choose Slide Setup from the File menu. In the Slide Setup dialog box, shown in Figure 15-1, you see options for the slide width and height, the slide number, and the slide orientation.

FIGURE 15-1.
The Slide Setup
dialog box.

Slide Size

From the Slides Sized for drop-down list in the Slide Setup dialog box, select one of the four preset slide sizes (On-screen Show, Letter Paper, A4 Paper, or 35mm Slides), or select Custom and then set a custom width and height in the Width and Height edit boxes.

> **NOTE:** When you select the Custom option, the default settings for the Width and Height are set to the printable area of the page for the current printer.

Slide Numbering

In the Slide Setup dialog box, the number shown in the Number Slides From edit box sets the slide numbering that appears both on the slides and in the slide number indicator at the bottom of the PowerPoint window. Keep in mind that before the number is actually displayed on a slide, you must enter the page number symbol on the slide master by choosing the Page Number command from the Insert menu.

You can start slide numbering at any number. For example, to number the first slide of the current presentation as 10, type *10* directly in the Number Slides From edit box or click the up arrow at the right end of the edit box to increase the setting to 10.

See Also: For more information about numbering slides, see "Adding the Date, Time, and Slide Number to the Background," page 238.

The Special Print Options

The options at the bottom of the Print dialog box let you make important changes to the way the presentation prints, although the defaults work well in most cases. You've already been introduced to the Collate Copies option; here are the other five options:

- The Print to File option prints the presentation to an output file on disk. You can then transport this output file to another system, and copy the file to the printer there.

- The Print Hidden Slides option prints slides that you have hidden using the Hide Slide command on the Tools menu.

- The Black & White option prints color slides properly on a black and white printer, such as a black and white laser printer. Black & White replaces fills in objects with white, and it replaces color patterns with patterns of black and white. This option also adds a thin black outline to objects that do not otherwise have borders, except text objects. If you've formatted the presentation with a template designed for black and white overheads from the BWOVRHD directory, you may not need to select the Black & White option.

- The Scale to Fit Paper option properly scales the slides to fit the printed page even if the slides have been set up for a different page size. For example, to print a slide that you sized for 35-mm slides (in the Slide Setup dialog box) on an $8\frac{1}{2}$ -by-11-inch page, you can use the Scale to Fit Paper option.

- The Pure Black & White option converts all color fills to white and all text and lines to black. Pure Black & White also adds outlines to filled objects, and it prints color pictures in shades of gray. Use this option to accelerate printing if you're willing to live with the loss of formatting.

Figure 15-3 shows three versions of a color slide printed on a black and white laser printer. The top left page was printed with the default print options. The top right page was printed with the Black & White option. The bottom page was printed with the Pure Black & White option.

FIGURE 15-3.

A page printed with three different print options: default (top left), Black & White (top right), and Pure Black & White (bottom left).

Printing Handouts and Speaker's Notes

To print audience handouts, select Print from the File menu or press Ctrl+P, and then select one of the three Handouts options from the Print What drop-down list in the Print dialog box. These options allow you to print two, three, or six slides per page. The orientation of the handouts is determined by the Orientation setting in the Slide Setup dialog box shown earlier. Figure 15-4 shows a handout page with three slides per page, which leaves audience members plenty of room to jot down notes about each slide.

FIGURE 15-4.

A handout page with three slides on the page.

To print speaker's notes, select Notes Pages from the Print What drop-down list. As with handouts, the orientation of the notes pages is determined by the Orientation setting in the Slide Setup dialog box.

Printing the Outline

To print the presentation outline just as it appears in Outline view, select Outline View from the Print What drop-down list box in the Print dialog box. The outline prints with as much detail as is currently displayed in Outline view. Collapsed entries do not print.

The size of the text on the printed page is affected by the zoom percentage in Outline view. If the zoom percentage is at 50%, for example, 40-point text in Outline view prints as 20-point text on the page.

Creating 35-mm Slides

If you're lucky enough to have a film recorder attached to your system and the Windows printer driver for the film recorder, you can select the film recorder as your printer and then print to the film recorder as if you were printing to any other printer. The film recorder creates an image of each slide on 35-mm slide film. You can then develop the film to produce 35-mm slides. You may need to refer to the documentation for the device for special instructions on using it with a Windows-based application such as PowerPoint.

Most people do not have large and expensive film recorders at their disposal, however. Instead, they rely on an outside service bureau that takes a PostScript file generated from PowerPoint and feeds it into a film recorder. Many service bureaus provide overnight service, returning the developed 35-mm slides by next-day delivery. A local service bureau may even provide same-day service.

PowerPoint comes with software that makes it especially easy to use a Genigraphics Service Center as your service bureau. When you install Power-Point, you can also install the Genigraphics printer driver, which automatically creates a PostScript file that Genigraphics can accept. When you install the Genigraphics driver, a communications program called GraphicsLink is also installed so that you can transmit the PostScript file to the nearest Genigraphics Service Center by modem.

To create a PostScript file to send to Genigraphics, follow these steps:

1. Make sure the Slides Sized for option in the Slide Setup dialog box is set to 35mm Slides.

2. Choose Print from the File menu, and when the Print dialog box appears, click the Printer button.

3. In the Print Setup dialog box, select Genigraphics Driver on GENI: as your printer, and then click Options.

4. Make sure Format is set to Presentation Format, and Reduce or Enlarge is set to 100%.

5. Click OK twice to return to the Print dialog box.

6. Click OK again to begin printing the slide file. When you click OK in the Print dialog box, the Genigraphics Job Instructions dialog box appears. Complete the options in the dialog box, and click OK. Then complete the options in the Billing Information dialog box, and click OK.

If you have a modem, you can launch the GraphicsLink software, which sends the file to Genigraphics over the telephone line, by double-clicking the GraphicsLink icon in the Windows Program Manager.

In the following chapter, you'll learn about an alternative method of presenting with PowerPoint that avoids printing: the electronic presentation, which displays your work in a slide show on the computer screen. However, even if you display a slide show, you may still want to print audience handouts so that your viewers can take home pages for future reference.

Creating Slide Shows

To assign a basic transition effect to a slide, click the slide and then select a transition effect from the Transition Effects drop-down list. Watch the slide carefully in Slide Sorter view, and you'll see that it previews the transition. If you want to see the preview again, click the small transition effect icon that has appeared just below the slide. Figure 16-1 shows these icons.

FIGURE 16-1.
Click a transition effect icon to preview the transition effect applied to the slide.

Transition effect icon ———

To apply the same transition effect to slides in a sequence, select the slides and then select an effect from the Transition Effects drop-down list. Remember, you can select multiple slides by holding down the Shift key as you click each slide or by drawing a selection box around a group of slides using the mouse pointer. To apply a single effect to all the slides, choose Select All from the Edit menu or press Ctrl+A, and then select an effect.

TIP   If you select the same transition effect for all the slides in a slide show, you might consider using a different transition effect for the title slides of each segment of your presentation. Simply select the title slides, and then select a different effect from the Transition Effects drop-down list.

By clicking the Transition button to the left of the Transition Effects box on the Slide Sorter toolbar, you can open the Transition dialog box shown in Figure 16-2. In the Transition dialog box, you can select not only a transition effect, but also a speed for the effect and the amount of time you want the slide to remain on the screen. The default Advance option, Only on Mouse Click, requires you to click the left mouse button or press the keys listed in Table 16-1 on page 395 during the slide show to advance to the next slide. Another way to get to the Transition dialog box is to select one or more slides and choose Transition from the Tools menu, or click the right mouse button and then choose Transition from the shortcut menu.

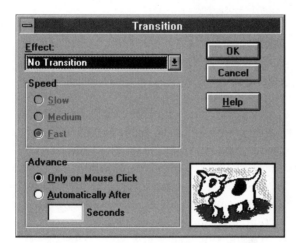

FIGURE 16-2.
The Transition
dialog box.

TIP Transition effects are undoubtedly snazzy, but don't let them detract from the content of your presentation by using too many different effects during a slide show or by setting them all to Slow to heighten the drama. Instead, use Fast for the transition speed whenever possible, and use one effect repeatedly, changing effects only for new presentation segments.

Assigning Build Effects

The bulleted text items on text slides can appear all at once or sequentially during a slide show. To have the bulleted text "build" on a slide, you must assign a build effect by selecting one or more text slides with bulleted items and then choosing an effect from the Build Effects drop-down list on the Slide Sorter toolbar or from the Build dialog box shown in Figure 16-3.

FIGURE 16-3.
The Build dialog
box.

 To open the Build dialog box, click the Build button to the left of the Build Effects box on the Slide Sorter toolbar, choose Build from the Tools menu, or click the right mouse button and choose Build from the shortcut menu. In the Build dialog box, you can select a muted color from the Dim Previous Points drop-down list to dim the bulleted items once they have been revealed and discussed. (The dimmed items remain readable on the screen.) Each newly revealed bulleted item then appears in the bright text color. From the Effect drop-down list at the bottom of the Build dialog box, you can also select a build effect to draw each new bulleted item. This list provides the same options as the Build Effects drop-down list on the Slide Sorter toolbar.

After you apply a build effect, a build effect icon—the same icon that appears on the face of the Build button—appears in Slide Sorter view next to the transition effect icon. Although you can click the transition effect icon to preview a slide's transition effect, you cannot preview a slide's build effect before you run the show. The build effect icon simply denotes slides with builds.

Hiding Slides

 To hide one or more slides during a slide show, select the slides, and click the Hide Slide button on the Slide Sorter toolbar or choose Hide Slide from the Tools menu or the shortcut menu. A slash appears through the slide number in Slide Sorter view to indicate that the slide is hidden. Although the hidden slide continues to display in Slide Sorter view, it does not appear in a slide show. Instead, when you move the mouse during the show, a hidden slide icon appears in the lower right corner of the previous slide to indicate that a hidden slide is available next. To show the slide, click the hidden slide icon. Figure 16-4 shows a slide with a hidden slide icon.

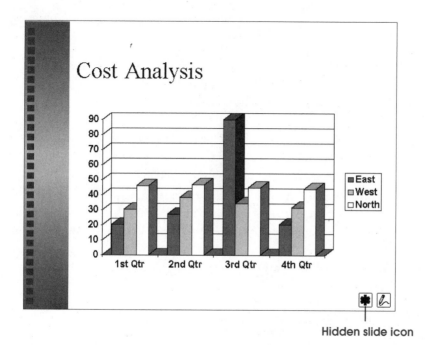

FIGURE 16-4.
A slide with a hidden slide icon.

Hidden slide icon

To unhide a hidden slide, select the slide and click the Hide Slide button again or choose Hide Slide again from the Tools menu or the shortcut menu.

NOTE: You can assign transitions, apply builds, and hide slides in Slide view by moving to a slide and then selecting Transition, Build, or Hide Slide from the Tools menu. But you cannot preview transition effects in Slide view, so you might prefer to create the show in Slide Sorter view.

Running a Slide Show in Slide Show View

As you know, when you develop a slide show in Slide Sorter view, you can preview the transition effects for individual slides. But to see the transitions full-screen and to see the builds in bulleted text slides, you must switch to Slide Show view, where the show takes place.

Starting the Slide Show

Before you actually start a slide show, you can designate the slide at which you want the show to begin. Simply select the slide in Slide Sorter view or turn to the slide in Slide view. Then, when you click the Slide Show button, the slide show starts at the currently selected slide. To advance to the next slide, click the left mouse button. To return to the previous slide, click the right mouse button. To discontinue the slide show and return to the previous view, press Esc, Ctrl+Break, or the minus key on the numeric keypad.

To run the entire show, select the first slide, and then click the Slide Show button or choose the Slide Show command from the View menu. When you choose the Slide Show command, the Slide Show dialog box shown in Figure 16-5 appears. You can then select All and click Show to run the entire show, or you can enter a starting and ending slide in the From and To edit boxes and click Show to view a segment of the slide show.

FIGURE 16-5.
The Slide Show
dialog box.

TIP   To run a slide show as an unattended demonstration (in a store window or building lobby, for example), click Run Continuously Until Esc in the Slide Show dialog box. The show will run as an ever-repeating loop that can only be interrupted when someone presses the Esc key. To make the Esc key unavailable, you can remove the keyboard and the mouse after you start the show and leave only the monitor and system unit.

Controlling the Slide Show with the Keyboard

We all like to control the show, but it's usually not as easy as PowerPoint makes it. During a slide show, you can use the keys listed in Table 16-1 to control various aspects of the show.

TABLE 16-1.
The Slide Show keyboard controls.

Press or Enter This	To Perform This Action
Spacebar, Right arrow, Down arrow, PgDn, or N	Advance to next slide
Backspace, Left arrow, Up arrow, PgUp, or P	Return to previous slide
Slide number+Enter	Go to slide number
B or period	Black screen/resume
W or comma	White screen/resume
A or =	Show/hide mouse pointer
S or + (numeric keypad)	Pause/resume automatic show

Rehearsing Automatic Slide Show Timings

To create a slide show that proceeds on its own from slide to slide, you can simply enter the amount of time you want each slide to remain on the screen in the Transition dialog box. A better method, however, is to practice giving the presentation first and have PowerPoint record the length of time you keep each slide on the screen. You can then use PowerPoint's findings to determine the amount of time to display each slide. You can also ascertain the overall length of the show.

To enter the display time manually for each slide, first select the slide in Slide Sorter view and click the Transition button on the Slide Sorter toolbar, or move to the slide in Slide view and choose Transition from the Tools menu or the shortcut menu. In the Transition dialog box, enter the number of seconds in the Advance section's Automatically After edit box.

To record the slide durations during a rehearsal of the slide show, click the Rehearse Timings button on the Slide Sorter toolbar; or choose Slide Show from the View menu, click Rehearse New Timings in the Slide Show dialog box, and then click Show.

When the slide show begins, practice giving the presentation, advancing the slides manually when needed. A button in the lower left corner of the slide show window counts off the seconds each slide displays. After you complete the last slide, a dialog box shows the total length of the show and gives you the option to place the new timings in Slide Sorter view. If you click Yes, the timing for each slide appears under the slide in Slide Sorter view. To run the show with the timings, choose Slide Show from the View menu, select the Use Slide Timings option in the Slide Show dialog box, and then click Show.

To remove slide timings, select one or more slides in Slide Sorter view, click the Transition button on the Slide Sorter toolbar, and then select Only on Mouse Click in the Advance section of the Transition dialog box.

TIP   You can also click the timing button in the lower left corner of the slide show window to advance slides during a rehearsal.

Marking Up Slides

To call special attention to a slide, or if you just don't know what to do with your hands during a slide show, you can use the mouse pointer to draw directly on slides. You can circle items, draw arrows, or add written comments, much like sportscasters who draw football plays on TV during a game.

To draw on a slide, move the mouse pointer to the lower right corner of the slide show window and click the drawing icon, which looks like a pencil in action. If the drawing icon is not present, it will appear as soon as you move the mouse pointer. Next, press the left mouse button while moving the mouse pointer on the slide to express yourself dramatically with scribblings. To clear everything you've drawn on a slide, press the E key (for erase). Figure 16-6 shows annotations drawn during a slide show.

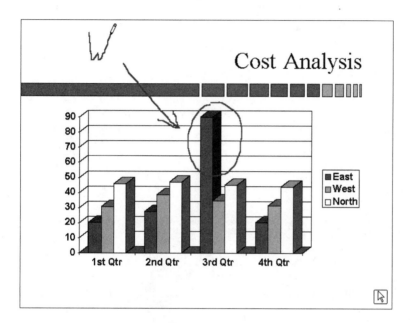

FIGURE 16-6.
Annotations drawn on a slide.

Using the PowerPoint Viewer

You don't need to have the entire PowerPoint program installed on a system to run a slide show. You can install only the PowerPoint Viewer, which displays your presentations just as if you were running the slide show in Slide Show view. The PowerPoint Viewer allows you to display PowerPoint slide shows on a portable computer where hard-disk space is too limited to install the entire PowerPoint application. It can also display slide shows created in PowerPoint for the Macintosh. In addition, you can copy a slide show to floppy disk and then send the show, along with the PowerPoint Viewer, to another location for viewing. (When you copy a slide show, you must also copy the viewer application, and the recipient of the disks must install the PowerPoint Viewer and the presentation on his or her system, because a presentation cannot be read and displayed fast enough from floppy disk.) ·

NOTE: Presentations cannot drill down to embedded documents when displayed in the PowerPoint Viewer if PowerPoint is not installed on the system. Nor can presentations branch to other presentations if PowerPoint is not present. For more information about drilling down to embedded documents, see "Adding Drill-Down Documents," page 401. For more information about branching to other presentations, see "Creating a Slide Show with Branching," page 402.

Before you can use the PowerPoint Viewer to display a slide show, you must add the transition effects, builds, and timings you want for the show; make sure the Use Slide Timings option is selected in the Slide Show dialog box; and save the presentation in a file. Then double-click the PowerPoint Viewer icon to start the PowerPoint Viewer application. The Microsoft PowerPoint Viewer dialog box appears, as shown in Figure 16-7.

FIGURE 16-7.
The Microsoft
PowerPoint Viewer
dialog box.

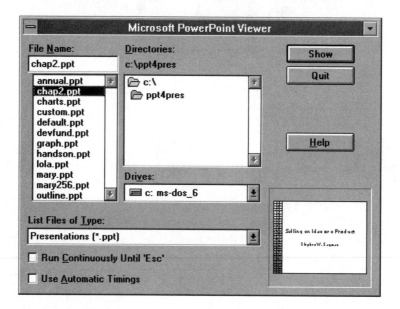

In the Microsoft PowerPoint Viewer dialog box, select the presentation file you want to display, and click Show or press Enter to run the slide show. You can also select the Run Continuously Until Esc option to display the slide show indefinitely, and you can select the Use Automatic Timings option to use the slide timings you recorded during a rehearsal. As the show progresses, you have all the mouse and keyboard control capabilities that you have in PowerPoint's Slide Show view. After the show, click Quit to exit the PowerPoint Viewer.

To prepare a slide show that can be viewed on a system not equipped with PowerPoint, first copy the floppy disk containing the PowerPoint Viewer (keep the original, of course), and then copy the presentation file to a floppy disk. Make sure the person giving the slide show knows that the VSETUP.EXE program on the floppy disk must be run from within Windows in order to install the PowerPoint Viewer on a local system. The presentation file must also be copied from the floppy disk to a directory on a local hard disk. You can copy and send the PowerPoint Viewer to as many recipients as you want, unlike the main PowerPoint application.

Special Slide Show Features

Special slide show features let you create basic multimedia presentations, add backup documents, and create interactive shows that can branch to other presentations. You can even instruct PowerPoint to run a series of slide shows, one right after the other.

Adding Sound, Music, and Video

Nothing brings a presentation to life like adding multimedia objects—sound, music, and video—to a slide show. As long as you have the objects available on your system and you have a Windows-compatible sound card installed, adding multimedia objects to a presentation is straightforward, and the effect is truly dramatic.

On any slide, you can embed one or more objects—perhaps a short music clip as the slide fades into view, followed by a video quote from someone involved with the project. These clips can play automatically when the slide appears, or after a set interval. A presenter can also double-click on a slide's sound, music, or video icon to start playing a particular object.

When you add a slide to a presentation, you can select any one of the nine autolayouts that has a *Double click to add object* placeholder. Double-clicking the placeholder leads to the Insert Object dialog box shown in Figure 16-8 on the next page. You can also add a multimedia object to any slide by moving to the slide in Slide view and then choosing Object from the Insert menu.

FIGURE 16-8.
The Insert Object
dialog box.

To select a multimedia object stored in a file, click the Create from File option in the Insert Object dialog box. Then click the Browse button to open the Browse dialog box, where you can locate the file you want. In the Browse dialog box, make sure you select All Files (*.*) from the List Files of Type drop-down list, and then use the Drives, Directories, and Source lists to select the multimedia file. The three most popular multimedia file types are WAV (sound files), MID (MIDI music files), and AVI (Video for Windows files).

After you select a file and click OK to close both the Browse dialog box and the Insert Object dialog box, an icon representing the multimedia object appears on the slide. If the object is a Microsoft Video for Windows clip, a sample frame, usually the first frame of the clip, appears. Select the icon or frame, and choose Play Settings from the Tools menu to determine how and when the clip will play. Figure 16-9 shows the Play Settings dialog box for a video clip.

FIGURE 16-9.
The Play Settings
dialog box for a
video clip.

In the Start Play section of the Play Settings dialog box, you can choose to play the clip when the presenter clicks the object, when the transition that draws the slide starts, or after the transition ends. You might want to set a music clip to play when the transition starts and a video clip to play two seconds after the transition ends, for example.

To prevent the multimedia object's icon from displaying on the screen during a slide show, click Hide While not Playing in the Play Settings dialog box. The object or its icon will still appear in Slide view, but won't be visible during the actual slide show.

If the object is a video clip, you might want to select the object and choose Scale from the Draw menu to get the best video playback quality. In the Scale dialog box, select the resolution that you'll use when displaying the slide show, and then click Best Scale for Slide Show. You can also increase or decrease the size of the video clip by entering a Scale To percentage, but the video may look jerky at other sizes.

To preview the multimedia object, double-click it, or click the object once with the right mouse button and choose Play Media Clip Object from the short-cut menu. By selecting Edit Media Clip object from the shortcut menu, you can use the capabilities of the Windows Media Player, provided with PowerPoint, to change how the object plays during the presentation. For example, if the object is a video clip, you can choose Options from Media Player's Edit menu, and then deselect the Caption option to remove the filename that appears below the video window.

A multimedia object will play during a slide show until its clip ends or until you move to the next slide.

Adding Drill-Down Documents

If you have data in another Windows-based application that can support an assertion you've made in a presentation or provide additional information, you can embed the data as an object on a slide so that it appears as an icon. During the slide show, you can then double-click the icon to "drill down" to the information and display the data in its original form. For example, you can embed a Microsoft Word document or a Microsoft Excel spreadsheet as a drill-down document. In fact, you can embed any file created by a Windows-based application that can act as an OLE server or an OLE2 object application. Most recent Windows-based applications can provide OLE objects for use in PowerPoint.

To embed an existing object, first choose Object from the Insert menu, and when the Insert Object dialog box appears, select Create from File and click the Browse button. In the Browse dialog box, select the file you want and then click OK. When you return to the Insert Object dialog box, select the Display As Icon option and click OK. The object appears on the current slide as an icon that you can double-click to open and work with the original object. Figure 16-10 shows an embedded Excel object on a slide.

FIGURE 16-10.

An embedded Excel object represented by an Excel icon.

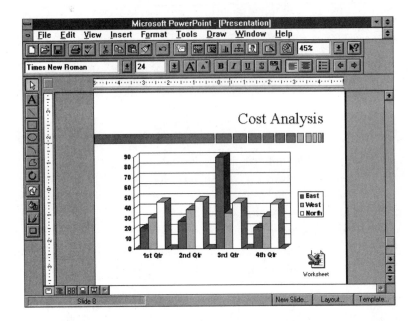

If the application from which the object came supports OLE2, Power-Point's menus and toolbars are replaced by those of the application. Otherwise, the application opens in its own window. Certain applications allow you to drag and drop files from the Windows File Manager to a PowerPoint slide. You'll have to test your application to see if it supports this feature.

Creating a Slide Show with Branching

By embedding a PowerPoint presentation as a drill-down object, you can branch to that presentation from within another slide show. The embedded presentation can provide detailed information on a topic covered by the main presentation. To embed a PowerPoint presentation, follow the procedure described in "Adding Drill-Down Documents" on the previous page, but select a PowerPoint presentation as the object you want to embed.

By adding embedded PowerPoint presentations, you can create an interactive training or informational presentation in which the viewer can select particular topics to review. Figure 16-11 shows a menu of topics within a presentation that you can present to a viewer. Double-clicking each topic's icon starts a different PowerPoint slide show.

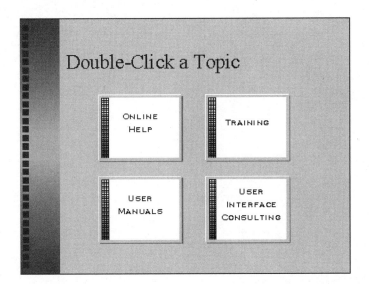

FIGURE 16-11.
A menu that a viewer can use to branch to other presentations.

Playing a Series of Slide Shows

To play a series of slide shows automatically, type the names of the PowerPoint presentations as a list in a text file. Be sure to type the full pathnames to the presentation files, such as C:\PPT4PRES\BOARD.PPT. Name the text file with the extension LST (for list), and then open the LST file using the Open command on PowerPoint's File menu. The slide shows in the presentations will play in sequence.

TIP   You can also double-click an LST file in the Windows File Manager. The PowerPoint Viewer will open automatically and display the presentations listed in the file.

Displaying slide shows can be the ultimate thrill in using PowerPoint, but you'll also appreciate some of the advanced topics covered next, in the final section of this book.

Advanced
PowerPoint

17

Using PowerPoint with Other Applications

A s you've seen, the developers at Microsoft made countless improvements in version 4 of PowerPoint. Many of the most critical improvements were designed to bring PowerPoint in line with two other highly sophisticated Microsoft applications: Word 6 for Windows and Excel 5. Word, Excel, Mail, and PowerPoint form the Microsoft Office bundle of applications. Word 6 is the word processor of the group, Excel 5 is the number cruncher, and Mail 3.2 is the messenger. PowerPoint 4 is the public voice of the Microsoft Office, telling the world your story with professionally and consistently designed images.

NEW!

Although each application is available separately, powers that are otherwise hidden emerge when you use two or more of the applications together. You first notice the common menus, dialog boxes, toolbars, and procedures that make switching from one application to another easy. But below the surface is a powerful object linking and embedding technology called OLE2 that lets you share information among applications as a natural extension of the way you work in one application alone. For example, not only can you move objects, such as passages of text or ranges of numbers, from place to place within a document, but you can also move them from application to application with the same ease. And when you move an object to a second application, an OLE2 feature called in-place editing gives you access from within the second application to all the menus, dialog boxes, toolbars, and procedures that you used to create the object. You can move a worksheet from Excel to PowerPoint, for example, and then gain access to Excel's menus and toolbars from within PowerPoint to edit the object. When you select the worksheet for editing, Excel's menus and toolbars appear temporarily within the PowerPoint window, and when you finish editing the object, PowerPoint's menus and toolbars reclaim the PowerPoint window.

Drag and drop is the key to embedding information in a Microsoft Office application. You can almost always select an item in one application and drag it to another application's window. And if you want a copy of the information to remain in the original application, you can hold down the Ctrl key as you drag. In this chapter, you'll learn how to select objects and drag them between applications. You'll also learn about a few considerations to keep in mind as you exchange information between the Office applications, and you'll learn about the menu alternatives that you can often use with other Windows-based applications that do not support the drag-and-drop procedure.

Using PowerPoint with Microsoft Word 6 for Windows

In Chapter 4, you learned how to exchange outlines between Microsoft Word 6 for Windows and PowerPoint; you can also exchange individual text objects and graphics with similar ease. Best of all, you can embed an entire PowerPoint slide show in a Word document, transforming a drab report into a lively, stimulating presentation complete with special effects, sound, music, and perhaps even video.

Of course, you can embed individual multimedia elements in a Word document without using PowerPoint, but embedding them in a PowerPoint presentation and then embedding the presentation in Word allows the multimedia objects and presentation to play collectively in a slide show.

Dragging Text from Word to PowerPoint

You'll appreciate dragging and dropping when you need to enter text in PowerPoint that you've already typed in Word. Rather than retype the text, you can simply drag it from Word to PowerPoint as easily as you drag it from place to place within a Word document.

To drag text from Word to PowerPoint, you must open the Word and PowerPoint windows and arrange them to share the screen, even if one window overlaps the other. Make sure the slide in which you want to embed the Word text is displayed in the PowerPoint window and that Slide view is active. Figure 17-1 on the next page shows how you might arrange the windows. Then, select the text in Word—a word, a paragraph, or anything else you've created in Word, including a Word table. Place the mouse pointer on the selection, and drag the selection to the current PowerPoint slide. To copy the text to PowerPoint rather than move it, hold down the Ctrl key as you drag the text.

It's important to understand that when the text arrives in PowerPoint, it appears as a picture of the text, with all of its Word formatting intact. When you stretch or compress the picture by dragging its handles, the text becomes distorted. By contrast, text that you've entered in a PowerPoint text box (using the Text Tool button on the Drawing toolbar) maintains its size and shape when you stretch or compress its text box but changes its word wrapping. Figure 17-2 on the next page illustrates the difference between text that has been dragged from Word and text that has been entered in a PowerPoint text box.

Embedding a Slide in a Word Document

By using the Insert Object command in Word, you can access the Microsoft Graph module just as easily as you can from within PowerPoint, so you don't need PowerPoint to create a graph for a Word document. In addition, PowerPoint gets its tables from Word, so you don't need PowerPoint's help there. But by dragging a PowerPoint slide to Word, you can place an image of the slide in a document, complete with a background design and a combination of foreground and background text and graphic objects. You can also copy and paste individual objects from a PowerPoint slide into a Word document using the Copy and Paste commands.

To drag a slide from PowerPoint to Word, you must arrange the PowerPoint and Word windows on the screen, and make sure the slide you want to drag is visible in PowerPoint's Slide Sorter view. Then simply drag the slide from PowerPoint to Word, holding down the Ctrl key if you want to copy the slide rather than move it.

After the slide appears in Word, you can drag and drop it within the Word window as you would a block of text. You can also drag a corner handle to resize the slide proportionally. By clicking the slide with the right mouse button, you can bring up a Word shortcut menu with commands that apply to the slide. For example, you can add a border, shading, and caption to the slide, or frame the slide so that you can wrap text around it and use other techniques that apply only to framed elements. Figure 17-3 shows the shortcut menu that appears in Word.

Also on the shortcut menu, you'll see a command called Edit MS PowerPoint 4.0 Slide. When you choose this command or double-click the slide, a special copy of PowerPoint opens in which you can edit the slide. After you finish, choose Update from PowerPoint's File menu, and then choose the Exit & Return to *Document* command from the File menu to return to Word, where the updated slide reappears.

TIP   To open one Microsoft Office application from within another, display the Microsoft toolbar, and then click the second application's button. If the Microsoft toolbar .is not present, click any toolbar with the right mouse button, and choose Microsoft from the shortcut menu.

FIGURE 17-3.

The shortcut menu for a slide dragged to a Word document.

You can try dragging and dropping a slide into any other Windows-based application in the same way, but if it won't budge, you must use the Cut or Copy command in PowerPoint's Slide Sorter view, switch to the other application's window, and then use the Paste command.

Transferring a Graphic to Word

To transfer a graphic from a PowerPoint slide to a Word document, select the graphic and then use the PowerPoint Copy command. In Word, use the Paste command to transfer a copy of the graphic. You can then edit the graphic directly in Word by double-clicking it to display Word's drawing tools, which work just like PowerPoint's drawing tools.

Embedding a PowerPoint Presentation in Word

To embed an entire PowerPoint presentation in a Word document, you must first select the entire presentation in Slide Sorter view by choosing Select All from the Edit menu or by pressing Ctrl+A. Then simply drag any one of the selected slides to Word. The first slide of the presentation appears in Word, and when you double-click the slide, the presentation displays as a full-screen slide

413

show. To edit the presentation, click the slide once with the right mouse button, and choose Edit MS PowerPoint 4.0 Presentation from the shortcut menu. After you make changes to the presentation, choose Update from the PowerPoint File menu to send the changes to Word, and then choose Exit & Return to *Document* from the PowerPoint File menu.

Linking a PowerPoint Presentation to Word

Rather than transfer a presentation to Word as an embedded object, you can link it to Word. The presentation's data is stored in PowerPoint rather than in Word, and only a representation of the presentation (the first slide) displays in Word. When you double-click the representation in Word, the presentation displays as a slide show, just as if you had embedded it.

Because you have linked the presentation, any changes you make to it in PowerPoint are reflected in the representation in Word. The advantage is that you don't have to update the presentation twice—once in PowerPoint and again in Word. The disadvantage is that you can't move the Word document to another computer without also moving the PowerPoint file. If you move the Word document without moving the PowerPoint file to the same destination, Word cannot access the PowerPoint data at the destination. Only when you drag and drop a presentation or use Paste Special to paste the presentation in Word as an embedded object can you transport the document and simultaneously transport the data.

To link a PowerPoint presentation, you must first save it in a file. Then, with the presentation displayed in Slide Sorter view, choose Select All from the Edit menu or press Ctrl+A, and choose Copy from the Edit menu. When you switch to Word, click an insertion point where you want the presentation to appear, and choose Paste Special from Word's Edit menu. In the Paste Special dialog box, shown in Figure 17-4, select the Paste Link option, and click OK.

To run the presentation, double-click its "representative" slide in Word. To edit the presentation, click the slide once with the right mouse button and choose Edit MS PowerPoint 4.0 Presentation Link from the shortcut menu; or select the slide, choose Linked MS PowerPoint 4.0 Presentation Object from Word's Edit menu, and then choose Edit from the submenu. After you make changes to the presentation in the PowerPoint window, save the presentation again. As soon as you save the file, the linked copy of the presentation in Word is updated with the same changes.

FIGURE 17-4.
The Paste Special
dialog box in Word.

Modifying the Link

When you save a PowerPoint presentation in a file, link it to Word, and then modify it in PowerPoint, the changes flow through to Word as soon as you save the modifications in the PowerPoint file. If Word is closed, the changes appear the next time you open the Word document that contains the linked presentation.

To prevent changes to a linked presentation from flowing through to Word, select the presentation's representative slide in Word, and choose Links from the Edit menu. In the Links dialog box, shown in Figure 17-5, select Manual rather than Automatic as the Update option. The linked presentation will only update when you click Update Now in the Links dialog box, or when you select the representative slide and choose Update Link from the shortcut menu or press F9. To prevent the presentation from updating even when you use the Update Now command, select the Locked option in the Links dialog box.

FIGURE 17-5.
The Links dialog
box in Word.

Other options in the Links dialog box are: Open Source, which opens the presentation in PowerPoint for editing; Change Source, which allows you to link a different object from another application; and Break Link, which severs the link and leaves a static presentation in Word that cannot be edited or updated in PowerPoint.

Using PowerPoint with Microsoft Excel 5

The vast majority of presentations relate information using words rather than numbers, but if you have numeric data, you are likely to accumulate it, calculate it, and analyze it in a spreadsheet program such as Microsoft Excel 5. You'll be glad to know that you can communicate between PowerPoint and Excel as easily as you can between PowerPoint and Word. In fact, you can create an Excel worksheet from within PowerPoint, drag a worksheet from Excel to PowerPoint, or drag a PowerPoint slide or presentation to an Excel worksheet using the same techniques you use with Word.

Embedding an Excel Worksheet in PowerPoint

By clicking the Insert Excel Worksheet button on PowerPoint's Standard toolbar, you can embed an Excel worksheet on a PowerPoint slide. While you are working with the worksheet, Excel's menus and toolbars appear in PowerPoint, and a framed worksheet window overlaps the PowerPoint slide. When you finish the worksheet and click outside of it, PowerPoint's menus and toolbars reappear, and a picture of the Excel worksheet is displayed on the slide.

> **NOTE:** It's best to format the worksheet while Excel's menus and toolbars are available so that the worksheet's picture looks just right when it appears in PowerPoint.

When you click the Insert Excel Worksheet button, a grid of empty cells appears. Drag across up to 15 columns and up to 5 rows of cells, and then release the mouse button. A worksheet frame opens on the current slide, displaying the number of columns and rows you specified. Using the Excel menus, toolbars, and procedures, create the worksheet within the worksheet frame. When the worksheet is complete, be sure all the cells that you want included in it are visible in the worksheet frame, and then click outside the frame to place a picture of the worksheet on the PowerPoint slide. You can move and stretch the picture by dragging its handles.

To edit an Excel worksheet that has been placed on a PowerPoint slide, first double-click the worksheet's picture. When Excel's menus and toolbars reappear and the worksheet is framed once again, you can make changes to it. When you are finished, click anywhere outside the frame to return to Power-Point with the modified picture in place.

If the worksheet already exists in Excel, you can drag it to PowerPoint. A picture of the worksheet will appear on the current PowerPoint slide. To drag any part of an existing worksheet, arrange the Excel and PowerPoint windows on the screen (be sure Slide view is active), and then select the worksheet range that you want to move or copy. Drag the border of the range to move the worksheet from Excel to the current PowerPoint slide. If you want to copy rather than move the worksheet, hold down the Ctrl key as you drag. Figure 17-6 shows a range of numbers in Excel and the same range copied to PowerPoint using drag and drop.

FIGURE 17-6.

An Excel worksheet that has been copied to PowerPoint using drag and drop.

Once again, because the Excel worksheet appears in PowerPoint as a picture, you can move and stretch the worksheet by dragging its handles.

TIP   To accentuate a worksheet on a slide, use the Shadow command on PowerPoint's Format menu. Adding a shadow gives the worksheet a slightly raised look.

To edit the worksheet, double-click it, or click it with the right mouse button and select Edit Worksheet Object from the shortcut menu. Like before, Excel's menus and toolbars appear in place of PowerPoint's, and the worksheet is surrounded by a frame. After you finish editing the worksheet, click outside the frame. To reopen the worksheet in a separate Excel window, select the worksheet, click the right mouse button, and choose Open Worksheet Object. When you finish editing, choose Update from Excel's File menu, and then choose Exit and Return to *Presentation* from the File menu.

TIP   You can crop a worksheet that has been placed on a PowerPoint slide by clicking the worksheet's picture with the right mouse button, choosing Crop Picture from the shortcut menu, and placing the cropping icon on one of the worksheet picture's side handles. Then drag the handle inward to reduce the width or height of the picture.

To link an Excel worksheet to a PowerPoint presentation, first make sure you've saved the worksheet in an Excel file. Then select the worksheet, and copy it using the Copy command on Excel's Edit menu (or using one of the shortcuts for copying items, such as clicking the Copy button on the Standard toolbar). Next, switch to PowerPoint's Slide view, and choose Paste Special from the Edit menu. Select the Paste Link option in the Paste Special dialog box, and click OK. The worksheet appears in PowerPoint. If you make subsequent editing changes to the worksheet in Excel, the changes will flow through to the linked PowerPoint presentation when you resave the Excel file. If you make changes to the Excel file when the linked presentation is closed, the changes will appear the next time you open the presentation.

Remember, when you link an Excel worksheet to a PowerPoint presentation and you move the presentation to another system, you must also move the Excel worksheet.

Displaying a PowerPoint Slide or Slide Show in Excel

To display a PowerPoint slide or slide show in an Excel worksheet, follow the same procedures you use to display a slide or slide show in Word. Simply drag a single slide from PowerPoint's Slide Sorter view to Excel, or select all the slides in PowerPoint's Slide Sorter view and then drag the entire presentation to Excel.

> **TIP**   After you drag a slide to Excel, you can resize the slide's width and height proportionally by dragging one of its corner handles.

If you've dragged a single slide to Excel, double-click the slide to place it in the PowerPoint window for editing. If you've dragged an entire presentation to Excel, double-click its representative slide to start the slide show. You can control the slide show as if you were displaying it in PowerPoint's Slide Show view. To edit an entire presentation, select its representative slide in Excel, click the right mouse button, and choose Edit MS PowerPoint 4.0 Presentation from the shortcut menu.

Mailing a Presentation with Microsoft Mail

If Microsoft Mail is installed on your system, the Send command appears on PowerPoint's File menu. When you complete and save a presentation, you can choose the Send command, fill out the Microsoft Mail dialog boxes to identify the recipient of the presentation, and click the Send button. The presentation is sent to another Microsoft Mail user as an attachment to a Microsoft Mail note.

Customizing PowerPoint

As PowerPoint guides you through the presentation-making process, you must follow the steps the software expects you to follow. But fortunately, you can also exert plenty of control over how PowerPoint works. You can customize the way PowerPoint looks, change the default choices it makes, and even circumvent some of the steps that it would otherwise have you follow in its quest to guide you through the process unharmed.

In this chapter, you'll learn how to customize PowerPoint from top to bottom, changing the defaults for everything from the blank presentation to the composition of the toolbars. Only when you've demonstrated your total domination over the program can you truly be considered a PowerPoint master.

Creating a Default Presentation

When you select Blank Presentation from the PowerPoint dialog box or the New Presentation dialog box, PowerPoint loads a default presentation called DEFAULT.PPT. By replacing DEFAULT.PPT with a customized presentation, you can change the look of the default presentation.

You might want to change the default presentation when you've taken the time to customize a presentation with your corporate colors, a corporate standard background design, your corporate logo, and special text. By saving the customized presentation as DEFAULT.PPT, you can start each new presentation with your customized look already in place. Of course, you can always change the presentation template to give the presentation a different look, but the default presentation can establish the appearance of many of your presentations.

As discussed in the next section, "Changing the Start-Up Defaults," you can set up PowerPoint to skip the PowerPoint dialog box that appears whenever you start the program. When you opt to skip this dialog box, PowerPoint loads the default presentation, and the Title Slide autolayout appears on your screen. The title slide is displayed with all the attributes of the default presentation, including the presentation's template, its background design and color scheme, the formatting of its slide master, and its Slide Setup dialog box settings (which determine the shape and size of the presentation pages). With the title slide on your screen, you can jump right in and enter the presentation's text and charts.

To set the default presentation, start a new presentation or open an existing presentation, and then change any or all of the following elements:

- The template attached to the presentation

- Any graphic objects on the slide background, such as logos

- Special text on the slide background, such as the date, time, and slide number

- The color scheme

- The formatting of the slide master

- The Slide Setup dialog box options

NOTE: You only need to format the slide master of the presentation. Special formatting that you apply to particular slide layouts is not applied to the default presentation.

When you complete the sample presentation, save it with the name DEFAULT.PPT in the same directory that holds the PowerPoint program files (POWERPNT—unless you specified a different directory when you installed PowerPoint).

WARNING: Instead of overwriting the default presentation that comes with PowerPoint, you should rename the DEFAULT.PPT file—to DEFAULT1.PPT, for example—before creating a new DEFAULT.PPT file. Then, you can always retrieve the original, blank default presentation.

When you next select Blank Presentation from the New Presentation dialog box, all the formatting of the sample presentation appears in the new presentation.

Changing the Start-Up Defaults

By removing the PowerPoint dialog box that appears each time you start PowerPoint, you can go straight to the New Slide dialog box, where you can select an autolayout whose placeholders you'll fill with text, charts, and graphics. You lose the opportunity to use the AutoContent Wizard or the Pick a Look Wizard as you start a presentation, and you get whatever formatting is applied to the default presentation. But you can always use the Pick a Look Wizard later by clicking its button on the Standard toolbar. You can also select a template by clicking the Template button or by choosing Presentation Template from the Format menu.

You might find it handy to skip the PowerPoint dialog box when you almost always use the same presentation design and you have the presentation's content worked out, such as when you use PowerPoint to prepare presentations that vary only slightly from day to day.

To set PowerPoint to skip the first dialog box, choose Options from the Tools menu. In the Options dialog box, shown in Figure 18-1, deselect the Show Startup Dialog option.

FIGURE 18-1.
The Options
dialog box.

By also deselecting the Show New Slide Dialog option in the Options dialog box, you can have a new PowerPoint presentation proceed directly to the Title Slide autolayout without stopping at the New Slide dialog box. Then, each time you click the New Slide button, the Bulleted List autolayout appears. To select a different layout, you can always click the Layout button at the bottom of the PowerPoint window, or hold down the Shift key as you click the New Slide button. This might be the ideal setup if you frequently create presentations that consist of series of text slides. The first slide of the presentation is a title slide, and successive slides are bulleted list slides, unless you choose otherwise when you add each slide.

Setting Other Defaults

The Options dialog box provides other options that you can use to change the PowerPoint defaults. For example, the three options in the Edit section of the dialog box let you change how text is handled.

- Replace Straight Quotes with Smart Quotes enters typographically correct quotation marks (opening and closing) when you type a passage of text enclosed in quotation marks.

- Automatic Word Selection selects the entire first and last words of a text passage even if you don't drag the mouse pointer across the beginning of the first word and the end of the last word.

- Use Smart Cut and Paste makes sure words are spaced properly when you cut and paste text. Smart Cut and Paste tries to ensure that there's only one space between words.

The Always Suggest option in the Spelling section of the Options dialog box lets you set whether the spelling checker will suggest alternatives to a misspelled word. Having the spelling checker suggest alternatives is slower than simply having it point out spelling errors.

To turn off the status bar at the bottom of the PowerPoint window, deselect the Status Bar option in the View section. As a result, the presentation window has a little more space on the screen, but you lose important information about the slide, such as the slide number. You also lose access to the New Slide, Layout, and Template buttons. You must click the Insert New Slide button on the Standard toolbar, choose New Slide from the Insert menu, or choose Slide Layout and Presentation Template from the Format menu to accomplish the same tasks.

Deselect the Prompt for Summary Info option in the Save section of the Options dialog box only if you do not want the Summary Info dialog box to appear when you save a presentation.

Finally, the Recently Used File List option lets you determine how many recently used presentations are listed at the bottom of the File menu for your convenience. You can click any of these presentation names to load the file.

Customizing the Datasheet Settings and Default Graph

When you start a graph, the Microsoft Graph module always displays a default set of data for you to modify in the datasheet. It also displays a default graph based on the data. You can modify the default data and graph so that a graph design more suited to your needs appears whenever you start Graph.

To modify the default data and graph, follow these steps:

1. Load Graph by clicking the Insert Graph button on the Standard toolbar or by double-clicking a *Double click to add graph* placeholder.

2. Modify the data in the default datasheet and/or change the graph type and formatting of the default graph. Also, close the datasheet window if you don't want it to open automatically when you start Graph.

3. Choose Options from Graph's Tools menu.

4. On the Chart tab of the Graph Options dialog box, shown below, click the Use the Current Chart button in the Default Chart Format section. A new option called Custom Default appears in the Default Chart Format box.

5. Click OK.

The next time you start a graph, the revised default graph will appear. To return to the original graph, select (Built-in) as the Default Chart Format in the Graph Options dialog box.

On the Chart tab of the dialog box, you can also specify whether empty cells of the datasheet should be omitted from the graph or plotted as zero. When empty cells are omitted, gaps may occur in the graph.

The Datasheet Options tab of the Graph Options dialog box offers two options that you can use to control the datasheet. The first option, Move Selection after Enter, determines whether the cell pointer moves to the next cell of the datasheet after you press Enter or whether it remains in the current cell. The second option, Cell Drag and Drop, turns drag and drop on or off within the datasheet window.

NOTE: The Color tab of the Graph Options dialog box displays the colors used to fill the markers (Chart Fills) and the colors used for the lines and outlines (Chart Lines) of the graph. These colors are set by the current color scheme of the presentation. You can override the colors of a graph by formatting its markers and lines directly, so you should not need to modify the colors on the Color tab.

See Also: For more information about graphs, see Chapter 6, "Adding Graph Slides," page 125.

Setting the Drawing Defaults

To change the default fill color, line style, and text style of objects you draw using PowerPoint's drawing tools, follow this procedure:

1. Draw an object and apply settings for the fill color, line style, text style, and other attributes.

2. Select the object.

3. Choose the Pick Up Object Style command from the Format menu or the shortcut menu.

4. Click somewhere else on the slide to deselect the object.

5. Choose Apply To Object Defaults from the Format menu.

Now when you draw any object, the new default settings are applied.

**See
Also:** For more information about drawing objects, see Chapter 13,
"Drawing Graphic Objects," page 329.

Customizing Toolbars

As you've seen, PowerPoint's toolbars give you easy access to the most popular
menu commands. But you may not find a toolbar button for every command
you use frequently. Fortunately, you can customize the toolbars. You can add
and remove buttons, move buttons from one toolbar to another, and create a
custom toolbar with your favorite buttons.

Displaying a Toolbar

The easiest way to display a toolbar is to click any visible toolbar with the right
mouse button. On the shortcut menu that appears, the toolbars accompanied
by check marks are already displayed. To bring any other toolbar to the screen,
click its name on the shortcut menu. Figure 18-2 shows the shortcut menu for
toolbars.

FIGURE 18-2.

The shortcut menu
for toolbars.

You can also choose Toolbars from the View menu to open the Toolbars
dialog box shown in Figure 18-3. In the dialog box, select the check boxes for
the combination of toolbars you want displayed, and then click OK.

FIGURE 18-3.
The Toolbars
dialog box.

Adding and Removing Buttons

To add a button to a toolbar, make sure the toolbar you want to customize is
visible, and then click it with the right mouse button. From the shortcut menu,
choose Customize. You can also choose Toolbars from the View menu, and
click Customize in the Toolbars dialog box. Either way, the Customize Toolbars
dialog box appears, as shown in Figure 18-4.

FIGURE 18-4.
The Customize
Toolbars dialog box.

In the Customize Toolbars dialog box, you see a list of categories that
corresponds to the PowerPoint menus, and a set of buttons that represents the

commands in the selected category. Simply follow the instructions in the dialog box by selecting a category, clicking a button to see its description, and then dragging the button you want to any toolbar. You can drag as many buttons from as many categories as you want, and you can drop the buttons in exact positions on the toolbars. When you're finished adding buttons, click Close to close the dialog box.

Removing a toolbar button is even easier. With the Customize Toolbars dialog box open, simply drag the button off its toolbar. The button is always available in the Customize Toolbars dialog box if you need it again.

 TIP   You don't have to open the Customize Toolbar dialog box to remove a button from a toolbar. Simply hold down the Alt key, and drag the button off its toolbar.

Moving Buttons Within and Between Toolbars

If you don't like the order of buttons on a toolbar or if you want to move a button to another toolbar, you can drag buttons within toolbars and between toolbars. You can drag a button up two positions in a vertical toolbar, for example, or drag a button from one toolbar to another. You can even choose to display the Custom toolbar, which starts with no buttons, and then drag your favorite buttons to it.

To move a button from one toolbar to another, hold down the Alt key and drag the button. To copy a button from one toolbar to another, hold down both the Alt key and the Ctrl key as you drag the button. As always, a small plus sign appears next to the mouse pointer to indicate that you are copying rather than moving an object.

To create a custom toolbar, first choose Custom from the toolbars short-cut menu or select Custom in the Toolbars dialog box. A small, empty toolbar appears floating on your screen, as shown in Figure 18-5.

FIGURE 18-5.
The Custom toolbar.

Custom toolbar

Now all you have to do is drag copies of your favorite buttons from the toolbars displayed on your screen or from the Customize Toolbars dialog box to the Custom toolbar. Then you can reposition the toolbar by dragging it to one side of the PowerPoint window.

With that final bit of customization, you've done it. You've achieved the coveted status of PowerPoint guru. You're now ready to go out and present to the world!

he figures in this appendix show printouts of the 55 black and white templates that come with PowerPoint. Each template has been applied to the same slide—a slide that uses the Text & Graph autolayout. The black and white templates shown here are ideal for pages that are printed with a black and white printer. They can be found in the BWOVRHD subdirectory in the TEMPLATE directory. All black and white templates have *B* as the last letter of their name.

Color versions of these templates with lighter colors that are especially suited for printing color overheads can be found in the CLROVRHD subdirectory. These templates have *C* as the last letter of their name.

Color versions of these templates with darker colors that are especially suited for 35-mm slides and on-screen slide shows can be found in the SLDSHOW subdirectory. These templates have *S* as the last letter of their name.

See Also: For more information about selecting a template, see "Selecting a Presentation Template, page 54, and "Applying a Different Template," page 218.

For information about how to customize a template, see "Modifying a Template," page 223.

AZUREB.PPT

BANNERB.PPT

BEVELB.PPT

BLACKB.PPT

BLSTRIPB.PPT

BLUDIAGB.PPT

BLUEBOXB.PPT

BLUEGRNB.PPT

433

BRKNBARB.PPT

BUBBLEB.PPT

CHECKSB.PPT

CHEERSB.PPT

COLORBXB.PPT

CONFETIB.PPT

DBLLINEB.PPT

DIAMONDB.PPT

DROPSTRB.PPT

EMBOSSDB.PPT

FIESTAB.PPT

FLAGB.PPT

FORESTB.PPT

GRIDWRKB.PPT

INTLB.PPT

ISLANDB.PPT

LINSBLUB.PPT

MARBLEB.PPT

MEDICALB.PPT

METLBARB.PPT

MOVNGLNB.PPT

MULTBARB.PPT

MULTBOXB.PPT

MUSICB.PPT

NEONLITB.PPT

PASTELB.PPT

PATCHWKB.PPT

REDLINE.PPT

SEASHORB.PPT

SHADBARB.PPT

Text & Graph Layout

- ◆ Bulleted text item
- ◆ Second bulleted text item
  - – Indented text item
  - – Second indented text item

SIDEBARB.PPT

Text & Graph Layout

- ■ Bulleted text item
- ■ Second bulleted text item
  - – Indented text item
  - – Second indented text item

SIDEFADB.PPT

Text & Graph Layout

- ● Bulleted text item
- ● Second bulleted text item
  - – Indented text item
  - – Second indented text item

SORINGB.PPT

Text & Graph Layout

- ◆ Bulleted text item
- ◆ Second bulleted text item
  - ◆ Indented text item
  - ◆ Second indented text item

SOUTHWSB.PPT

Text & Graph Layout

- ➤ Bulleted text item
- ➤ Second bulleted text item
  - ➤ Indented text item
  - ➤ Second indented text item

SPARKLEB.PPT

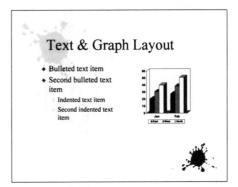

Text & Graph Layout

- ◆ Bulleted text item
- ◆ Second bulleted text item
  - Indented text item
  - Second indented text item

SPLATB.PPT

TABLEB.PPT

THEATREB.PPT

TOPLINEB.PPT

TRAVELB.PPT

TRIDOTSB.PPT

TRIUMPHB.PPT

TROPICB.PPT

TWINKLEB.PPT

VIVIDLNB.PPT

WATERCOB.PPT

WORLDB.PPT

Index

Numbers

3-D charts
  area, 133, 135, 148–49, 283–84
  bar, 133, 135, 148–49, 282
  column, 133, 135–36, 148–49
  floor, 277–78
  formatting, 272–79
  graph objects, 276–79
  gridlines, 278–79
  line, 133, 136, 148–49, 151–52, 282, 283–84
  pie, 292
  surface, 134, 136, 148–49, 293, 294
  walls, 277–78
35-mm slides, 36, 385–86, 388

A

accent colors, 228
Add Clipart dialog boxes, 367
addresses, cell, 137
ADI files, 369
Align command, 356
aligning
  graphic objects, 356–57

aligning, *continued*
  paragraphs, 111–12
Alignment command, 111
Always on Top command, 24
annotations. *See* text annotations
Apply Color Scheme command, 314
Apply Object Style command, 348
Apply Style button, 349
Apply Text Style command, 119
Apply To Object command, 427
Apply To Object Defaults command, 349
arcs, drawing, 336–37
Arc Tool button, 336
area charts, 132, 134, 148–49, 283–84
Arrange All command, 16, 310
Arrow button, 299
Arrowheads button, 334
arrow keys, 68
arrows
  adding to graphs, 299–300
  drawing, 333–34
ASCII text files, 159–61
AutoCAD Format 2-D file format, 369
AutoCAD Plot File format, 369

Index

Steve Sagman   Since 1988, Steve Sagman has written half a dozen books on graphics and presentation graphics and has contributed to several more. Half a million readers worldwide know his best-selling *Using Harvard Graphics*. He is also the author of *Using Freelance Graphics 2.0 for Windows, Harvard Graphics 2.0 for Windows: Visual Quickstart Guide, 1-2-3 Graphics Techniques, Using Windows Draw*, and *Getting Your Start in Hollywood*. In addition, he has contributed to *Mastering CorelDraw!, Using 1-2-3 Release 4 for Windows*, and *The PC Bible*.

Along with book writing, Sagman gives classes and seminars on graphics and presentation graphics. His company provides training, courseware, user interface consulting, and user documentation for PC hardware and software.

The author welcomes feedback at:

CompuServe: 72456,3325
Internet: wmgroup@phantom.com
MCI Mail: 315-0779
Postal: 140 Charles St., New York, NY 10014

The manuscript for this book was prepared and submitted to Microsoft Press in electronic form. Text files were prepared using Microsoft Word 6 for Windows. Pages were composed by Online Press using Ventura 4.1.1 for Windows, with text in Garamond and display type in Avant Garde Demi. Composed pages were delivered to the printer as electronic prepress files.

Cover Designer
Rebecca Geisler

Interior Graphic Designers
Kim Eggleston, Carolyn Davids, Lynne Faulk

Illustrator
Mark Monlux

Layout Artist
Bill Teel

Editor
Polly Fox Urban

Proofreader
Christina Dudley

Indexer
Julie Kawabata

Printed on recycled paper stock.

Running Microsoft® Software

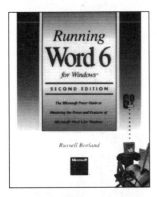

Running Word 6 for Windows™
Russell Borland

Master the power and features of Microsoft Word 6 for
Windows with this updated edition of the bestselling guide for
intermediate to advanced users. This example-rich guide contains
scores of insights and tips not found in the documentation and
includes in-depth, accessible coverage of Word's features.

832 pages, softcover $29.95 ($39.95 Canada)   ISBN 1-55615-574-3

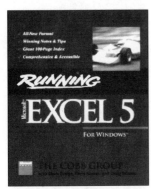

Running Microsoft® Excel 5 for Windows™
*The Cobb Group with Mark Dodge,
Chris Kinata, and Craig Stinson*

Here's the most comprehensive and accessible book for all levels of spreadsheet
users. It includes hundreds of tips and practical shortcuts for using the powerful
new features of Microsoft Excel 5 for Windows. In addition to the step-by-step
tutorials, straightforward examples, and expert advice, this updated edition
features a new and improved format designed to help you find answers faster!

1184 pages, softcover $29.95 ($39.95 Canada)   ISBN 1-55615-585-9

Running Microsoft® Access® 2
for Windows™
John L. Viescas

Here is the best source of information on Microsoft Access for
all levels. Packed with winning tips, notes, and strategies, this complete
and thorough tutorial runs you through all the ins and outs of data access,
the program's powerful tools, and its robust development environment.
The bound-in disk includes a fully functional database that illustrates
the examples in the book, as well as additional sample databases
that show you efficient table designs for common applications.

**960 pages, softcover with one 3.5-inch disk
$39.95 ($53.95 Canada)   ISBN 1-55615-592-1**

*Microsoft*Press

PowerPoint Toolbars

(continued from the inside front cover)

Drawing Toolbar

Selection Tool

Line Tool

Ellipse Tool

Freeform Tool

AutoShapes

Line On/Off

Text Tool

Rectangle Tool

Arc Tool

Free Rotate Tool

Fill On/Off

Shadow On/Off

Drawing+ Toolbar

Fill Color

Shadow Color

Dashed Lines

Bring Forward

Group

Rotate Left

Flip Horizontal

Line Color

Line Style

Arrowheads

Send Backward

Ungroup

Rotate Right

Flip Vertical

AutoShapes Toolbar

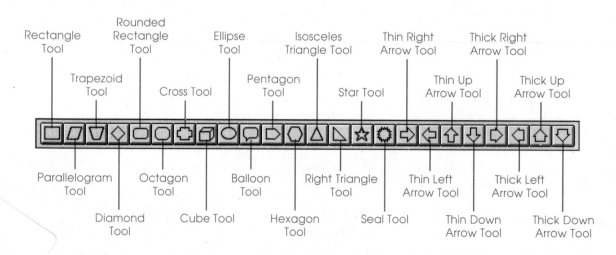

Rectangle Tool

Trapezoid Tool

Rounded Rectangle Tool

Parallelogram Tool

Diamond Tool

Cross Tool

Octagon Tool

Cube Tool

Ellipse Tool

Balloon Tool

Pentagon Tool

Hexagon Tool

Isosceles Triangle Tool

Right Triangle Tool

Star Tool

Seal Tool

Thin Right Arrow Tool

Thin Up Arrow Tool

Thin Left Arrow Tool

Thin Down Arrow Tool

Thick Right Arrow Tool

Thick Up Arrow Tool

Thick Left Arrow Tool

Thick Down Arrow Tool